A HISTORY OF THE WORLD

A HISTORY OF THE WORLD

FROM PREHISTORY TO THE 21ST CENTURY

JEREMY BLACK

ARCTURUS

For Alan Newman

Author's Acknowledgements:
Lecturing for many years in World History courses helps shape ideas. I have also benefited from an invitation to speak on related topics at Stillman College, and would like to thank William Gibson and Heiko Whenning for their comments. I owe much to the editorial help of John Turing. This book is dedicated to Alan Newman after over fifty years of friendship.

This edition published in 2018 by Arcturus Publishing Limited
26/27 Bickels Yard, 151–153 Bermondsey Street,
London SE1 3HA

ISBN: 978-1-78828-090-7
AD005920UK

Printed in Malaysia

CONTENTS

INTRODUCTION

The interplay of change and continuity is a condition of human life, one that is as insistent as the passage of the years, the rhythm of the seasons and the passing of generations. Alongside the continuities stemming from earlier adaptation, from established practices and from the cultural and psychological habits of referring to the past and being reverential of it, human history shows a continuing capacity to adapt to the environment, displays the mechanics and settings of life, indicates the power and structure of society and reflects the ways humans think and are taught about life.

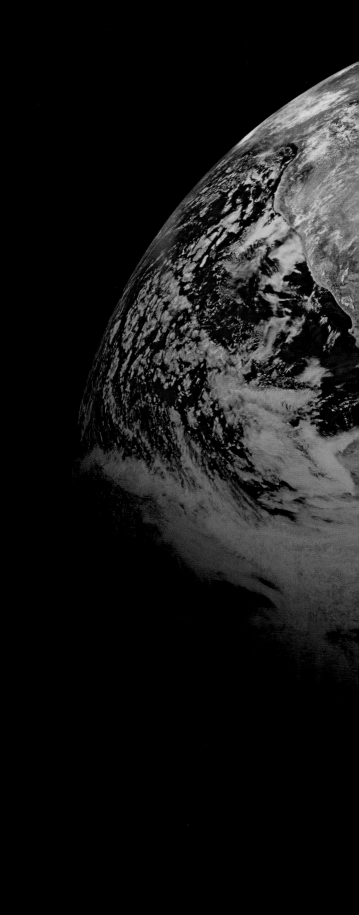

Above: Memorials to history, like this one from Charleroi, reflect human reverence for the past

Right: Much of the earth is unsuitable for human life. Only human ingenuity in adapting to their environment has allowed them to thrive

Above: Deserts like the Sahara have too little rainfall to support much life, but humans have nonetheless found a way to survive in them

Humans need this ability to adapt because they are not well-suited to live on most of the planet without the help of technology. They cannot fly unaided, nor can they live under the water which covers the majority of the earth. Although fish and rainwater can be obtained while on boats, it is difficult to live permanently on the water surface. Part of this water is frozen as ice, and humans cannot stop more of this water freezing in the winter. This is true in particular of the Arctic Ocean.

Much of the land surface is intractable because it is too cold or hot, or arid or mountainous for habitation. Antarctica, a large and very cold continent, was uninhabited until recent scientific stations were established. It was not until 1912 that the Norwegian Roald Amundsen became the first human to reach the South Pole, three years after the American Robert Peary had been the first to approach the North.

A lot of the world's land surface does not support much vegetation, or enough animal life for more than a small population of hunters. In deserts, of which the largest is the Sahara in Africa, there is too little rainfall or soil to support abundant life, plant or animal. Large ones can be found elsewhere, including the Gobi in Asia, the Atacama in South America, the Gibson and Simpson deserts in the interior of Australia and the deserts of the south-west of the United States. Europe is exceptional in not having deserts. Humans do live in deserts and have adapted to them. The populations involved are generally small and the problems posed, notably of water availability, very serious, although the very large city of Los Angeles grew with the help of water from Owens Valley.

Beyond supplying water through irrigation and cutting down trees,

Below: Roald Amundsen was the first person to reach the North Pole, in 1912

humanity's ability to change the environment on a large scale was restricted for much of history. It was not until the late 19th century that the advent of more powerful explosives made tunnelling under the Alps possible, the first example of such significant man-made change to the environment. Projects of truly great magnitude, such as the Panama Canal, showed that humanity lacked the necessary organizational sophistication even into modern times: the French began the construction of the canal in the 1880s, but it was only finished by the Americans in 1914, after the loss of many lives to malaria and yellow fever. Until recently, humans have also had scant ability to understand changes in the climate and weather, let alone to try to change them.

Separately, humans have long faced challenges created by the organization of our species as social creatures. Humans need to be social in order to have children and to protect them during their long period of vulnerability. Tasks such as competing with other animals that are physically stronger,

for example lions, and providing protection from them, require co-operation. Agriculture and warfare, later developments, need an even higher level. The structures of society which developed are inherently competitive with other human groups. The idea that humans were originally peaceful, and only became warlike due to social conditioning, is no longer widely held. Such a view is more reflective of the Biblical aspirations focused on the Garden of Eden and the utopian thoughts of the 1960s and 70s than of the surviving evidence.

In turn, this competition, and the social structures that result from it, shape the norms that guide human assumptions and actions. What is the purpose of life? How are the gods, or God, to be satisfied? How should rival gods and humans be treated? These norms, expressed in religious beliefs and social practices, help humans understand their environment and, in

Below: The Panama Canal was completed in 1914 – an instance of humans radically changing the world around them

Rght: We cannot always understand the adaptions made in the past, including their understanding of the world, so mysteries like the Nazca lines of Peru remain

particular, determine how best to respond to the social aspects of existence. There has never been universal agreement on these points and that they have led to widely varying political ideas and practices only makes them more significant.

Returning to 'prehistory' (which itself is very much a present-day concept), adaptation to the environment rapidly became supplemented by attempts to mould it to suit human requirements and those of the crops and animals used by humans, a process that was in turn driven by the need for resources and space. The moulding came to be shaped by ideologies and accelerated by the development of information storing and transmitting systems such as writing. The movement of early peoples shows clearly the need for resources and space, such as in the hunting of animals across long distances or in patterns of seasonal migration. Humans, though, did not only seek to modify their environment, but themselves were changed by it. For example, humans in areas with relatively low levels of sunlight developed genes linked to lighter skin to absorb more Vitamin D. This led to changes in Europe to lighter skin pigments around 7–8,000

years ago, a change which appears to have occurred first in Northern Europe.

Humans were not the only species adapting and evolving, but their greater development of social skills, notably in communication and organization, made that adaptation particularly successful. In one sense, the modern era began when humans became the most successful mammals. Birds had a greater range and could readily organize to act in groups, but humans acquired the power to dominate. They also became the species with the largest colonies of omnivores, no longer bound to a specific food source like most other carnivores or herbivores. The increasing size of those colonies, from prehistoric bands to modern mega-cities, and the power that it has given to our species to shape our destiny is one of the most underestimated aspects of human history.

Consider the related effectiveness of species and its consequences. This book will work if it makes you think – think not only about what is written here, but also about what you have experienced, and the world around you. If you disagree with the views presented, think why, and contribute to understanding by articulating your view.

TIMELINE

Shaded boxes = 1000 years

| 10 million years ago | 1 million years ago | 100,000 years ago | 50,000 years ago | 10,000 years ago | 2000 BCE |

7 million years ago Division between human ancestors and those of chimpanzees

315,000 years ago Appearance of Homo Sapiens

6 million years ago Early hominids begin to walk

3.3 million years ago Evidence of human tool use

2.4 million years ago Appearance of *Homo habilis*

*c.*100,000–11,700 years ago Ice Ages

AFRICA

c.220,000–190,000 years ago Humanity begins to spread out of Africa

3400 BCE The first walled towns appear in Egypt

5000 BCE Grain cultivation spreads to the Nile Valley

6500 BCE Domestication of cattle in North Africa

2575–2134 BCE Old Kingdom of Egypt

AMERICAS

c.10,000 BCE Humans reached South America

2500 BCE Temple mounds appeared in the Supe Valley in Peru

14,500 years ago Human occupation of Huaca Prieta began in northern Peru

5000 BCE Domestication of grains in Central America

c.16,000 years ago Humans cross the Bering Land Bridge into the Americas

ASIA AND OCEANIA

50,000 years ago Humans arrive in Australia

2500 BCE Major settlements emerged at Harappa, Mohenjo-Daro and Kalibangan in the Indus Valley

2800 BCE The first ploughs are used in Kalibangan, India

4,500 years ago Cities emerge in the Indus Valley

MIDDLE EAST

23,000 years ago Wild cereal gathering in the Middle East

2300 BCE Sargon established the empire of Sumeria in southern Mesopotamia

3500 BCE Emergence of the city state of Uruk

*c.***8000 BCE** Emergence of agriculture in Mesopotamia

EUROPE

*c.***65,000 years ago** Modern humans arrive in Europe

4000 BCE Horses are domesticated on the steppes of Russia

3100 BCE A settlement is established at the Ness of Brodgar in Orkney.

SCIENCE AND CULTURE

150,000–50,000 years ago Development of language

*c.***2700 BCE** The Pyramids are built in Ancient Egypt

*c.***3100 BCE** Development of cuneiform script in the Sumerian civilization in Mesopotamia

*c.***3500 BCE** The first wheels are made in Mesopotamia

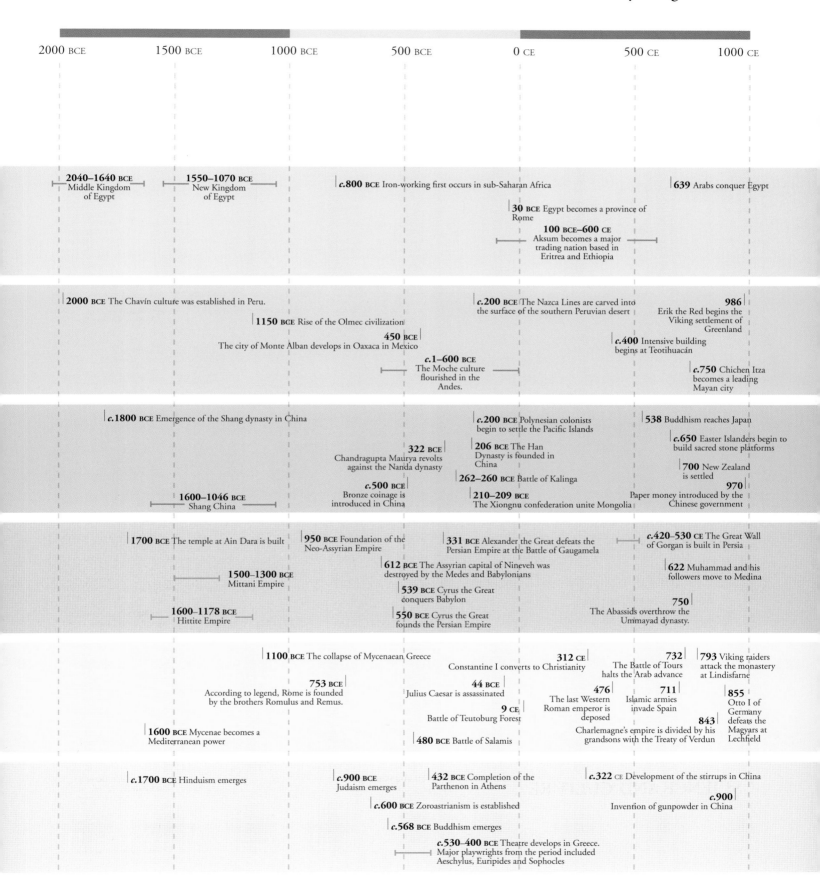

2000 BCE   1500 BCE   1000 BCE   500 BCE   0 CE   500 CE   1000 CE

2040–1640 BCE
Middle Kingdom
of Egypt

1550–1070 BCE
New Kingdom
of Egypt

***c.*800 BCE** Iron-working first occurs in sub-Saharan Africa

639 Arabs conquer Egypt

30 BCE Egypt becomes a province of Rome

100 BCE–600 CE
Aksum becomes a major
trading nation based in
Eritrea and Ethiopia

2000 BCE The Chavín culture was established in Peru.

1150 BCE Rise of the Olmec civilization

450 BCE
The city of Monte Alban develops in Oaxaca in Mexico

***c.*200 BCE** The Nazca Lines are carved into
the surface of the southern Peruvian desert

***c.*1–600 BCE**
The Moche culture
flourished in the
Andes.

986
Erik the Red begins the
Viking settlement of
Greenland

***c.*400** Intensive building
begins at Teotihuacán

***c.*750** Chichen Itza
becomes a leading
Mayan city

***c.*1800 BCE** Emergence of the Shang dynasty in China

322 BCE
Chandragupta Maurya revolts
against the Nanda dynasty

***c.*500 BCE**
Bronze coinage is
introduced in China

1600–1046 BCE
Shang China

***c.*200 BCE** Polynesian colonists
begin to settle the Pacific Islands

206 BCE The Han
Dynasty is founded in
China

262–260 BCE Battle of Kalinga

210–209 BCE
The Xiongnu confederation unite Mongolia

538 Buddhism reaches Japan

***c.*650** Easter Islanders begin to
build sacred stone platforms

700 New Zealand
is settled

970
Paper money introduced by the
Chinese government

1700 BCE The temple at Ain Dara is built

950 BCE Foundation of the
Neo-Assyrian Empire

1500–1300 BCE
Mittani Empire

1600–1178 BCE
Hittite Empire

331 BCE Alexander the Great defeats the
Persian Empire at the Battle of Gaugamela

612 BCE The Assyrian capital of Nineveh was
destroyed by the Medes and Babylonians

539 BCE Cyrus the Great
conquers Babylon

550 BCE Cyrus the Great
founds the Persian Empire

***c.*420–530 CE** The Great Wall
of Gorgan is built in Persia

622 Muhammad and his
followers move to Medina

750
The Abassids overthrow the
Ummayad dynasty.

1100 BCE The collapse of Mycenaean Greece

753 BCE
According to legend, Rome is founded
by the brothers Romulus and Remus.

1600 BCE Mycenae becomes a
Mediterranean power

Constantine I converts to Christianity

44 BCE
Julius Caesar is assassinated

9 CE
Battle of Teutoburg Forest

480 BCE Battle of Salamis

312 CE

476
The last Western
Roman emperor is
deposed

Charlemagne's empire is divided by his
grandsons with the Treaty of Verdun

732
The Battle of Tours
halts the Arab advance

711
Islamic armies
invade Spain

843

793 Viking raiders
attack the monastery
at Lindisfarne

855
Otto I of
Germany
defeats the
Magyars at
Lechfield

***c.*1700 BCE** Hinduism emerges

***c.*900 BCE**
Judaism emerges

***c.*600 BCE** Zoroastrianism is established

***c.*568 BCE** Buddhism emerges

432 BCE Completion of the
Parthenon in Athens

***c.*530–400 BCE** Theatre develops in Greece.
Major playwrights from the period included
Aeschylus, Euripides and Sophocles

***c.*322 CE** Development of the stirrups in China

***c.*900**
Invention of gunpowder in China

TIMELINE

	1000	1100	1200	1300	1400	1500	1600	1700	1800

AFRICA

1498 Portuguese begin trading in Mozambique

1250 Mamluks overthrow the Ayyubid dynasty in Egypt

1578 Portuguese forces are defeated in Morocco

1517 The Ottomans conquer Egypt

***c*.1000** Work begins on the stone walls of the Great Zimbabwe

1562 Serse-Dingil becomes king of Ethiopia

***c*.1100** Timbuktu is settled

1324 Mansa Musa, emperor of Mali, makes pilgrimage to Mecca

1591 Moroccan forces defeat the Songhay empire at the Battle of Tondibi

AMERICAS

***c*.1200** Incas settle in Andean valley near Cusco

1492 Columbus reaches the West Indies

1519–21 Spanish conquest of the Aztec empire

1775 American Declaration of Independence

1532-5 Spanish conquests of Inca empire

1607 English begin permanent settlement of Virginia

1000 A small Viking settlement is founded in Newfoundland

1224 Chichen Itza is abandoned

1536 Manco Inca leads a rebellion against Spanish forces and establishes a rebel state in Vilcabamba

1572 Tupac Amaru, the last Inca ruler, dies

1050 Construction of large mounds along the Mississippi Valley

1325 Tenochtitlan is founded

1539–42 Hernando de Soto leads an expedition into the Mississippi valley

1756–1763 The Seven Years' War

ASIA AND OCEANIA

1340–51 Black Death

1405–1433 Zheng He leads the Chinese treasure fleets on expeditions through the Indian Ocean

1757 British forces establ[...] East India Company rule [...] Bengal at the Battle of Pla[...]

1206 The Mongol Empire is established

1361 Timur establishes an empire in central Asia

1467–77 The Onin War begins the Sengoku period in Japan

1639 The Portuguese are expelled from Japan

1227 Chinggis Khan dies

1598 The Tokugawa Shogunate is established in Japan

1044 Establishment of the first Burmese state at Pagan

1279 Khubilai Khan completes the Mongol conquest of China

1368 Establishment of the Ming Dynasty

1526 Mughals capture Delhi

1644 The Manchu conquest of China

1498 Vasco da Gama completes the first sea voyage from Europe to India

MIDDLE EAST

1258 Mongols capture Baghdad

1739 Nadir Shah of Persia invades northern India

1260 Mamluk soldiers defeat the Mongol invaders in Syria

1071 Byzantine forces are defeated by the Seljurk Turks at the Battle of Manzikert

1099 Crusaders capture Jerusalem

1401 Timur sacks Baghdad

EUROPE

1095 The Council of Clermont calls for the First Crusade

1453 Constantinople is conquered by the Ottomans

1618–1648: The Thirty Years' War

1241 Mongol forces invade eastern Europe

1492 Granada is conquered by Christian forces

1756–1763 The Seven Years' War

1204 Crusaders sack Constantinople

1066 William the Conqueror invades England

1789 Start of the French Revolution

1340–51 Black Death

1529 The Siege of Vienna

1085 Castile conquers the city of Toledo

1571 The Ottoman navy suffers a major defeat at the Battle of Lepanto

1683 The second Ottoman siege of Vienna

1086 The Almoravids invade Moorish Spain

SCIENCE AND CULTURE

1517 The Protestant Reformation begins when Martin Luther presented his 95 theses

1783 First manned balloon flight

***c*.1045** Movable type printing is invented in China

***c*.1250** Building of stone mosques in Swahili city-states of East Africa

1519–1522 Ferdinand Magellan makes the first circumnavigation of the world

1543 Copernicus publishes his heliocentric theory

1660 Foundation of the Royal Society

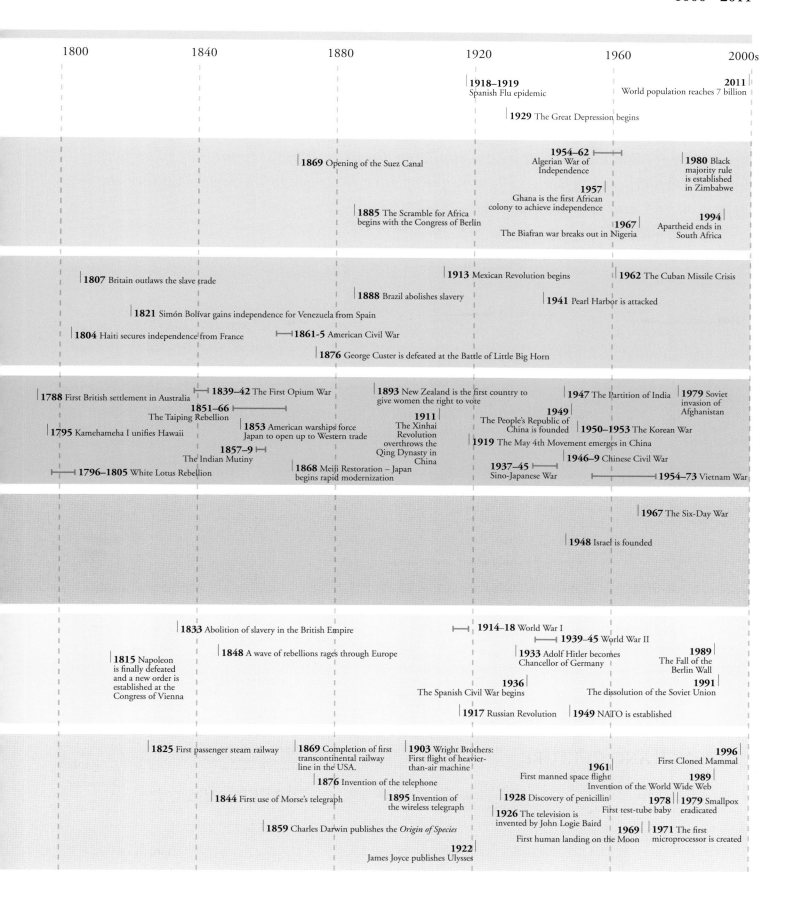

1000 - 2011

1800   1840   1880   1920   1960   2000s

1918–1919 Spanish Flu epidemic

2011 World population reaches 7 billion

1929 The Great Depression begins

1869 Opening of the Suez Canal

1954–62 Algerian War of Independence

1980 Black majority rule is established in Zimbabwe

1957 Ghana is the first African colony to achieve independence

1885 The Scramble for Africa begins with the Congress of Berlin

1967 The Biafran war breaks out in Nigeria

1994 Apartheid ends in South Africa

1807 Britain outlaws the slave trade

1913 Mexican Revolution begins

1962 The Cuban Missile Crisis

1888 Brazil abolishes slavery

1941 Pearl Harbor is attacked

1821 Simón Bolívar gains independence for Venezuela from Spain

1804 Haiti secures independence from France

1861-5 American Civil War

1876 George Custer is defeated at the Battle of Little Big Horn

1788 First British settlement in Australia

1839–42 The First Opium War

1893 New Zealand is the first country to give women the right to vote

1947 The Partition of India

1979 Soviet invasion of Afghanistan

1851–66 The Taiping Rebellion

1949 The People's Republic of China is founded

1795 Kamehameha I unifies Hawaii

1853 American warships force Japan to open up to Western trade

1911 The Xinhai Revolution overthrows the Qing Dynasty in China

1950–1953 The Korean War

1919 The May 4th Movement emerges in China

1857–9 The Indian Mutiny

1946–9 Chinese Civil War

1796–1805 White Lotus Rebellion

1868 Meiji Restoration – Japan begins rapid modernization

1937–45 Sino-Japanese War

1954–73 Vietnam War

1967 The Six-Day War

1948 Israel is founded

1833 Abolition of slavery in the British Empire

1914–18 World War I

1939–45 World War II

1815 Napoleon is finally defeated and a new order is established at the Congress of Vienna

1848 A wave of rebellions rages through Europe

1933 Adolf Hitler becomes Chancellor of Germany

1989 The Fall of the Berlin Wall

1936 The Spanish Civil War begins

1991 The dissolution of the Soviet Union

1917 Russian Revolution

1949 NATO is established

1825 First passenger steam railway

1869 Completion of first transcontinental railway line in the USA.

1903 Wright Brothers: First flight of heavier-than-air machine

1996 First Cloned Mammal

1876 Invention of the telephone

1961 First manned space flight

1989 Invention of the World Wide Web

1844 First use of Morse's telegraph

1895 Invention of the wireless telegraph

1928 Discovery of penicillin

1978 First test-tube baby

1979 Smallpox eradicated

1926 The television is invented by John Logie Baird

1859 Charles Darwin publishes the *Origin of Species*

1969 First human landing on the Moon

1971 The first microprocessor is created

1922 James Joyce publishes Ulysses

PREHISTORIC HUMANS
10 Million Years Ago–10,000 BCE

Early hominids lived among the stalactites and stalagmites of Kent's Cavern, the impressive cave system at Torbay in Devon, England. The caves gave them shelter from the wet of south-west winds and opened to the light from the east. Now the caves offer an inspiring visit for tourists and a challenge for artists; but, for most of their long human history, they reflected the struggle of man to adapt to the land and face the opportunities and problems it posed.

Early Humans

Most of the earth's history, and that of life on earth, was over long before the appearance of humans. When the magma cooled to form the earth's crust, when the amphibians developed and left the primeval oceans, and as geological ages succeeded one another, there were no humans. Nor, as the dinosaurs dominated and then lost their sway, were humans among

Right: First Neanderthals and then Stone Age humans made their homes in Kent's Cavern in Devon

the first of the mammals to evolve. While the first reptiles appeared about 310 million years ago, the first true mammals emerged about 220 million years ago. They were like rats and shrews.

Humans are primates, an order (or sub-division) of mammals, warm-blooded creatures whose infants feed on their mother's milk. The first primate-like creatures emerged about 66 million years ago, about the time the dinosaurs disappeared, but the first apes did not appear until about 23 million years ago. Their relatively large brains, dexterity and social characteristics gave primates particular advantages. Originally primarily forest tree-dwellers, primates made significant adaptations for life on the ground. Early humans were faced with more open ground cover and began to walk on their hind legs, rather than on all-fours.

Above: The first hominids evolved from apes, with larger brains and the ability to walk on two legs

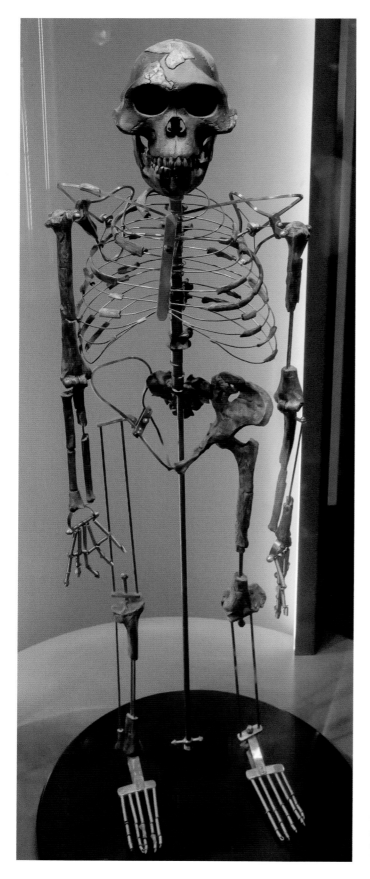

Combined with the development of sweat glands to cool bodies after exertion, this increased human mobility on the ground and made it possible to live in different climate zones. Human brains also have a relatively large cerebral cortex, which is linked to increased intelligence, one of the keys to their success. Humans also have highly dexterous hands, which enabled them to develop and use tools much more effectively than other animals.

The development of upright locomotion was an enormous step in human evolution. With its long sole and five forward-pointing toes without claws (including a big toe), the human foot provides balance and enables greater mobility. Its evolution can be traced in the fossil record in Africa: whereas the 4.4 million-year-old *Ardipithecus ramidus* from Ethiopia, the earliest hominin known from nearly complete fossils, has an ape-like foot, the 3.7 million-year-old Laetoli footprints from Tanzania, which are thought to have been made by *Australopithecus*, another hominin species, are similar to those of human footprints. Evidence for hominins (early members of the human lineage) outside Africa has also begun to emerge, strengthened by analysis of the fragmentary 7.2 million-year-old primate *Graecopithecus* from Greece and Bulgaria. It was from these ancestral species that modern humans evolved, first as *Homo habilis* and then into more recognizable human-like specimens in the forms of *Homo erectus, Homo heidelbergensis, Homo neanderthalensis* and, finally, *Homo sapiens*.

Left: Lucy is the most complete skeleton of an *Australopithecus afarensis*, one of the ancestors of Homo sapiens

Above: The use of tools dates back approximately 2.6 million years. Handaxes, like the one pictured above, were meta-tools, that could be used to make other tools

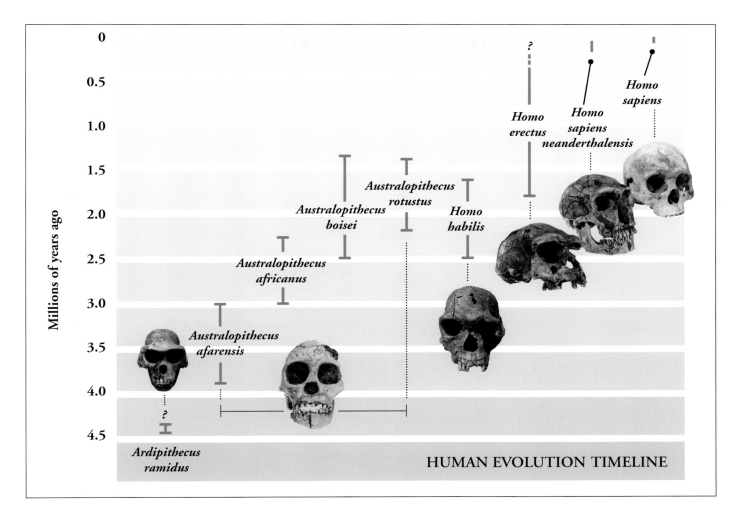

HUMAN EVOLUTION TIMELINE

The pace of discovery and analysis in archaeology and genetics is such that theories of human origins and spread are both rapidly changing and controversial. For example, recently-discovered human-like footprints from Crete (not then an island in the Mediterranean but part of the main landmass), analysed in the 2010s, test the established narrative. Approximately 5.7 million years old, they were made two million years earlier than the footprints discovered at Laetoli in Tanzania, Africa. Their discovery has challenged the earlier notion that hominins originated in East Africa and remained there before eventually dispersing to Europe and Asia, or at least led to calls for the re-dating of that dispersal.

By about four million years ago, when a change of climate had led to the disappearance of large forests, walking on two feet had become the norm for early humans. The demands of walking upright led the legs to be developed to increase speed, range and ease of mobility, and to support the body weight. The arms instead became focused on tool-use, which appeared from about 3.3 million years ago and was vitally important to the development of humans. The first tools were simply whatever could be found, and only later became worked and specialized for particular purposes. Stone, wood and bone were the basic materials. Simple tools were followed by composite ones, which increased their usefulness and also showed a level of adaptability in humans greater than in other species. This was notably so with 'meta-tools' – tools used to make other tools; for example, a very hard stone employed as a kind of hammer to open nuts (rather like a hammer on an anvil) and to make stone spear tips and, eventually, metal tools. Chimpanzees can use meta-tools, as in nut-cracking, but not move further along. Human ingenuity greatly developed the potential for such tools.

Theories of Human Origins and Spread

Traditionally, anthropologists proposed that modern *Homo sapiens* – our own species – first arose in Africa (around 315,000 years ago) and developed fully there. It then migrated outwards, replacing other existing species, notably *Homo erectus* and the Neanderthals, with only limited interbreeding between species. The degree to which there was competition and conflict between the species is unclear. DNA analysis does, however, indicate some interbreeding, with Neanderthal DNA found in modern humans.

This 'Out of Africa' theory has been challenged by recent discoveries. Today, scholars debate between ideas of a single source for human evolution against a more complex multi-regional evolution with gene flows occurring between regions. In this second version, there is an overall evolution toward the modern *Homo sapiens*, but with significant regional differences occurring.

Early *Homo sapiens* who migrated – whether from Africa or from several regional centres – faced landscapes and shorelines very different from those today. There was also land between South-east Asia and modern Indonesia which made movement possible between the two, as also between mainland Australia and Tasmania, and a land-bridge across the Bering Strait. In this period, humans lacked boats and, when they did develop (around 50,000 BCE), they were limited in their ability to confront currents and winds.

Those first boats were probably used by modern humans to reach Australia about 50,000 years ago. By 45,000 years ago *Homo sapiens* had reached Europe. The timing of the human settlement of the Americas has proved especially controversial. The mainstream thesis is that the first arrivals in the Americas came from Asia about 36,000 years ago, crossing a land bridge over the Bering Straits during the Ice Age, but there is an alternative argument of a spread north from South into North America. The general view is that people spread mainly from north to South, reaching Central America about 11,000 BCE

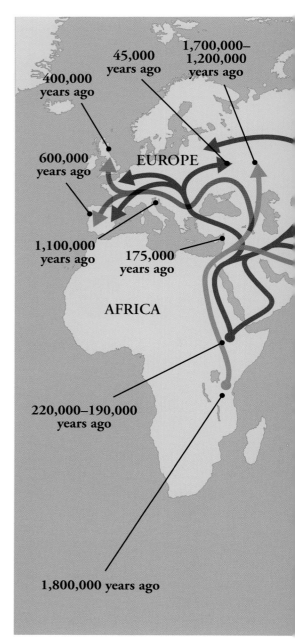

400,000 years ago

45,000 years ago

1,700,000–1,200,000 years ago

600,000 years ago

EUROPE

1,100,000 years ago

175,000 years ago

AFRICA

220,000–190,000 years ago

1,800,000 years ago

Left: The discovery of a 175,000-year-old bone fragment in Misliya Cave, Israel, is rewriting the timeline of humanity's move out of Africa

Above: Any map of the spread of humanity offers a misleading precision, not least because the meaning of distance was very different for people who had to walk everywhere

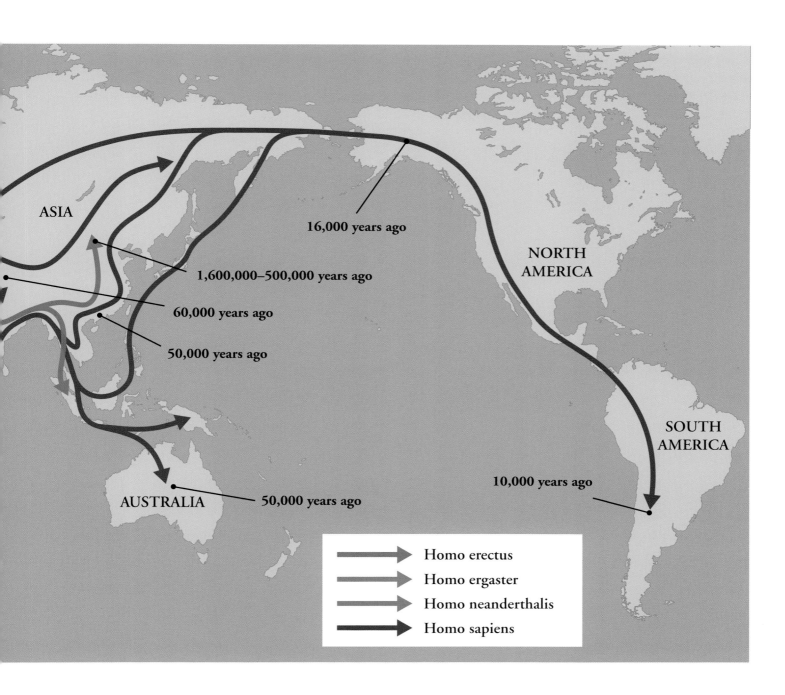

ASIA

16,000 years ago

NORTH
AMERICA

1,600,000–500,000 years ago

60,000 years ago

50,000 years ago

SOUTH
AMERICA

10,000 years ago

AUSTRALIA   **50,000 years ago**

→	Homo erectus
→	Homo ergaster
→	Homo neanderthalis
→	Homo sapiens

and the far south by *c.*10,000 BCE.

Evidence which pushes back the dates for the spread of humans continues to be found, suggesting that changing climatic conditions were a factor in promoting a move out of Africa about 190,000–220,000 years ago. In 2017, palaeontologists discovered *Homo sapiens* remains in Moroccan rock dating to about 300,000 years ago, 100,000 years earlier than the point when the species was generally credited with developing from *Homo erectus*. In the Misliya cave in Israel, a 175,000-year-old bone fragment from *Homo sapiens* has been discovered, alongside evidence of the ability to control fire and use stone-working technology.

Life as Hunter-Gatherers

Early humans were omnivores, hunter-gatherers whose varied diets and skills enabled their spread across the world. The development of weapons and the refinement of hunting techniques permitted them to hunt, and perhaps to hunt-out, large mammals such as mastodons and mammoths. In 10–9,000 BCE, early settlers in North America armed with large stone points were able to kill mammoth by piercing their hide and then to cut up their bodies and thus eat them. The diet of these early humans

Hunting large mammals like mammoths provided the main source of food for early humans

was supplemented by hunting other animals and fishing. A burial pit found in Alaska in 2010 revealed the bones of an infant girl and another baby who died about 9500 BCE, laid on a bed of antler points and weapons, and covered in red ochre. In Central America, sloths, mastodons and giant armadillos were hunted. In Europe, large mammals, such as mammoths, mastodons, sabre-toothed tigers, giant deer and the woolly rhinoceros, became extinct in the same period.

The ability to communicate through language and to organize into groups was significant in hunting these and other animals and was part of a broader pattern of social development. The use of fire was important to the human advance as it could provide protection, for example in caves, against other animals. Humans also retained useful objects for future use and performed tasks entailing a division of labour. Stone-blade technology gradually improved, culminating in microlithic flints mounted in wood or bone hafts which could be used as knives or as arrowheads.

This skill in hunting helped ensure that humans were better able than other animals to adapt to the possibilities created by the retreat of the ice sheets at the end of the last Ice Age in around 10,000 BCE, the last stage of the several advances and retreats that characterized the Ice Ages. Humans were increasingly able to confront other carnivores. They gradually drove bears, wolves and other competing predators away from areas of human settlement and into mountain and forest vastnesses.

A general global warming at the end of the Ice Age assisted in the spread of humans. Forest and wildlife zones moved closer to the poles, with the trees of a cold climate – birch, pine and hazel – replaced by oak, elm, ash and lime. These deciduous forests, with their far greater undergrowth, were rich in plant and animal life. In Europe, red and roe deer and wild pigs moved north, providing sources of food which helped the spread of hunter-gatherers. An increase in seafood was also exploited, aided by the development of harpoons and boats. In coastal areas, such as in Japan, the gathering of shellfish increased. By exploiting the wider range of food resources available to them, in time the human species spread round much of the

CAVE ART

Hunting clearly played a key role in early human society. Depictions of humans fighting animals appear widely in early rock paintings in caves, notably in Spain. Those in Cueva de la Vieja show men with bows hunting stags; those in Altamira (from around 34,000 BCE) include bison as well as a wild boar; the paintings in the Cueva de la Pileta show panthers, goats and a large fish. Rock art from the Tassili n'Ajjer plateau in the Sahara, dating from about 6000 BCE shows the hunting of giraffes. In Kashmir, the Burzahama site from about 4300 BCE depicts hunters and a bull. The bones of animals in early human settlements provides other evidence of the human use of weapons and tools to fight, kill and cut up animals.

world, even colonizing less hospitable areas at the edges of deserts and on the polar fringes.

The meat which humans obtained from hunting provided protein which did not require the long processing needed to digest raw vegetables and fruits. The use of fire – probably widespread by about 80,000 years ago – to cook further increased the human ability to gain energy efficiently. Despite these advances and the spread of humanity across the globe, early humans remained few in numbers, grouped insto small bands and possessing technology whose advances were measured in many thousands of years.

THE ANCIENT WORLD
12,500 BCE–1000 BCE

As human societies developed, so did their interaction with the natural environment. Agriculture, and the food surplus it produced, allowed great civilizations to emerge alongside the world's most fertile river valleys. Animals were domesticated for agriculture, used for food and transport. Humans established systems of belief to explain what otherwise could seem a violent and mysterious environment.

The Birth of Agriculture

Humanity's long apprenticeship in the hunter-gatherer lifestyle began to change at the end of the last Ice Age. The first stage of this new Neolithic period was the harvesting, grinding and storing of wild grains for food. These wild grains were very plentiful in many areas, notably in warm, fertile river valleys, such as the Nile and Niger valleys in Africa, and in the Middle East,

Right: The fertile Nile Valley was the perfect location for the birth of agriculture

12,500 BCE	4000 BCE	2500 BCE
		2575–2134 BCE Old Kingdom (Egypt)
12,500–4000 BCE early Peruvian civilization		**2334–2154 BCE** Akkadian Empire
		2600–1100 BCE Minoan Civilization

where they provided a useful supplemental food source. The transition to cultivating them deliberately, and so to the beginning of agriculture, was a slow one. Large-seeded grains such as emmet and einkorn, early forms of wheat, were domesticated by about 9000 BCE in northern Syria, and there is evidence of them in Jericho in Palestine by 8000 BCE. By about 7000 BCE, farming, as opposed to hunter-gathering, had become the leading form of subsistence in South-west Asia. Agriculture developed in other areas, notably northern China by about 7000 BCE and Central America by 5000 BCE.

In a classic instance of human adaptability, particular crops were developed in different areas. Wheat and barley were domesticated and cultivated in the Middle East, and spread from there, including into Egypt by 5000 BCE; while millet was domesticated in northern China; rice in the

Above: The domestication of crops and animals allowed the growth of more complex societies and it was reflected in artwork, as seen in this 11th century BCE painting from an Egyptian tomb in Luxor

2000 BCE	1500 BCE	1000 BCE	400 BCE

2040–1640 BCE Middle Kingdom (Egypt)

1550–1070 BCE New Kingdom (Egypt)

1600–1178 BCE Hittite Empire

1600–1046 BCE Shang China

2500–1500 BCE Harappan Culture

1500–1300 BCE Mittani Empire

1250–400 BCE Olmec Civilization

1500–600 BCE Vedic India

1800–539 BCE Babylonian Empire

2000–850 BCE Chavin culture

1600–1100 BCE Mycenaean Civilization

950–609 BCE Assyrian Empire

Yangtze Delta and the Yellow River valley; maize, potatoes, manioc, chili pepper, squash and beans in South America; maize, yuccas and yams in Central America; millet, sorghum and yams in Africa; and taro in New Guinea. Responses to the requirements of moisture, drainage, temperature range and soil acidity showed the skill and resourcefulness of humans. Knowledge spread within social groups, both kinship groups and more widely, and crops spread across vast regions; beans from Central America reached into the Mississippi Valley and the American South-West.

Crop domestication provided important advantages in cultivation and storage. While the wild einkorn strain had brittle stalks, making it hard to harvest, wheat – its domesticated counterpart – had larger seeds and a tougher stalk. As early farmers selected more productive strains of cereal crops, the yield became far greater and more predictable,

Below: During the Neolithic period, fixed settlements developed, as in the Ness of Brodgar in Orkney

THE RISE OF RITUAL

The religious practices of pre-literate societies are obscure, but astronomical knowledge clearly played a major role. For example, the midsummer sun rises along the axis of the Neolithic stone circle at Stonehenge. Ritual centres would have required at least hundreds of thousands of man-hours to construct, and are evidence of large-scale communal activity and organization. Such centres can be found in many parts of the world, for example on the Andean coast of South America from about 2600 BCE.

Above: Stonehenge required immense labour and reflected the increasing importance of ritual in society

compared to that from wild strains.

This greater yield, and the development of agricultural tools, encouraged the clearing of forest, a process which can be detected in the archaeological record by a drop in surviving tree pollen.

The spread of agriculture promoted the development of other new skills. Apart from those required for cultivation and harvesting, expertise was needed for grinding grain into flour, and then for providing storage in order to prevent loss to weather and animals. Stone querns became important for grinding and pottery containers for storage and cooking were widespread by 7000 BCE.

The Neolithic period also saw the beginning of fixed settlements as human populations increased and cultivation required extended periods of habitation in a single spot. These were not simple dwellings and often show considerable sophistication. During the Neolithic period in Europe (*c*.4000–*c*.2000 BCE), 'causewayed' camps – a form of earthwork enclosure – ritual monuments and burial chambers were constructed. At the Ness of Brodgar in Orkney, an impressive Neolithic site, the large buildings in the settlement from about 3100 BCE were enclosed by a massive stone wall.

The population growth which agriculture allowed had other consequences. The farming lifestyle was less healthy, and the nutritional intake of early farmers may actually have been lower than that of their hunter-gatherer predecessors, while new diseases emerged in the more crowded and less sanitary conditions of agricultural settlements. However, agriculture also allowed the creation of a food surplus, which in turn provided opportunities for the growth of specialist elites, including craftsmen, warriors, priest and aristocrats. Human society was becoming more differentiated.

Domesticating Animals

Alongside the domestication of crops, a similar process took place as humans domesticated animals. The key drive was to supplement the food that was obtained from hunting and gathering, but animals could serve a variety of other purposes. The physical environment played a crucial role, but so too did the existing distribution of animals and the changing nature of humans themselves. A human mutation in about 5500 BCE ended lactose intolerance and ensured that drinking milk became common in some areas (although far from universal, as lactose intolerance remains an issue in the Far East). Milk was an important source of nutrition and the ability to drink milk greatly increased the value of cattle, sheep and goats, providing a major addition to the use conferred by their meat. The hides and wool of domesticated animals also became valuable as sources of clothes and footwear.

Human development depended in large part on the exploitation of other animals, not only as prey

Below: This painting from the Egyptian tomb of Nebamun, *c.* 1350 BCE reflects the importance of domesticated cattle in ancient society

Above: Ploughing began in India from 2800 BCE, as evidence from Kalibangan in the Indus Valley indicates

but also as allies or rather servants in a mutually-beneficial partnership. This was particularly true of dogs – descended from trained wolves – which were used not as pets, but for guarding and hunting. More commonly, domesticated animals provided crucial additions of calorific power, notably in providing the energy necessary to carry goods and draw ploughs. Animals were effort-multipliers. The spread of the plough, replacing hand-held digging sticks, and hoes, in turn helped increase crop yields.

Cattle appeared to have been successfully domesticated in the Middle East around 8500 BCE and in North Africa in about 6500 BCE, while goats, hardier beasts and therefore useful across a greater range of environments, were the key animals in the Middle East by about 7000 BCE. The pig, another sturdy animal, occupied a similar niche in China by the same date. Although diseases, such as influenza and tuberculosis, jumped from animals to humans, selective breeding enhanced useful traits in a process that has continued to the present. Cattle came to be domesticated all over Eurasia, where sheep, goats and pigs were also widespread; in the Andes in South America the principal domesticated animals were alpaca, guinea pigs and llamas; in North America, dogs, honey bees and turkeys; in South-east Asia, banteng (a type of cattle); in the Himalayas, yaks; and in Central Asia, Bactrian camels.

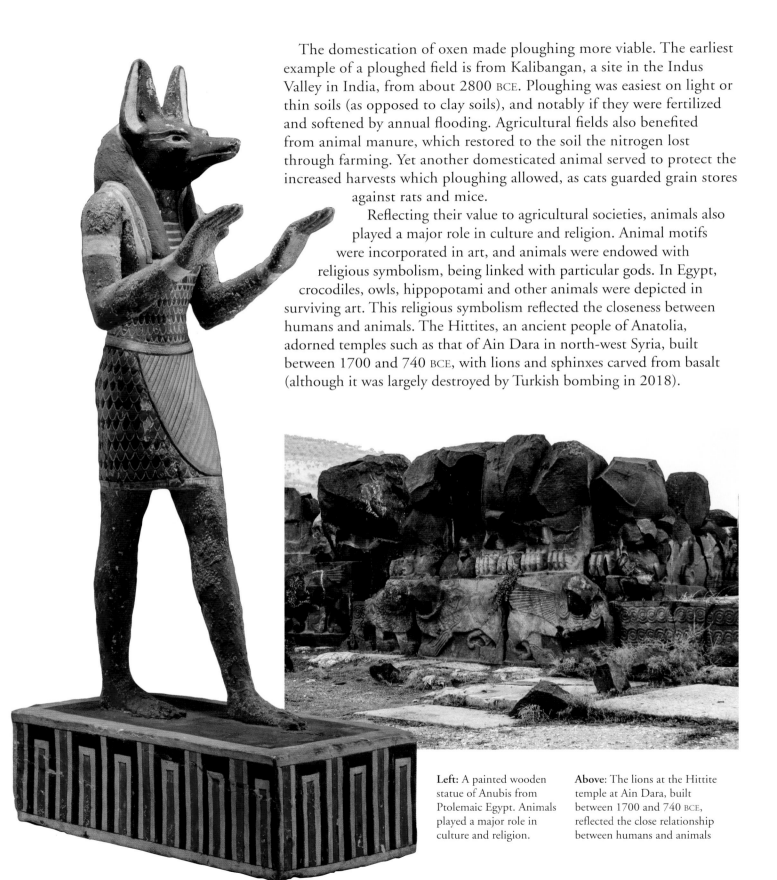

The domestication of oxen made ploughing more viable. The earliest example of a ploughed field is from Kalibangan, a site in the Indus Valley in India, from about 2800 BCE. Ploughing was easiest on light or thin soils (as opposed to clay soils), and notably if they were fertilized and softened by annual flooding. Agricultural fields also benefited from animal manure, which restored to the soil the nitrogen lost through farming. Yet another domesticated animal served to protect the increased harvests which ploughing allowed, as cats guarded grain stores against rats and mice.

Reflecting their value to agricultural societies, animals also played a major role in culture and religion. Animal motifs were incorporated in art, and animals were endowed with religious symbolism, being linked with particular gods. In Egypt, crocodiles, owls, hippopotami and other animals were depicted in surviving art. This religious symbolism reflected the closeness between humans and animals. The Hittites, an ancient people of Anatolia, adorned temples such as that of Ain Dara in north-west Syria, built between 1700 and 740 BCE, with lions and sphinxes carved from basalt (although it was largely destroyed by Turkish bombing in 2018).

Left: A painted wooden statue of Anubis from Ptolemaic Egypt. Animals played a major role in culture and religion.

Above: The lions at the Hittite temple at Ain Dara, built between 1700 and 740 BCE, reflected the close relationship between humans and animals

How we travelled – The Horse

Horses were first domesticated as early as 4000 BCE in southern Russia, at about the same time oxen, castrated male cattle, began to be employed as draught animals in Europe and the Middle East. Horses proved more flexible than oxen, being used both as beasts of burden to pull carts, ploughs and carriages, but also as animals which could provide speed. They could be used to carry men – important for sending messages – a crucial advantage in both governance and warfare.

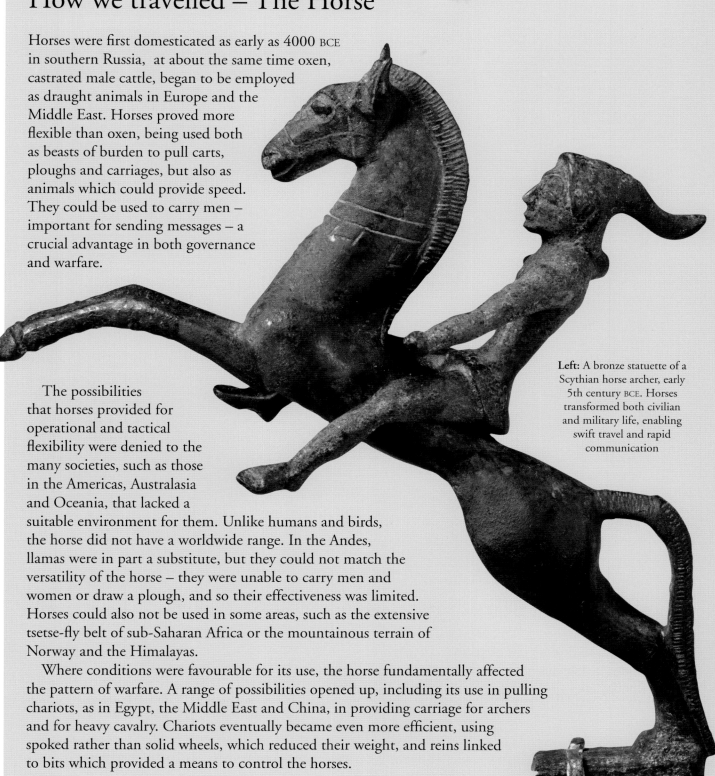

Left: A bronze statuette of a Scythian horse archer, early 5th century BCE. Horses transformed both civilian and military life, enabling swift travel and rapid communication

The possibilities that horses provided for operational and tactical flexibility were denied to the many societies, such as those in the Americas, Australasia and Oceania, that lacked a suitable environment for them. Unlike humans and birds, the horse did not have a worldwide range. In the Andes, llamas were in part a substitute, but they could not match the versatility of the horse – they were unable to carry men and women or draw a plough, and so their effectiveness was limited. Horses could also not be used in some areas, such as the extensive tsetse-fly belt of sub-Saharan Africa or the mountainous terrain of Norway and the Himalayas.

Where conditions were favourable for its use, the horse fundamentally affected the pattern of warfare. A range of possibilities opened up, including its use in pulling chariots, as in Egypt, the Middle East and China, in providing carriage for archers and for heavy cavalry. Chariots eventually became even more efficient, using spoked rather than solid wheels, which reduced their weight, and reins linked to bits which provided a means to control the horses.

A key invention in increasing the horse's usefulness was the stirrup, originally developed in Central Asia. It is possible that the Scythians used leather loops in the fourth century BCE, although these may simply have been to help in mounting horses. The use of rigid metal stirrups offered a better fighting platform, provided stability in motion, helping both in shock action and in making firing or throwing projectiles from horseback easier. The earliest Chinese figurine which depicts two stirrups probably dates from about 322.

Aside from stirrups and saddles, cavalry benefited from the adoption of more effective edged weapons and from heavy armour. This ensured that shock, mobility and firepower could all be exploited. Horses remained a key enabler of human effectiveness until the use and spread in the 19th century of new technologies such as locomotive steam power and the internal combustion engine largely superseded them.

Above: Chariots, and later mounted soldiers, were a devastating new weapon of warfare. This relief shows the war chariot of the pharaoh Ramesses II, whose reign represented a period of major territorial expansion.

The Origins of Fortification

At the most basic of levels, humans always had to protect themselves against the claws and teeth of predators. Humans, though, behaved differently from animals. The human need for protection often instead led to a kind of 'permanent' rest or 'shelter'.

In this context, many of the earliest 'fortifications' were simply natural features that provided shelter or enhanced strength. Caves, ridges, thickets of vegetation and marshlands were all natural fortifications in which men on foot could protect themselves from more mobile opponents. Caves provided both shelter from the weather and protected their residents against outflanking. In Gibraltar, the same cave systems were used by successive human species, both Neanderthals and early *Homo sapiens*. In Africa, thorn bushes long acted as palisades.

In flat regions, artificial fortifications were developed where natural features were lacking or inadequate.

Natural fortifications were eventually enhanced by constructing barricades of stones and earth. Fire was used to deter animals and provide light for fighting. Wooden palisades were created to both protect and control domestic animals. In the absence of wood, stone or even earth could be used. As well as protecting against animal predators – particularly wolves, bears, tigers and lions – fortifications had to guard against other human bands, who sought to seize livestock and the land to raise them on. Livestock proved much easier to protect by impounding it in a small shelter or fortress, than large fields of crops. However, the development of the granary or silo, a large building in which to store the product of the fields, created a kind of fortress for agricultural products, which both offered protection against pests and weather, and provided a site to defend against raiders.

Fortifications of a more sophisticated type followed the development of states around 4000 BCE. States clashed over the need to protect or acquire resources which led to large-scale conflict and encouraged the walling of settlements. Yet the growth of agriculture, and the social and state developments that came with it, in turn allowed the accumulation of surplus resources and its allocation to large-scale fortification and the establishment of armies.

Right: Caves were natural fortifications that protected men and women from both the elements and predators

Cities of God

The appearance of a warrior class was just one aspect of the specialization that the surpluses made possible by the shift to crop cultivation allowed; lifestyles became more varied, as people had time to think and to create new things. As agriculture developed, settlements grew larger, from villages to early towns such as Jericho in Palestine and Çatal Höyük in Turkey, and then into cities. This urban development rested on agrarian systems that were able to support substantial populations, found first in fertile river valleys of Mesopotamia and elsewhere (see pages 35–41). These societies were dependent on the flow of the rivers – a flow easily explained in religious terms as reflecting divine favour.

Religion was a key element in the urban societies which developed from around 4000 BCE. The observance of public rituals became significant in establishing political identity and cementing the power of the city's ruling class. The sacred enclosure of a raised, mud-brick, ziggurat temple complex was an important feature of cities in Mesopotamia, where the earliest urban culture arose. The priests of the temples which were built in the cities deployed information, both divine and human: divination enabled them to understand what the gods wanted. They

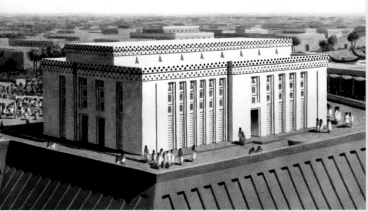

Above: This reconstruction shows the ancient city of Uruk in Sumeria, founded *c.*5000 BCE. Its ziggurat temple complex was a symbol of the city's religious significance

provided a sacral base for the power of the ruling elite, administered much of the city's land and, possessed of literature and acting as the guardians of state archives, they could record production and store products.

Early cities each tended to have their own patron gods. In Mesopotamia, the city-state of Uruk developed in about 4500 BCE. The nearby holy city of Nippur was sacred to Enlil, the most revered deity in the Sumerian pantheon, with the city's first temple to the god built for the ruler of Ur in about 2100 BCE. In what is now Peru, large temple mounds appeared along the Pacific coastal river valleys, in places such as the Supe Valley, from *c.*2500 BCE.

THE BIRTH OF TRADE

The wealth of many early urban cities depended vitally on trade, and long-distance commercial networks grew by sea and land. These included Mediterranean ports, such as Byblos (Lebanon), founded in *c.*3100 BCE, and other Phoenician settlements including Beirut, Tyre, Sidon and, eventually, Carthage. Dilmun (Bahrain) and Ras al-Junayz (Oman) linked the Mediterranean world to Eastern maritime centres. There were also trading cities and colonies across the South Asian inland hinterland, such as Shortughai on the Oxus River in northern Afghanistan in about 2500 BCE.

Long-distance trade routes developed across even longer distances by sea in the first millennium BCE. In particular, trade linked China to India and the Middle East. Among the most valuable products traded were spices, which were transported from Indonesia as far as the Roman empire. Such high-value, low-bulk goods continued to be the easiest to trade until large, steam-powered ships were launched in the 19th century. By the third millenium BCE, the merchants' horizons were rapidly expanding.

'Cradles of Civilization'

I. ANCIENT EGYPT

The fertile soil of the Nile valley became the basis of one of the world's first civilizations. By about 3300 BCE, walled towns had begun to be built along the Nile in Egypt, with the earliest being Nekhen or Hierakonpolis, and Naqada. Struggles for domination between these cities led to the building of massive mud-brick walls. Finally, the country was unified in c.3100 BCE by Narmer, the ruler of Upper Egypt, who became the first pharaoh or ruler of Egypt. Regarded as a living god, he founded the mud-brick walled city of Memphis as his capital on the west bank of the Nile, south of the delta, not far from modern Cairo. Egypt consolidated and the united kingdom proved very durable, surviving in the shape of the successive Old (c.2575–c.2134 BCE), Middle (c.2040–c.1640 BCE) and New (c.1550–c.1070 BCE) kingdoms.

Among its greatest surviving legacies are the massive and imposing pyramids, built as royal burial places about 2700 BCE by thousands of workers.

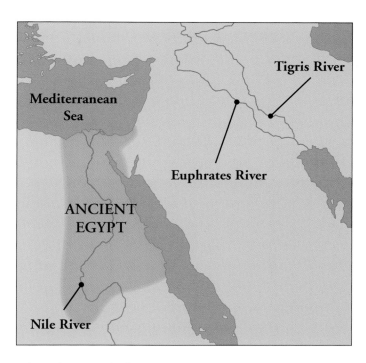

Below: The Pyramids of Giza are ancient Egypt's most striking creation

Above: The sarcophagus of Tutankhamun is representative of the elaborate lengths the ancient Egyptians went to send the pharaohs into the afterlife

There are also astonishing carvings, funerary remains (notably mummies) and hieroglyphics, the Ancient Egyptian writing system which adorns temple walls, tombs and papyrus manuscripts.

At the same time, helped by the use of bronze weapons (which became common from around 2000 BCE), compound bows and chariots, Egypt became a major power that long dominated its region. In the 15th century BCE, an expanding Egypt challenged the Mitanni empire of Mesopotamia for dominance of the region west of Mesopotamia proper; the climax being the dramatic, daring victory of Thutmosis III of Egypt over a Syrian coalition at Megiddo in *c.*1460 BCE. In the 13th century BCE, however, Egypt had to give ground before a revitalized and expanding Hittite kingdom (based in Turkey) that asserted its dominance in the Syrian region. There was another climax of sorts at Kadesh in about 1274 BCE, where Rameses II narrowly escaped defeat. Egyptian forces also conquered land in Nubia in modern Sudan, although Egypt's southern frontier proved a persistent source of conflict.

Egypt's power waned at the end of the New Kingdom and it was to be conquered by a number of invaders, including the Assyrians in 671–663 BCE, the Persians under Cambyses II in 525 BCE and Alexander the Great of Macedon, who captured it from the Persians in 332 BCE. After rule by the Ptolemies, a dynasty established by one of Alexander's generals, it became a province of Rome in 30 BCE, then lost its independence to a succession of imperial systems.

II. MESOPOTAMIA

Mesopotamia, where the first cities had arisen, also saw the founding of the first empire in about 2300 BCE by Sargon, who united the city-states of Sumer (southern Mesopotamia in modern Iraq) and conquered neighbouring regions of modern Syria, Turkey and Iran. This empire was in turn conquered by the neighbouring Gutians in about 2150 BCE, but their control was short-lived. An empire based on the Mesopotamian city of Ur followed. Protected by encircling walls and a fortress, Ur was linked to the Euphrates River by canals. It was destroyed by Elam (a state in south-west Iran) in about 2000 BCE. Later, a new empire arose under Hammurabi of Babylon, a key lawgiver (reigned 1790–1750 BCE). Babylon, like other leading Mesopotamian cities before it, became a centre for learning, culture and the law, before its destruction by a Hittite raid in 1596 BCE.

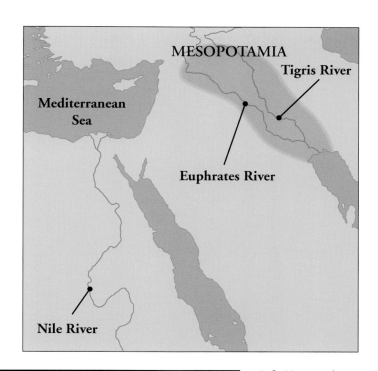

MESOPOTAMIA

Tigris River

Mediterranean Sea

Euphrates River

Nile River

Left: Hammurabi, who ruled c.1790–1750 BCE, provided a code of laws with which people were was expected to comply

Other civilizations followed in Mesopotamia. The neo-Assyrian empire, founded further north in modern Iraq in 950 BCE, and greatly strengthened under Assurnasirpal II (r. 883–859 BCE), created the first empire to span from the Persian Gulf to the Nile. The first people to make systematic use of iron in military technology, the Assyrians were formidable warriors and experts in siege-craft. They also were the first to make real use of cavalry. Their gods were warlike beings, and the Assyrians worked hard to spread the domain and worship of their chief deity, Ashur. Their terroristic style of rule, which involved mass killings, torture and deportation ultimately failed because it bred hatred and fostered rebellions. The debilitating attempt to take and hold Egypt, a rebellion by the Babylonians and the rise of the neighbouring Medes, who aligned with Babylon to destroy the Assyrian capital, Nineveh, in 612 BCE, were responsible for the rapid downfall of Assyria.

Above: The Babylonian map of the world from the 6th century BCE represents the world as a disc with a ring-shaped river surrounding it

III. THE INDUS VALLEY

The development of urban civilizations in the fertile Indus Valley, in modern Pakistan and north-west India, produced the Harappan culture (*c*.3300–*c*.1500 BCE) which spread east and south. In the Indus Valley, walled settlements were followed, in *c*.2500 BCE, by major cities, notably Harappa, Mohenjo-Daro and Kalibangan. Built over 148 acres (60 hectares), the latter had a population of perhaps 50,000. Its urban infrastructure included a sophisticated sewage system which was necessary to limit deaths from disease, a constant problem with ancient urban life, which led to many cities depending on continual immigration from the countryside.

From *c*.1500 BCE, the Vedic Aryans spread over much of northern India, a development which may be linked to the decline of the Indus civilization, though environmental factors also played a key role in its demise. By the early first millennium BCE, fortified settlements reappeared in the Punjab. India also experienced the spread of iron technology from *c*.1000 BCE and religious changes, with the emergence of Hinduism and Buddhism about four hundred years later.

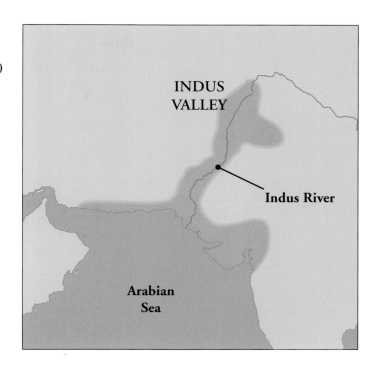

Below: Mohenjo-Daro, built *c*.2500 BCE, was one of the largest settlements of the Indus Valley

IV. SHANG CHINA

The Yellow River was the basis for the Shang, the first Chinese state supported by archaeological evidence. The loess soils of the Yangtze river provided fertility, and made it possible to support cities, as at Erlitou,

founded in about 1900 BCE, and Yin (modern Anyang), as well as a sophisticated culture, including writing, which mostly takes the form of divinations inscribed on oracle bones. These indicate the importance of religion to the Shang culture. Based on agriculture, this Bronze Age civilization practised human sacrifice, invented musical instruments and took part in astronomical observations.

Left: Oracle bones were an early form of divination in Shang China

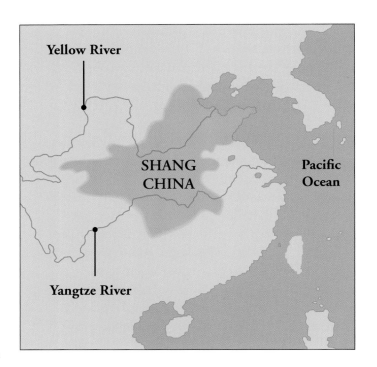

V. PERUVIAN COAST

Just as in Eurasia, the Americas saw the development of complex cultures. In South America, the Peruvian coastline was especially important. It brought together a range of domesticated crops, notably maize, as well as the rich seafood resources of the Pacific. At Huaca Prieta in northern Peru, which was occupied from about 14,500 to about 4,000 years ago, seafood was crucial, while corncobs that may date from as early as 4700 BCE were discovered in 2012, and evidence of avocados dates back possibly 15,000 years. Cotton fabric dyed with an indigo dye from 6,000 years ago was discovered there in 2016. There were also basket weavings and decorated gourds. Large temple mounds appeared on the coast of central Peru from about 2500 BCE, many built by the Chavín culture which flourished 900–200 BCE and the Moche culture that followed in c.1–c.600.

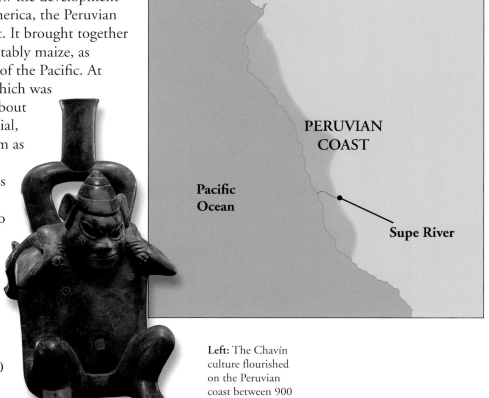

Left: The Chavín culture flourished on the Peruvian coast between 900 and 200 BCE

VI. MESOAMERICA

The earliest civilization in Mesoamerica, that of the Olmecs, developed in the coast of the Gulf of Mexico in about 1150 BCE and lasted until the end of the first millennium BCE . Major traders, the Olmecs built substantial settlements, and produced stone sculptures and ceramics, as well as developing a calendar and a writing system. As they began to decline from about 400 BCE , other civilizations developed and expanded, including the Maya, who were already significant by 1000 BCE , as well as the Zapotecs of the Oaxaca Valley.

Right: The Olmecs were the first major civilization in Mesoamerica, emerging *c.*1150 BCE

THE ADENA CULTURE

In North America, although there are human sites from c.15,000 BCE and pottery from c.2500 BCE, cultures leaving burial mounds and extensive earthworks did not emerge until later than in Central America. Known as the 'Woodland Period', there are few significant remains from this era for archaeologists to pore over.

In c.700 BCE – c.400 BCE the Adena culture was found in the upper Ohio Valley from which it spread to north-eastern parts of the modern United States. The region is littered with complex earthworks which may have been used as gathering places or as burial sites. It was to be followed from c.100 CE by the Hopewell culture in the Mississippi valley. It is distinctive for animal sculptures.

Right: The Hopewell culture of the Mississippi Valley is renowned for its distinctive animal sculptures

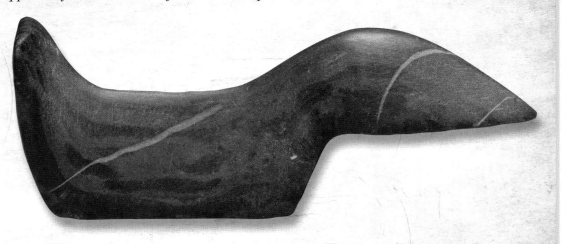

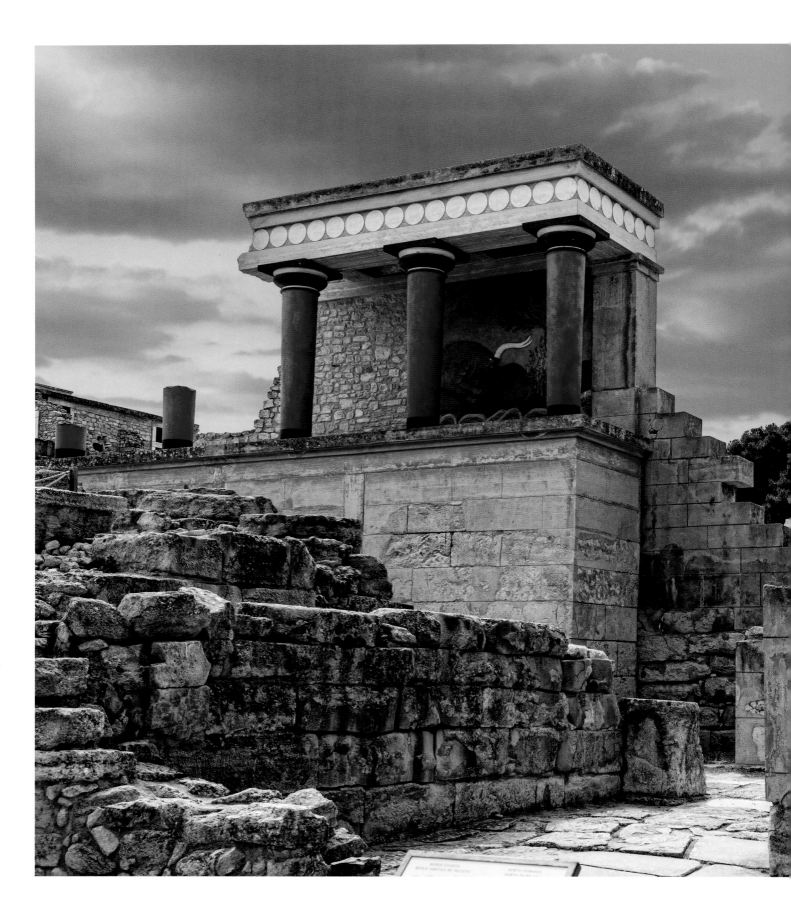

Outside the Cradles

BRONZE AGE CIVILIZATIONS OF THE MEDITERRANEAN

Civilization soon spread to (or emerged separately in) a number of centres outside the main cradles. In Greece a series of societies emerged in the Bronze Age that traded widely in the Mediterranean, notably the Minoan civilization of Crete and the Mycenaean culture of mainland Greece. Palace-based societies emerged on Crete in about 2000 BCE, but were destroyed, possibly by a volcanic explosion, in about 1450 BCE. The extensive ruins of the palace at Knossos are a testimony to the sophistication of this society. Mycenae, which dominated the main road between the two great ports of Argos and Corinth, had already become prominent in about 1550 BCE, and, as Minoan culture went into decline, it then took over control of Crete.

Left: The Palace of Knossos reflected the sophistication of Minoan Crete

Above: The Mask of Agamemnon, found at the citadel of Mycenae, reflected the wealth and sophistication of the ancient civilization of the same name.

Mycenaean Greece is the basis for the story of the *Iliad*, the account by Homer of an expedition by the Greeks to besiege the city of Troy near the Dardanelles (in modern Turkey). This epic is important as a myth in which the gods played a role, but humans, such as Achilles, also had an independent part. Homer continued the story with the *Odyssey*, an account of the later travels of the royal Greek warrior Odysseus. The strange beasts encountered by Odysseus, such as the one-eyed giant Polyphemus and the enchantress Circe, underline the extent to which the Greeks, like other ancient peoples, populated their cosmos with dangerous creatures. Other major examples included harpies and the Sphinx, the author of a deadly riddle which was solved by Oedipus.

Mycenaean civilization collapsed in about 1100 BCE, possibly as a result of invasion. This formed part of a more widespread collapse that affected the eastern Mediterranean, which included the fall of Troy, of the Hittite empire and of the Syrian and Canaanite cities. The collapse was triggered partly by obscure invaders, known sometimes as the Sea Peoples, and by internal rebellions, and the resulting crises in international trade and political control. It may also be linked to environmental crises, and the effect of the entry of iron weapons into the region, which marked the end of the Bronze Age and the beginning of the Iron Age around 1100 BCE.

Below: Homer's tale of the siege of Troy in the *Iliad* blurred the boundaries between myth and history, as do modern illustrations

DISCOVERING TIME

Ideas of space and time depended on the relationships between the human and the sacred that helped explain the linked significance of astronomical observation, astronomical record-keeping and calendrical systems.

The development of calendars is somewhat obscure but was closely linked to religious practice and institutions, and notably to the need to predict days of ritual significance. Astronomical observation and record-keeping both played a major role and, as a result, numeracy and writing were significant. Lunar and solar systems were particularly important. Calendars spread, both within imperial systems and between them. The Julian calendar of Rome proved particularly important as did that of China.

The separation of past from present did not have particular weight for societies that put an emphasis on cyclical theories of time, which were common among peoples who focused on the rhythms of the seasons which dominated agriculture, fishing and forestry. The interplay of winds and currents, the melting of the ice and snow, and the beginning of the growth of grass (for draught animals) all set the terms for the timing of long-range trade by sea and land.

Societies that looked to the past for example and validation focused instead on the sacred spaces, the works of divine providence, prophets, priests, sages, soothsayers, oracles, and sibyls, or diabolical forces and their earthly intermediaries such as witches.

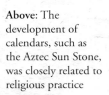

Above: The development of calendars, such as the Aztec Sun Stone, was closely related to religious practice

'NON-ARCHITECTURAL' CIVILIZATIONS

In thinking of early civilizations, there is a strong tendency to consider those that left major structures and for which state forms are readily apparent. This preference can lead to an underplaying of civilizations that did not have stone readily available and, in particular, were located in forested regions. Wood rots, notably in the tropics, but valuable evidence survives in the form of mud or adobe structures for early civilizations in areas such as the forests of Central and South America. The archaeological holdings in the Museo Nacional de Costa Rica in San Juan, amply demonstrate the significance of the cultures in the region. So also in South America, where sites containing early ceramics in the heavily forested lower valleys of the Amazon and Orinoco rivers indicate considerable development. As with the earlier diffusion of *Homo sapiens*, it is clear that the spread of 'civilization' was more complex than a simple model might suggest. Much work remains to be done on such civilizations.

Organized Religion

Religion developed in all cultures across the world, as peoples sought to make sense of their position in the world and to improve it through divine intervention. Many ancient cults were linked to burials and to the memorialization of the dead, as in the chambered tombs in Neolithic Orkney, and with calendrical systems that made it possible to locate dates of ritual significance.

Their rites often encouraged gift-giving to the gods, which promoted a sense of civic unity, as did rituals such as the Phoenicians' child-sacrifice cult of Baal Hammon. The Greeks also had oracles, like those at Delphi in Greece and Cumae in Italy, which provided a way to understand and propitiate divine intentions.

As civilization grew more complex, religions also diversified, with the appearance of new gods – often by absorbing those of conquered peoples – and of new belief systems and religious practices. By the 5th century BCE, the religious landscape included Buddhism in South Asia, Taoism in China, the Greek and Egyptian cults and Judaism in the Mediterranean, and ceremonial-centred religions in American cultures, such as the Chavín in South America. Many religions of the period, such as the Etruscan, Hittite and Phoenician religions do not survive today and were not well documented. Our knowledge of them is limited and their beliefs remain obscure.

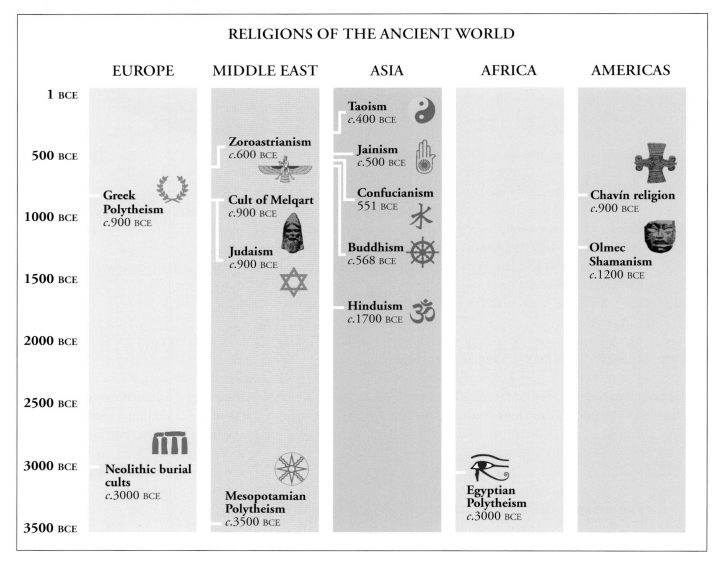

RELIGIONS OF THE ANCIENT WORLD

	EUROPE	MIDDLE EAST	ASIA	AFRICA	AMERICAS
1 BCE			Taoism *c.*400 BCE		
500 BCE		Zoroastrianism *c.*600 BCE	Jainism *c.*500 BCE		
1000 BCE	Greek Polytheism *c.*900 BCE	Cult of Melqart *c.*900 BCE	Confucianism 551 BCE		Chavín religion *c.*900 BCE
		Judaism *c.*900 BCE	Buddhism *c.*568 BCE		Olmec Shamanism *c.*1200 BCE
1500 BCE			Hinduism *c.*1700 BCE		
2000 BCE					
2500 BCE					
3000 BCE	Neolithic burial cults *c.*3000 BCE			Egyptian Polytheism *c.*3000 BCE	
3500 BCE		Mesopotamian Polytheism *c.*3500 BCE			

Goods that changed the world – Metals

Right: Bronze was an alloy of copper that was more suitable for weapons, and was widely embraced from 2200 BCE onwards

For millions of years, humans' prime tool-making material remained stone. In 7000–5000 BCE this changed. In both West Asia and south-east Europe it was discovered that heating could isolate metals from ore-bearing deposits. Soft metals, which melt at low temperatures, were the first to be used, and so copper, rather than iron, became the first basis of metal technology. At first, there was a considerable overlap of flint tools (including weapons) with copper, then copper with bronze, and then bronze with iron. Ötzi, a corpse from c.3100 BCE found frozen in the ice of the European Alps, had a copper axe, a flint knife and flint-tipped arrows with bow, and he was wounded, if not killed, by similar weapons. Metals offered greater potency than stone, not least because they provided stronger penetration and weight, while their reduced bulk aided ease of use and mobility. Metal weapons generally favoured more complex societies as metalworking required the gathering of a wider range of resources. Bronze demanded copper and usually long-distance trade for tin. The Copper Age was followed, from c.3300–800 BCE, by that of bronze, a harder alloy of copper that was more effective in tools and weapons as it could hold its shape under greater pressure. Bronze in turn was supplanted by iron, whose smelting and forging spread from West Asia into Europe. The first iron working in sub-Saharan Africa dates from about 800 BCE, with the Nok Iron Age culture developing in Nigeria in the sixth-fifth centuries BCE. Iron offered many advantages. The use of iron hoes and nails brought a new flexibility to agriculture and construction. Iron made wagons more durable. It also helped create stronger, sturdier weapons, especially when carbon was added to produce steel. Blacksmiths became key figures in the local economy.

The Birth of Writing

As civilizations became more complex, they needed a means to keep records, codify regulations or to pass on religious traditions or other learning. The invention of writing answered this need, when it appeared in various forms, with representation of language through graphic means developing differently across the world, with particular contrasts between hieroglyphs (picture writing), as used in Egypt and in Chinese pictographic writing, and alphabetic writing. Full writing systems first appeared in Sumer (Mesopotamia) and Egypt around 3100 BCE, and in China around 1200 BCE.

Currency

As ancient cultures came to depend on trade, they needed systems for representing and storing value. Tokens were created from valuable metals, such as gold and silver, and when validated by public authorities as of constant weight and certain value they became coins. The Greeks of Asia Minor created the first coinage in the 7th century BCE. This confidence provided by rulers' validation of coinage was important for the ease of both trade and taxation, and notably so as trade networks ranged more widely and covered more goods. To levy taxes in food was not helpful if the taxation raised needed to be used at a distance. The movement of coins removed this obstacle. All these currencies benefited from the increasing sophistication of mathematical systems. Most of the latter employed base 10 as the basis for units, but some (such as the Maya of Mesoamerica) used base 20 and others (like the Babylonians) base 60.

Left: The use of metal coins greatly facilitated trade and replaced the earlier barter economy

CLASSICAL CIVILIZATIONS
1000 BCE–500 CE

Imperial states became more wide-ranging in the mid-first millennium BCE, in part as a result of the use of iron technology for both agriculture and weapons manufacture, which enabled successful conquests. Other important factors included more sophisticated organizational methods, especially coins, writing, and organized religion, and the adoption by governments of useful concepts, such as Confucian teaching in China. The interaction of these factors varied, which helped create the diversity of systems, but their confluence helped make each more potent.

The Rise of Empires and the Development of Politics

Zhou China (1046–246 BCE) and the Persian empire created by Cyrus the Great in 525 BCE were some of the first great imperial states, and were followed in 500–250 BCE by several others, including the empire of Alexander the Great of Macedon, the Mauryan empire in India, the Qin empire in China, and that of Carthage in the western Mediterranean. In turn, the defeat of Carthage and of the empires that succeeded that of Alexander was crucial to the rise of Rome, an empire that for a long time was ruled not by a dynasty of monarchs, but by a republican system.

Empires relied on co-operation as well as conquest. This co-operation was economic and cultural, as well as political and military. As well as co-operation with their own subjects, empire had to work with outsiders, 'barbarians' from beyond the future, where the careful politics of mutual advantage and the ability to create a sense of identification was more useful than bureaucratic organization. Chinese relations with nomadic and semi-nomadic peoples of the steppe combined military force with a variety of diplomatic procedures, including *jimi* or 'loose rein,' which permitted the incorporation of 'barbarian' groups into the Chinese realm. Their chiefs were given Chinese administrative titles, but continued to rule over their own people in traditional fashion.

Right: The 'Gate of All Nations' at Persepolis, the capital of the Persian Empire from *c.*550 to 330 BCE when it was destroyed by Alexander the Great

The Birth of the Chinese State

During the Warring States period in China (475–221 BCE), the Zhou dynasty, originally a frontier power to the west that had overthrown the Shang dynasty (*c.*1600–*c.*1050 BCE), finally succumbed, to the Qin (221–206 BCE), the most successful of a number of regional warlords. Qin undertook a major series of conquests, which ended with its ruler Zheng taking on a new title, as the first Emperor (when he became known as Qin Shi Huangdi). His success rested on large armies that were made possible by the extension of state authority over rural populations. Zheng was able to project his power south of the Yangtze River and to the South China Sea; in contrast the Shang and the Zhou had only loose hegemonies limited to north China. Near his tomb in Xi'an, thousands of large-size terracotta soldiers were buried.

Zheng's death was followed by conflict in the ruling family, military disaffection and popular uprisings. The eventual civil war was won by Gaozu, who took the title King of Han. The Han dynasty (206 BCE–220 CE) extended Chinese power even further, including into Korea, Vietnam and Central Asia, where in 101 BCE an army forced Ferghana to acknowledge Chinese overlordship, and another was sent beyond the Pamir Mountains in 97 CE. This westward expansion was linked to the opening up of the Silk Roads, a series of trading routes into Central Asia. Further south, Yunnan was made a tributary state in 109 BCE.

The Han expanded and consolidated the Chinese position in the south, securing a southward migration of settlers that was of great importance to the reshaping of China as a larger society. Although non-Han Chinese groups such as the Miao remained in the south, they became minority peoples of no political consequence, although they engaged in periodic rebellions into the 19th century.

Right: Zheng, ruler of the princely state of Qin, conquered his rivals and established control over all China by 206 BCE, when he took the title of emperor and the name Qin Shi Huang

China Battles the Steppe People, 210 BCE–600 CE

On their northern flank, the Han faced challenges by the formidable Xiongnu confederation of nomadic tribes, which became unified in 210–209 BCE, and was the first empire to control all of Mongolia. Large-scale Han offensives against them in 201–200 BCE and 133–87 BCE failed. A few victories could not compensate for heavy costs and it proved impossible to destroy the coherence of the Xiongnu. Instead, the Han relied for their security on paying off the nomads.

Instability in China ultimately led to the replacement of the Han dynasty by the Age of the Three Kingdoms and then by the Western Jin dynasty whose capital, Luoyang, was stormed by the Xiongnu in 311. The capital then moved to Nanjing.

By 500, Turkic-speaking peoples had overrun much of north China and established the Northern Wei dynasty (439–534). The success of the Wei owed much to winning support from other groups, including the Chinese who lived in their domains, and the adoption of Chinese administrative practices. Emperor Xiaowen (r. 471–99) created a hybrid regime in which the Northern Wei elite became sinicized, a conscious policy of conforming to Chinese practices which would be adopted as late as the Qing dynasty – of Manchurian origin – in the 17th century.

Many Wei, particularly soldiers, resisted this sinicization and in the resulting rebellion, the Northern Wei split, to be reunited by Yang Jian, a general, who founded the Sui dynasty (581–618).

THE RELIGIONS OF ASIA
Organized religion took many forms in Asia. A key characteristic was a linkage to particular political circumstances. Differences included whether rulers were worshipped, the extent of ancestor worship, the degree of monotheism, and the presence of animist beliefs. In China, ancestor worship was important, notably in Taoism. In Persia and in Israel, monotheistic religions (Zoroastrianism and Judaism) proved durable. Religions offered a sense of continuity, explanation and community including of the living and the dead.

Left: The Xiongnu confederation of Mongolian tribes were a serious threat to Han China

Africa in the Ancient World

The formation of states in Africa faced far more formidable obstacles than in China. Trade routes provided links within Africa, but the scale of the continent and the diversity of its environment led to varying levels of development in different parts of the continent. In sub-Saharan Africa, the migration south of Bantu-speakers from around 1000 BCE helped diffuse agriculture. Farming and the use of iron provided the Bantu with a major advantage over the hunter-gatherers of the area, such as the Khoisan peoples of the Orange River region. Their spread was a fundamental change in the human geography of the continent, one comparable to the movement of the Han Chinese in East Asia. It is an important reminder of the range of human movements before the great migrations of the last two centuries and that migration is a constant strand in human history. The movement of people in the Classical period was a continuation of the process of adaptation to the environment seen in the earlier movement of humans, although just as in those earlier migrations, it also led to the displacement of other human groups.

Below: The Khoisan hunter-gatherers of southern Africa gradually gave way to Bantu speakers, who brought agriculture and iron with them

To the north of the Bantu, on the fringes of the Sahara, there lived peoples about whom relatively little is known, such as Chadians and Nilotic peoples. More coherent states also developed in this region, such as those of the Berbers in North Africa. Imperial Rome conquered these states by the mid-1st century CE, which they called Numidia and Mauretania, and Egypt, part of an expansion which brought the whole southern shore of the Mediterranean under Roman control. Evidence of the breadth of this control is provided by the extensive archaeological remains which the Romans left, notably at Leptis Magna (Libya) and at Thysdrus (Tunisia).

There were also important states to the south of Egypt, both in the Nile Valley and in Eritrea and northern Ethiopia. Axum became a significant commercial force from 100 BCE to 600 CE, co-operating with Rome in trade along the Red Sea, just as the kingdom of Kush was important to trade along the Nile valley. Each of these trade routes supplied slaves to Rome. The stone stelae (monuments) built by the kings of Axum remain impressive. In time, Christianity and then, from the 7th century, Islam spread into northern Africa, producing new alignments and tensions.

North Africa had long been a conduit, both to the Sahara, and through it to the Sahel region to the south, and northwards across the Mediterranean, a link continued while the Roman and then the Byzantine (eastern Roman) empires occupied it. The eventual outcome of the religious warfare that accompanied the Islamic conquest of the 7th century left North Africa in Islamic hands and Southern Europe under Christian control, changing the Mediterranean from a route of cultural transmission into a barrier.

Above: The stelae, or stone pillars, of the kingdom of Axum in Eritrea, remained long after the state had fallen

Below: The Romans left impressive remains at Leptis Magna in Libya, an earlier city they greatly expanded in 193–211 CE

Empires of South-west Asia

The destruction of the Assyrian empire at the close of the 7th century BCE was followed by its replacement by a Babylonian empire, whose most powerful ruler was Nebuchadnezzar II (r. 605-652 BCE). This, in turn, was overthrown in 539 BCE by the far more wide-ranging empire of the Persian Achaemenids, founded by Cyrus the Great (r. 559–30 BCE). He united the kingdoms of the Medes with Persia, and went on to defeat the Lydians in Anatolia (547 BCE) and to conquer Babylon (539 BCE). Cyrus died on campaign in Central Asia against the nomadic Massagetae, but his successor, Cambyses II, conquered Egypt in 525 BCE. Under Darius I, the Great (r. 522–486), the Achaemenid empire expanded further, including the invasion of Scythia (513 BCE) and Macedonia (492 BCE).

The vast Persian empire was administratively sophisticated, although in the end its success depended on military strength.

Below: Babylon fell in dramatic fashion to the forces of Cyrus the Great as successive victories by the Persians created a new order in Mesopotamia

Right: The Battle of Salamis was a decisive naval encounter between the Greek and Persian fleets that helped prevent further Persian advances into Greece

THE BATTLE OF SALAMIS, 480 BCE

Faced by a much larger Persian fleet (about 800 ships to the Greek 300), the Greeks decided to fight the Persians in the narrows of Salamis, rather than in open water, a move which nullified the Persians' numerical advantage. The Persians found their ships too tightly packed, and their formation and momentum were also disrupted by a strong swell. The Greeks attacked when the Persians were clearly in difficulties, throwing their formation into confusion. The Persians retreated having lost over 200 ships; their opponents lost just 40 vessels.

It was knit together by a road network, which included the Royal Road from Sardis, near the Aegean, to Susa near the Persian Gulf, that helped unite the provinces into which it was divided. The Achaemenids also built a major palace complex at Persepolis (in modern central Iran).

The Persians used their conquests of Phoenicia and Egypt to build up a formidable navy, becoming a major force in the Aegean. Yet their attempts to conquer Greece in 490 and 480–479 BCE failed, ending in defeat at Marathon (490 BCE) and Salamis (480 BCE), battles that became crucial to the sense of special destiny of Athens, the leading Greek city-state. At Salamis, the Athenians' victory owed much to their use of the trireme, a particularly effective war galley.

The Persian empire succumbed to invasion by Alexander of Macedon, who invaded modern Turkey, which was part of the Achaemenid empire and heavily defeated larger Persian armies at Issus (333 BCE)

and Gaugamela (331 BCE). By the time of his early death in 323 BCE in Babylon, aged 32, Alexander had conquered an empire reaching to the River Indus and including Egypt as well as modern Turkmenistan. It is unclear what Alexander would have achieved had he lived longer. His attempt to conquer India had already failed: he had advanced through Afghanistan into the Indus Valley in 326 BCE, but had experienced firm resistance in both, while his troops had rebelled at the Hyphasis River against his plans to push further into northern India.

After Alexander's death, his generals established a number of rival kingdoms from his empire, including Macedon (ruled by the Antigonids), Egypt (the Ptolemies), and Syria, Iraq, Persia and southern Turkey (the Seleucids). This period of extensive Greek cultural and political influence is known as Hellenistic. While the Seleucid kingdom soon lost much of its territory, the rule of the Ptolemies

Left: Alexander the Great established an empire that stretched from Egypt to India

Below: After his conversion to Buddhism, Ashoka built stupas across the Indian subcontinent and established a firm foundation for the religion

IF ALEXANDER HAD TURNED WEST?

In his influential history of Rome, Livy (Titus Livius, c.59 BCE–17 CE) considered an early counterfactual: what would have happened had Alexander, the greatest conqueror known to Antiquity, turned west and invaded Italy. Livy felt able to reassure his Roman readers that the might of Rome would have proved invincible. He commented on the quality of Roman generalship, claimed that Alexander had become degenerate as a result of his absorption of Persian culture, and contrasted the achievements of one man with those of the Romans, a people who had fought for centuries.

in Egypt lasted until the conquest by Rome in 30 BCE. Independent Hellenistic kingdoms also developed, notably Bactria in what is now Central Asia. Hellenistic Greek culture diffused widely in Egypt, as well as in large parts of Asia, where it merged with Asiatic influences.

After the death of Alexander, the Mauryan empire (321–181 BCE) quickly came to dominate the Indian subcontinent. Chandragupta Maurya founded the empire after raising an army against the Nanda dynasty of the north-east in 322 BCE. Successful wars against the Seleucids (305–303 BCE) and Kalinga (262–260 BCE) followed. Ashoka, the young general responsible for the victory over Kalinga and grandson of Chandragupta, converted to Buddhism in c.260 BCE and attempted to rule in accordance with its principles. He built stupas across India and carved edicts inspired by Buddhist precepts into a series of rock pillars. His influence helped Buddhism to spread throughout India and into the surrounding areas of South-east Asia.

The Greek World

Compared to the empires such as those of the Assyrians or Persians, the Greeks (and after them the Romans) were initially minor powers, although they grew to become major influences on the development of Western civilization. Both the Greeks and the Romans had to see off external attacks, the Greeks defeating Persian attempts at conquest in 490 BCE and 480–479 BCE. The Greek city states survived through their use of citizen militia in the form of hoplites (heavy infantry) who fought in phalanx formation, providing a disciplined force which their opponents struggled to match.

Below: The ancient Greek city states relied on citizen militias and hoplites fighting in phalanx formation to protect against invasion

Subsequently, the powerful cities of Sparta and Athens formed leagues of cities, but were unable to convert these into durable empires. The autonomy of the divided Greek city-states fell victim in 338 BCE to a new imperial power, that of Macedon, led by Alexander the Great's father Philip II. Greece had, though, provided important models of political organization, such as the democracy of Athens, established by reforms in 508 BCE which gave power over important decisions to an assembly of the citizenry.

Not all Greeks were empowered to take part in the life of the city. In Sparta, long the leading adversary of Athens among the Greek city-states (and against whom the Athenians fought the bruising Peloponnesian War in 431 to 404 BCE, ending with defeat and the temporary dismantling of their democracy), a narrow military elite ruled. More generally, women had few political rights, and to an extent that they generally preferred to ignore, the Greeks also made much use of slavery, for example in mining. Near Athens, the great silver mines at Laurium contained approximately 35,000 slaves who worked in small tunnels underground, the cramped conditions forcing them to crawl and kneel.

Aristotle (384–322 BCE), one of the leading Greek philosophers, argued in his *Politics* that slavery was natural, like the use of horses. To Aristotle, the simple village was a community in which ox was the slave of the poor man, whereas the more advanced and benign Greek *polis* (or city-state) offered a place where public culture and virtue was possible in part because slavery allowed those higher in the social hierarchy the leisure to pursue it.

Above: Aristotle, one of the great philosophers, saw the Greek polis as the ideal location for the pursuit of virtue

GREEK THEATRE
Originating in religious festivals for the gods, the development of theatre was among the most important of the Greeks' cultural advances. Major playwrights included Aeschylus (c.525–c.456 BCE), the father of tragedy, whose works included the Oresteia *and* The Persians, *Euripides (c.480–c.406 BCE), whose plays included* Medea, Electra *and* The Trojan Women, *and Sophocles (c.497–c.406 BCE), who wrote* Antigone, Oedipus Rex *and* Electra. *These playwrights were remarkable in their ability to innovate, developing complex characterization that marks the beginning of Western drama.*

Rome

It was the Romans who would ultimately conquer the Greek city-states. Initially a small settlement in the lower Tiber valley, Rome was founded, according to legend, in 753 BCE by Romulus and Remus, descendants of Aeneas, a royal refugee from the fall of Troy. Archaeological evidence of a village on Rome's Palatine Hill by 850 BCE suggests that earlier settlements were present. Rome faced opposition to its expansion from neighbouring peoples such as the Latins and Etruscans. Its first rulers were kings, among them the Tarquins, who were Corinthian Greeks (and possibly also Etruscan) by origin, until the last was driven out by Latin nobles who created a republic in 509 BCE. As was the case with cities elsewhere in the ancient world, this republic was ruled in practice by an oligarchy. Tensions between this oligarchy and the plebeians, the wider citizenry, would bedevil the history of the Roman Republic.

Below: According to legend, Romulus and Remus were raised by wolves and founded the city of Rome in 753 BCE

Left: The Roman legionaries were a force to be reckoned with. Equipped with short swords, javelins and shields, their discipline and training enabled them to overcome opponents across the Mediterranean world

The Romans proved formidable warriors. Equipped with short, stabbing iron swords, heavy javelins and shields, the training and discipline of the main army formations, the legions, enabled them to march at a formidable rate and to deploy in a variety of planned formations, including the *testudo* (or tortoise, in which the soldiers used their shields to form a protective shell against missiles). The Roman army also possessed the means to conduct sieges, and to perform complex and effective manoeuvres on the battlefield, as well as to deploy and operate in a range of physical and military environments, in part by fort and road-building. They were adept at constructing marching camps every time they stopped. These generally occurred at 24-km (15-mile) intervals, the average daily rate of march expected of a legion. Many (such as Vienna) would eventually grow into towns and cities.

In the north of Italy, the Etruscans were the dominant force for nearly five centuries. It was not until 275 BCE that Rome unified the Italian peninsula after defeating Pyrrhus, the king of Epirus, in costly battles at Heraclea and Asculum. Incessant warfare helped ensure that Rome's culture, public memory, public spaces, religious cults, society and political system were intensely militaristic. Rome praised martial values and promoted and honoured politicians accordingly.

The Romans eventually triumphed in the three Punic Wars against Carthage, a maritime empire based near modern Tunis that ruled Sardinia, Sicily, parts of Spain and much of modern Tunisia. These were wide-ranging struggles that involved conflict in mainland Italy, Sicily, Spain and North Africa. In the First Punic War (264–241 BCE), which focused on Rome's struggle with Carthage for control of Sicily, the Romans won after a bitter conflict in which they had to learn how to operate as an effective naval power.

Subsequently Carthage and Rome came to compete over southern and eastern Spain. This rivalry, which touched off the Second Punic War (218–201 BCE), reflected Rome's increasing ambition. Hannibal (247–183 BCE), the key Carthaginian general, marched across southern France, crossed the Alps in 218 BCE and attacked the Romans in Italy.

That Hannibal brought his war elephants across the Alps helped posterity to see this as an epic struggle, although only one survived the crossing and it died soon after. Hannibal's arrival in Italy created an acute crisis for Rome. His highly-professional force was ably led and gained control of the dynamic of campaigning. Hannibal defeated major Roman armies at the River Trebia (218 BCE), Lake Trasimene (217 BCE), Cannae (216 BCE) and Herdonea (210 BCE).

In the event, Hannibal failed not because of defeat in battle in Italy, but through his inability to translate victory in battle into his intended outcome: the collapse of Rome and its territorial system. Hannibal's army was small and lacked a siege train, and Rome's allies stood firm. The Carthaginian system was brought down when the theatre of war moved to North Africa in 204 BCE, where Hannibal was defeated by Scipio Africanus at Zama in 202 BCE. Rome's victory left it dominant in the western Mediterranean.

Above: The Carthaginian general Hannibal marched his army across the Alps and inflicted great defeats on the Romans at the River Trebia, Lake Trasimene and Cannae before he was obliged to withdraw

How we travelled – Wheels and Roads

Left: The development of the wheel and the spread of roads allowed faster movement of both troops and trade goods

Originally developed in about 3500 BCE in Mesopotamia in the form of potters' wheels, the wheel was used for wheeled vehicles from about 3200 BCE. In China, the wheel was certainly present from about 1200 BCE. It was more efficient to move goods in a horse or oxen-drawn cart, with its four wheels, rather than on pack animals and so larger loads could be moved and fewer draught animals were required. This efficiency also reduced the amount of forage needed for pack animals.

Wheeled travel depended on surfaces. The Romans provided an impressive system of roads, such as the Appian Way in Italy and Watling Street in Britain, that helped link their empire, complementing maritime links such as the route from Alexandria to Ostia, the port for Rome. Built to a regulation pattern, and designed to resist freezing and the rain, the major roads were well paved and drained, the latter achieved by cambers and by drainage ditches. Accurate surveying ensured that the roads were straight and bridges played a major role in the system. The road system enabled the rapid movement of troops as well as trade. Many routes survived long into the post-Roman period.

The large size of the army of republican Rome which had enabled it to defeat Hannibal derived from the organization of the peoples of Italy into various citizen and allied statuses, all of which were required to provide military service. Like the Han rulers of China, the Romans believed in a mass army based on the adult males of the farming population, which provided huge reserves of manpower. Perhaps up to a quarter of a million Italians were in the Roman army in 31 BCE, nearly a quarter of all men of military age.

The Romans had used this superior manpower, together with resources, willpower and organization to take control of the eastern Mediterranean, Egypt, Gaul (France), and Spain by 19 BCE, following up with most of Britain and the Balkans by 100 CE. Julius Caesar was the key figure in the conquest of Gaul, most dramatically by overcoming Vercingetorix, his major opponent, in 52 BCE.

However, in places the Roman expansion stalled. Defeat in Germany in 9 CE at the Teutoburg Forest led to the loss of three legions and an abandonment of Roman ambitions to reach the Elbe. In the 110s CE Roman staying power also proved to be lacking east of the River Euphrates in modern Iraq. These failures led to a shift from expansionism toward a policy of consolidation and fixed, defensive frontiers. This involved formidable systems of walls and fortresses designed to provide both sites for defence and bases for attack and the establishment of large garrisons along the borders, notably on the Rhine and Danube rivers and in Asia.

The Roman Republic collapsed in the 1st century BCE, as competing military commanders, first Marius and Sulla, and then Pompey and Julius Caesar, used force to establish primacy and settle their political differences. Ambitious politicians such as Caesar sought military command on the frontiers, and then tried to have resources directed to their campaigning. Caesar, although himself a patrician, very much associated with the plebeians (ordinary people), while his opponents, most prominently Brutus and Cassius, favoured a republic directed by the aristocracy. This division, as well as personal ambition, led to Caesar's

Left: Vercingetorix, the famous military leader of the Gauls, was finally overcome by Julius Caesar in 52 BCE

Above: Julius Caesar was an ambitious general who parlayed military successes into political prominence

ROMAN MAPPING

The Romans inherited Greek knowledge about the world. Their realization that their known world was only a small portion of the globe meant that the Greeks appreciated that the world needed exploring and mapping. In 150 BCE, the Greek philosopher Crates of Mallos made a large globe in Rome at least three metres (nine feet) in diameter that depicted four balancing continents, one in each quarter of the world, but all separated by water. The idea that the world had to balance would encourage the long-standing belief in a great Southern Continent. Ptolemy (c.90–c.168 CE), a Greek geographer who worked in Alexandria under Roman rule, drew up a world gazetteer that included an estimate of geographical co-ordinates.

The Romans were prolific surveyors and quite capable of drawing to scale. There was a close connection in the Roman world between mapmaking and imperial conquest; and between world maps and Roman pretensions to world power.

Some Roman mapping has survived. The Tabula Peutingeriana, *a 12th-century copy of a 4th-century Roman road map, was a route planner, not a topographical map, and represents the terrain in a strip form. The map depicts the mountains and shows roads centring on particular cities, such as Taranto. A less well-known source is the* Ravenna Cosmography, *a list of more than 5,000 place names covering the empire, drawn up in about 700 by an anonymous cleric at Ravenna.*

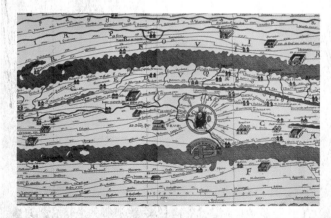

Above: The *Tabula Peutingeriana* mapped the many roads of the Roman empire

assassination in Rome on the Ides of March (15 March) in 44 BCE, and then to a civil war in which a triumvirate of Caesar's supporters defeated his assassins at Philippi (42 BCE) in Greece.

In turn, the triumvirate fell out. Mark Antony allied with Cleopatra, ruler of Egypt, who became his lover; only to be defeated in 31 BCE at a great

SLAVE REBELLIONS

There were frequent slave revolts against the Romans, the most famous being that of the Thracian-born Spartacus, who was enslaved for desertion from the army and became a gladiator before leading a major uprising in 73 BCE. He built up an army, possibly 90,000 strong, advancing along the length of the Italian peninsula, devastating the great landed estates. He vanquished a number of Roman forces, before being defeated and killed in 71 BCE in Lucania by Marcus Licinius Crassus. To deter other slave rebels, Crassus had large numbers of Spartacus' followers crucified along the Appian Way. Other slave revolts occurred in Sicily in 135–132 BCE and 104–100 BCE, but they were all crushed. When the last 20,000 rebel slaves surrendered in 132 BCE they were slaughtered in a fit of anger.

Above: Spartacus' revolt was the most serious of a long line of slave rebellions

Right: Aqueducts were part of the standard infrastructure of Roman cities

DECISIVE BATTLES OF THE CLASSICAL WORLD

naval battle at Actium, on the west coast of Greece by Caesar's heir, Octavian. The victor gradually gathered all the levers of power in the Roman republic to himself, and acquired the title Augustus, becoming the first Roman emperor in 27 BCE. Pressing on to seize Egypt, Augustus boasted of bringing peace to Rome, and his period in power was far more stable than the preceding half-century.

The success of the Roman system rested on the idea of citizens. Citizenship provided a number of rights, but not true equality. Free tenant farmers, who had to pay rents and taxes, were in a weak position economically compared to major landowners and tenants-in-chief. Citizenship, at first severely restricted, was extended to all adult male Italians in the 1st century BCE, and eventually to all males who were not slaves in 212.

Aspects of the Roman system mean that when Christianity appeared and began to spread in the 1st century CE, it posed a threat. The equality propounded by Jesus Christ was particularly subversive. As Christianity was monotheistic (believing in one God), it also challenged the

traditional Roman pantheon of the Olympian gods, a system of multiple deities that allowed the revering of the emperors as gods. In this context, it is not surprising that Christians were persecuted and sometimes martyred in the Roman empire, most notably under the emperor Diocletian (r. 284–305).

The Romans produced a replica infrastructure in the lands they conquered of solidly-built roads and aqueducts, as well as amphitheatres, forums, theatres, public baths and other public buildings. Much is still visible by tourists, for example the great aqueduct at Segovia in Spain, though in general Roman towns survive as stone husks and fragments that do not capture the life, energy and rituals centred on these buildings, nor their splendour when new and decorated.

The Fall of Rome

The causes of the decline of Rome have been the subject of a historical debate ever since it occurred. Attacks from 'barbarians' outside the empire were a key element. From the late 2nd century, when the Marcomanni and Quadi invaded northern Italy in 167–70 CE, Rome was an attractive target for these groups. A particularly serious invasion crisis in the 250s led to the territorial division of the empire as a means to provide local solutions for its defence. This system eventually led to a permanent division between the eastern and western parts of the empire. The centre of power moved to the new capital of Byzantium (later Constantinople), now Istanbul,

founded by Constantine I in 330. He had converted to Christianity in 312. This conversion greatly disrupted notions of continuity, and the divisiveness that resulted weakened the empire at a time it needed to concentrate on external threats. Byzantium became the city of the new, and Rome that of the old.

Economic problems in the Roman empire mounted and by the later 2nd century, agricultural production, industry and trade were all in decline. Imperial finances suffered, and the weight and precious metal

Below: Rome faced attacks from many directions in the 5th century as Goths, Vandals and Huns among others migrated west and south, putting immense pressure on the western empire, leading to its fall in 476.

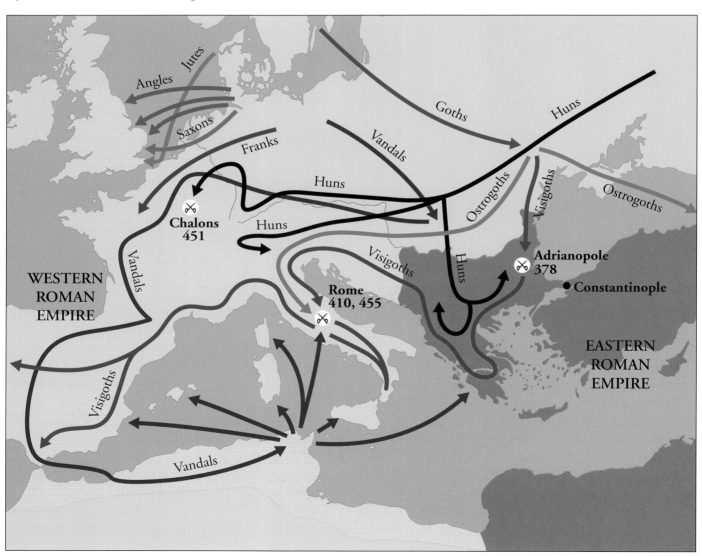

Above: The Madaba mosaic map from the mid-6th century showed the vibrancy of the Eastern Roman Empire after its western counterpart had collapsed

content of Rome's currency fell, which made it harder to win support from allies, both locally and abroad. As the costs of running the empire continued to expand, Rome was increasingly unable to pay.

Disease was a problem – plague swept through the empire in the 160s and 170s CE, as did a haemorrhagic fever epidemic in the 3rd century, while tuberculosis and smallpox were ongoing problems. The very large crowded cities, notably Rome, Milan, Alexandria and Constantinople, were particularly susceptible to disease and relied on a vulnerable food chain, while the empire's exposure to large networks of trade, travel and migration exposed it to greater risks.

The poorer and less populous western half of the empire proved less able to cope with 'barbarian' attack, especially as mistrust between the two divisions grew. The failure to hold the Rhine and Danube frontiers created pressure on Italy, pressure that was difficult to meet as so much of the army was committed to the frontiers. The army itself was smaller than in the period of the Roman Republic and unable to cope with the barbarian influx.

Under pressure from the Huns further east, the Visigoths, a Germanic group led by Alaric, sacked Rome in 410 after the city was starved into submission. Italy was then ravaged by invaders: Huns, Goths and Vandals, the last a Germanic tribe who plundered Rome in 455 and seized Sicily in 468. The Vandal capture of Tunisia in 439 was a turning point as it deprived Rome of an important source of grain.

Linked to the invasions, the Roman empire also suffered intense political instability including civil wars, with 14 emperors ruling in the West between 394 and 476. Power was generally held by military leaders, several of whom, including Odoacer, were 'barbarians'. Indeed, there was overlap and co-operation as well as opposition between Rome and the 'barbarians.' As the empire lost provinces to barbarian occupation, military, political and administrative links ended, and the empire became even less able to raise the taxation to defend itself against further incursions. Finally, Odoacer deposed Romulus Augustulus, the last Roman emperor in the West, in 476.

Below: The Visigoths were the first of many barbarian invaders that troubled Rome during the 5th century

Right: Alaric the Visigoth sacked Rome in 410. It was the first time the city had fallen to an invader in nearly a millennium.

Left: The Eastern
Roman Empire had
its own issues to
deal with. Repeated
attacks by the
Sassanids of Persia
prevented it from
aiding the Western
Empire against
invasions by the
Goths and Vandals

Below: In 476 the
last Roman empire,
Romulus Augustulus,
abdicated to
Odoacer, marking
the end of the
Western Roman
Empire

In the East, the Roman (or Byzantine, as it came
to be called) empire survived. It experienced pressure
on its own eastern frontier by the Sassanids who took
control of Persia in the 3rd century and then pressed
westward. Despite losing control of their trade in the
Indian Ocean, and then much of the Middle East
and North Africa to Arab Muslim invaders in the 7th
century, the Byzantine empire lasted until 1453, when
its capital, Constantinople, fell to the Ottoman Turks.

Rome remained a key influence in Western thought
and activity, most prominently with the role of the
Catholic Church. Later state-formation frequently
looked back to Roman examples, as with the
American constitution and its Senate.

Imperial Cities

In Zhou China (1046–403 BCE), the principles of urban design were based upon a holy square system derived from a mixture of cosmology, astrology, geomancy and numerology. During the Qin dynasty (221–206 BCE), the imperial capital of Xianyang presided over a series of lesser administrative centres. This was also the case in the Han era (206 BCE–220) with its successive capitals of Chang'an and Luoyang, as well as thriving coastal maritime cities such as Fuzhou.

Roman civilization was primarily an urban culture. At its head was the imperial capital, Rome, whose population may have reached one million in the second century CE. The supply of goods to support this population was a major economic, governmental and logistical achievement, notably in the shipping of grain from Sicily, Tunisia and Egypt, with Alexandria operating as a key entrepôt. Major warehouses along the River Tiber in the south-west of Rome testify to the importance of trade.

Cities also developed in the Americas, notably the hilltop Zapotec city of Monte Albán in central Oaxaca (southern Mexico) in about 450 BCE, and El Mirador, the largest early Maya city by about 250 BCE. In central Mexico, Teotihuacan, a grid city with temple-topped pyramids, had 125,000–200,000 inhabitants by 500 CE. In South America, Tiwanaku (Tiahuanaco) on the shore of Lake Titicaca in modern Bolivia, had up to 40,000 inhabitants and was a centre of religious activity.

Below: Teotihuacan in central Mexico had a population of *c.*200,000 by 500 CE.

THE MIDDLE AGES
500–1500

From the 15th-century onwards Western commentators repeatedly separated out the earlier Middle Ages in order to disparage them, and so create a clear basis for proclaiming the novelty of what came later. This approach provides on overly static account of a millennium of human history. The Middle Ages were instead an important and significant period of considerable development. They began with the so-called 'Dark Ages', when Europe underwent barbarian assaults and ended with very different societies and states.

Below: The Magyars were part of a second wave of 'barbarian' attacks that swept across Europe between the 8th and 10th centuries

Left: The White
Huns repeatedly
attacked the Gupta
dynasty in India
during the late 5th
century, leading to
the division of the
subcontinent into a
number of regional
powers

PROTECTING AGAINST BARBARIANS

*The 195-km-(120-mile-)
long Great Wall of Gorgan,
the 'Red Snake,' is the longest
Persian (Iranian) defensive
work. Reaching from the east
of the Caspian Sea into the
Elburz Mountains, it appears
to be a work of the Sassanian
rulers that was designed to stop
invasions by the White Huns.
Constructed and maintained
in the 5th to 7th centuries,
this wall was matched by the
Iron Gates to the west of the
Caspian Sea.*

The Second Wave of 'barbarians'

A second wave of 'barbarian' attacks struck Europe in
the 8th, 9th and 10th centuries, whose main assailants
were the Arabs, the Vikings and the Magyars. The
last invaded and conquered the Hungarian plain only
to be stopped by the Emperor Otto I at the battle
of the Lechfield in 955 as they tried to advance into
Germany. As in the earlier wave, barbarians also
attacked China: the Kitans from Mongolia took over
the area round Beijing in the 10th century, while the
Tanguts gained control of the north-west around
Gansu. In turn, the early Tang dynasty (618–907)
became interested in territorial expansion in Central
Asia, notably into Xinjiang, the Tarim Basin and the
Tibet borderlands.

THE WHITE HUNS

India, too, suffered from significant 'barbarian'
incursions. Much of northern and central India had
been united in the 4th century by the Gupta dynasty,
but it was put under great pressure by the White Huns
(also known as Hephthalites), invaders from Central
Asia. The Battle of Herat in 484 saw the reconfiguration
of power in the region as the White Huns inflicted
a humiliating defeat on the Sassanid Empire. Their
attacks in the 480s, 500s and 510s greatly weakened
Gupta power. This prepared the way for the division of
India from the mid-6th century among a large number
of regional powers, a fragmentation which remained the
case until the 13th century.

VIKING EXPANSION

The limited land available for settlement in Scandinavia, notably in mountainous Norway, led the Vikings (or Norsemen), traders, colonisers and fighters, to engage in raiding from the late 8th century. They invaded the British Isles and France, spread east to Russia and west across the northern Atlantic, searching for opportunities for trading and settlement in more prosperous and fertile lands. Viking longboats, with their sails, stepped masts, true keels, and steering rudders, although shallow and open to the rain, were effective oceangoing ships able to take to the Atlantic, but also, thanks to their shallow draught, easily rowed in coastal waters and up rivers such as the Thames in England, the Seine in France and the Shannon in Ireland. The Vikings reached Iceland in about 860, settled Greenland from 986 and, in about 1000, established a small settlement in Newfoundland. Evidence for settlement further south in North America is problematic, although Americans who did not like the idea of being explored first by Spain would later claim that the Vikings reached New England.

Beyond Iceland, Viking expansion was very small-scale, and the failure to seek co-operation with the Inuit of Greenland was a major flaw. Disease, remoteness, and the problems of global cooling in the high Middle Ages, also helped bring the Viking Greenland settlements to a close in the mid-15th century, while that in distant Newfoundland only lasted for two or three decades.

In France and England, the Vikings established more lasting settlements. The Vikings who settled in northern France founded what would become the Duchy of Normandy in 911 and eventually became the Normans. From Normandy, they conquered England under William the Conqueror in 1066 and, from there, overran much of Wales and Ireland. Other Normans took over Sicily and southern Italy. In the Viking homelands of Scandinavia, powerful kingdoms developed in Denmark, Sweden and Norway by the 11th century, which sought to project their power both into the British Isles and to the eastern Baltic. They also converted to Christianity, marking a significant change from the early Viking period, when their raids had often targeted Christian centres such as monasteries, including that at Lindisfarne in north-eastern England, the site of their first dated raid in 793.

Left: The Vikings travelled across Europe as raiders, traders and settlers and had turned their sights further afield to Greenland and North America by the end of the 10th century

Below: The Normans, descendants of Viking settlers in northern France, invaded England in 1066 under William the Conqueror

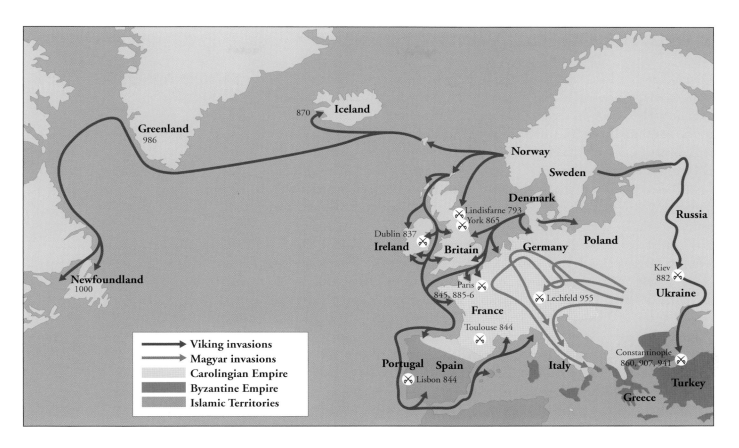

Viking invasions
Magyar invasions
Carolingian Empire
Byzantine Empire
Islamic Territories

Greenland
986

Iceland
870

Norway

Sweden

Russia

Denmark

Lindisfarne 793
York 865

Dublin 837
Ireland

Britain

Germany

Poland

Kiev
882

Ukraine

Newfoundland
1000

Paris
845, 885-6

Lechfeld 955

France

Toulouse 844

Constantinople
860, 907, 941

Portugal Spain
Lisbon 844

Italy

Greece

Turkey

Above: The Vikings expanded rapidly from the late 8th century, exploring as far afield as Newfoundland in the West and Kiev in the East

Right: Kievan Rus was founded by Viking traders in the mid-ninth century and its history was documented in the *Radziwiłł Chronicle*

KIEVAN RUS

In the mid-9th century, Viking traders based in Kiev (in modern Ukraine) founded the state of Kievan Rus. This expanded greatly in the 10th century, aided by its commercial activity and by the links with Byzantium which were strengthened by the conversion of the Rus to Greek Orthodox Christianity after 988, This helped give what became Russia a heritage from Byzantium, encouraging the idea that Moscow was the 'Third Rome'. The Kievan state dissolved after the death of Vladimir I (r. 980-1015) who was succeeded by sons who ruled separate principalities based on Novgorod, Polotsk and Chernigov. In the early 13th century, Mongol conquerors devastated the region, eventually leading to the rise of Muscovy (Moscow) as the leading Russian principality.

Empires of the Mediterranean

Divided and in part conquered, the Roman world survived in the Eastern Mediterranean as the Byzantine empire, which held out against Islamic attacks until its capital, Constantinople (Istanbul), finally fell to the Muslim Ottoman Turks under Mehmed II in 1453. Earlier still, Byzantium had lost North Africa and the modern states of Syria, Lebanon, Israel and Palestine to Muslim Arab forces in the 7th century.

In Western Europe, the 'barbarian' Germanic tribes established new, competing, kingdoms after the fall of Rome: the Ostrogoths in Italy and the Visigoths in Spain. Other 'barbarian' groups included the Suevi in north-west Spain, the Burgundians, and the Angles, Saxons and Jutes who invaded England. The most important kingdom which emerged was of the Franks, who consolidated control over modern France and, in 732, at Tours, defeated Islamic invaders who had moved north after defeating the Visigoths and conquering Spain and Portugal.

In the late 8th and early 9th century, the Frankish state, under its new Carolingian dynasty, expanded greatly. Charlemagne (r. 768–814) conquered northern Italy, where he defeated the Lombards, and absorbed much of modern Germany and Austria, crushing the Saxons in Germany. In 800, he was crowned Holy Roman Emperor by Pope Leo III, an event which linked the imperial legacy of Rome, the power of the Carolingian empire, and the rising prestige of the Papacy. With his capital at Aix-la-Chapelle (Aachen), Charlemagne united most of Western Christendom, but it was divided among his grandsons by the Treaty of Verdun (843), and then further fragmented, while also coming under pressure from Magyars, Vikings and Arabs. The kingdom of Germany came to be the key element and its ruler, Otto I, was crowned Emperor in 962, acquiring a title which came to compete with that of the Byzantine emperors.

Below left: Was the Battle of Poitiers a turning point? Edward Gibbon thought so, but modern historians are more sceptical

Above: Charlemagne established Frankish power over much of Western Europe, but his empire was divided by his grandsons

THE BATTLE OF TOURS, 732

The historian Edward Gibbon argued in the late-18th century that had the Arabs defeated Charles Martel and the Franks at Tours, it might have led to the conquest of Christian Europe. While some modern historians have suggested the expedition was simply a raid, the invading army was a substantial force and its victory could have reinforced the pattern of Christian co-operation with the Arabs and helped the latter maintain a strong presence in France. As with many battles, Tours was more significant for one side (the Franks) than the other. The Arabs never repeated their advance so far north in France.

THE BATTLE OF RELIGIONS

Beginning in the 7th century, the struggle between Islam and Christendom (and in South Asia between Islam and Hinduism) became a major strand in world history. A rapid period of Muslim conquest in the 7th and 8th centuries was accompanied by serious divisions. The Abbasids, who claimed descent from the Prophet Muhammad's uncle, rebelled in 747 in Persia and defeated the Umayyads in 750, achieving primacy in the Islam world. Based in Baghdad, they would rule as caliphs until 1258 when they were overthrown by the Mongols.

THE ARAB CONQUESTS

The most effective of the invasions of the Classical world were mounted by Arabs converted to the new religion of Islam. Launched by Muhammad, this movement rapidly came into conflict with the

Above: The Arab forces moved quickly to assert their military might from the 7th century. By the middle of the 8th century, Islamic rule extended from Spain to central Asia

paganism that prevailed in most of Arabia, and his forces captured Mecca in 630. His successors, known as caliphs, united Arabia, defeated the Byzantines and the Sassanians of Persia, and conquered South-west Asia and Egypt by 642, going on to advance across Persia into modern Afghanistan, as well across North Africa, both in the 640s. Arab forces benefited from mobility and high morale. In 711, they invaded Spain, and in 751 defeated a Chinese army near Lake Balkhash, a victory which drove forward the Islamicization of Central Asia. The Muslim advances helped to mould the modern world. It was a cultural as much as a military advance and its progress was to be reversed in relatively few areas.

The Muslim world was itself increasingly fractured by rebellions and civil wars. The political unity of Islam ended when the Abbasid governor of Spain was overthrown by a member of the Umayyad family in 756. In addition, the Fatimids, who were Shi'ites (followers of an Islamic tradition that believed political power should be held by the descendants of Muhammad's son-in-law Ali) established a caliphate in Tunis in 910 and conquered Egypt in 969. These and other divisions led to repeated conflict: in the second half of the 11th century the Seljuk Turks defeated the

Abbasids and the Christians of Byzantium, while the Fatimids, based in Egypt, competed with the Seljuks for control over the Holy Land.

THE CRUSADES

The advances by the Seljuks against the Christian Byzantines, whom they defeated at Manzikert in 1071 – and concerns about access for Christian pilgrims to the holy city of Jerusalem – led Pope Urban II in 1095 to preach a holy war against Islam that became the First Crusade. It was the first of a series of Christian

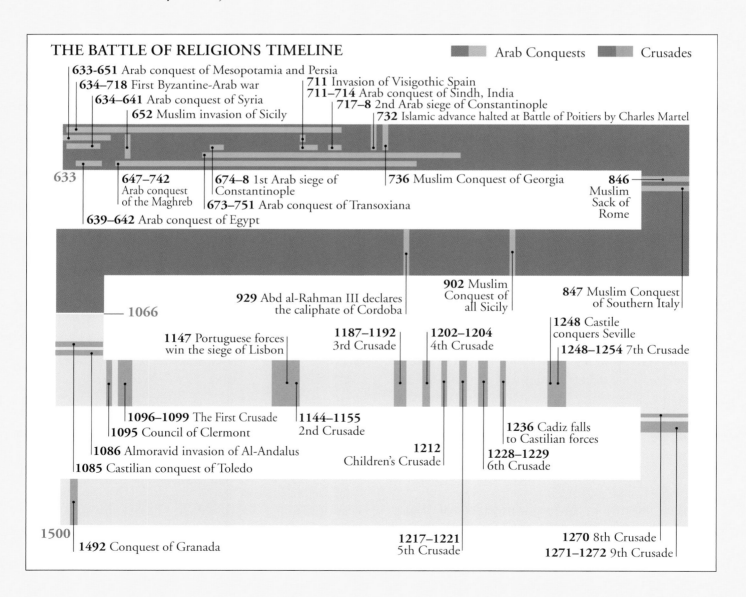

THE BATTLE OF RELIGIONS TIMELINE

Arab Conquests   Crusades

633-651 Arab conquest of Mesopotamia and Persia
634–718 First Byzantine-Arab war
634–641 Arab conquest of Syria
652 Muslim invasion of Sicily
711 Invasion of Visigothic Spain
711–714 Arab conquest of Sindh, India
717–8 2nd Arab siege of Constantinople
732 Islamic advance halted at Battle of Poitiers by Charles Martel

633

647–742 Arab conquest of the Maghreb
674–8 1st Arab siege of Constantinople
673–751 Arab conquest of Transoxiana
736 Muslim Conquest of Georgia
846 Muslim Sack of Rome

639–642 Arab conquest of Egypt

929 Abd al-Rahman III declares the caliphate of Cordoba
902 Muslim Conquest of all Sicily
847 Muslim Conquest of Southern Italy

1066

1248 Castile conquers Seville

1147 Portuguese forces win the siege of Lisbon
1187–1192 3rd Crusade
1202–1204 4th Crusade
1248–1254 7th Crusade

1096–1099 The First Crusade
1144–1155 2nd Crusade
1095 Council of Clermont
1236 Cadiz falls to Castilian forces
1086 Almoravid invasion of Al-Andalus
1212 Children's Crusade
1228–1229 6th Crusade
1085 Castilian conquest of Toledo

1500

1492 Conquest of Granada
1217–1221 5th Crusade
1270 8th Crusade
1271–1272 9th Crusade

The most famous Muslim warrior of the High Middle Ages, Saladin (c.1138–93) was a Kurd who rose to prominence in the service of his uncle the governor of Egypt, whom he succeeded in 1169. Two years later, Saladin deposed the Egyptian sultan and founded his own Ayyubid sultanate. His forces pushed west to Tunisia and south into Sudan and Yemen. He also took Syria and northern Iraq, capturing Damascus in 1174. This was an age-old goal of the Egyptians, one that Saladin successfully achieved. He ably linked military, political and diplomatic strategies. In 1187, Saladin proclaimed a jihad (holy war) and crushed the Christian kingdom of Jerusalem.

holy wars, inspired by the potent ideal of fighting against the external or internal foes of Christendom. The crusaders captured Jerusalem in 1099 and they founded a number of states in the Holy Land. Their movement led to the creation of a novel organization that had political overtones: the Military Orders. The Templars and Hospitallers, warriors who had taken religious vows, had troops and castles and were entrusted with the defence of large tracts of territory.

When their Muslim neighbours were restored to political unity, the crusaders found it difficult to sustain their position. By 1144, they had lost most of the County of Edessa, which led to the calling of the unsuccessful Second Crusade. Saladin's victory against the crusaders at Hattin in 1187 made matters worse and was followed by the capture of Jerusalem. The crusaders lost their remaining strongholds one-by-one. Acre, their last major position (which they had taken in 1104), fell to the Mamluks in 1291.

Above: Detail from a 13th-century French manuscript depicting the Siege of Antioch (1097–8). The Middle Ages saw an unforgiving battle for supremacy between Christianity and Islam

Right: Saladin defeated the crusader kingdom of Jerusalem in 1187

THE FOURTH CRUSADE

Under Venetian influence, the Fourth Crusade (1202–4) attacked not
the Muslims, but, first, the Hungarian-ruled city of Zara and, then,
Constantinople itself. Alexius Angelus, the son of the deposed Byzantine
emperor Isaac II, offered money, help with the crusade and the union of
the Orthodox Church with Rome (from which it had been divided since
1054) if his uncle was removed. This was secured by the crusaders in
1203, but the new Emperor, Alexius IV, was unable to fulfil his promises
and was deposed in an anti-Western rising. This led the crusaders in
1204 to storm the city, crown Count Baldwin of Flanders as emperor,
and partition the Byzantine empire between them. However, the new
situation was far from stable. In 1261, the Greeks retook Constantinople,
bringing this brief Latin Empire to an end.

Below: A medieval miniature showing the
crusader attack on the Byzantine capital of
Constantinople in 1204

Right: Rodrigo Díaz de Vivar, better known as El Cid, was a mercenary who fought for both the Christians and Moors, and has since become the iconic figure of the Spanish *Reconquista*

THE *RECONQUISTA*

The Christians had far more success in reversing Islamic gains in Spain and Portugal where a gradual advance known as the *Reconquista* (Reconquest) drove the Muslim rulers out of the Iberian Peninsula, which returned to Christian rule after centuries of Muslim occupation. Toledo fell in 1085, Lisbon in 1147 and Granada, the last city controlled by the Muslims, in 1492.

The Christians also successfully recovered a series of islands in the Mediterranean from the Muslims, including Crete and Sicily. These successes, along with greater Christian maritime effectiveness, were crucial to the development of European trading systems centred on the Italian cities of Pisa, Genoa and, most successfully, Venice, which created an overseas empire including Crete, Cyprus and the coastal regions of modern Croatia.

In 1415, the *Reconquista* moved into north-west Africa with the capture of Ceuta. Portugal and Spain both made conquests in the region, with Portugal only abandoning its attempt to dominate Morocco after a heavy defeat there in 1578 in which its king, Sebastian, was killed.

EL CID AND HEROISM

A soldier of great ability and ambition, Rodrigo Díaz de Vivar, known later as El Cid, was a Castilian noble who fell out with Alfonso VI of León and Castile and became a mercenary. His nickname El Cid comes from the Arabic sayyid, *or lord, or derives from a form of the Arabic word* asad *(lion). El Cid fought both Christians and Muslims, derived much income from tributes, and ruled Valencia himself from 1094 until his death in 1099, fighting off the Almoravid Berbers. His widow was finally forced to surrender Valencia to the Almoravids in 1102.*

El Cid was later presented as a role model, but his actions reflected the opportunities and opportunism of frontier society. This pattern of entrepreneurs of power occurred elsewhere in Spain during the Reconquista, *in the mountains north-west of Málaga, where the church of Bobastro is all that remains of the stronghold of Umar b. Hafsun (c.850-917), a brigand who successfully defied the caliphate at Córdoba before converting to Christianity. Bobastro was finally reconquered by the Umayyads in 927.*

The World Conquerors

The light cavalry of the peoples of Central Asia proved repeatedly successful as conquerors from the 5th to the 15th centuries, helping to bring down the Roman Empire in the West and, most spectacularly, in the conquests of the Mongols under Chinggis Khan (c.1160–1227) and his successors, from China to Hungary. A subsistence crisis in the steppe caused by a temperature drop that affected grass growth proved the catalyst for their invasions, but the Mongols were able to operate successfully in a range of environments. Major centres, such as Beijing in 1215, Bukhara in 1219, Kiev in 1240 and Baghdad in 1258 all fell to the Mongols. In 1241, they successfully invaded Poland and Hungary.

The Europeans were never able to defeat the Mongols and were fortunate that Chinggis had concentrated on China and then Central Asia. In 1241, the Mongol invaders of Europe only turned back when news arrived of the death of Ögedei, Chinggis' successor as Great Khan. Mongol expansion elsewhere was halted by their defeat by the Mamluks of Egypt (originally slave-soldiers from Central Asia) when they invaded Syria in 1260 and by the Japanese (helped by a storm) in 1281.

The Mongol empire, the largest contiguous land empire ever in world history, has been claimed as the starting point for continuous global history. It created exchange circuits of information, technologies, ideas and even, with the Black Death of the 14th century, of diseases. Drawing on the different cultural traditions of the societies with which they came into

Above: Chinggis Khan was the founder of the largest contiguous land empire in world history

MARCO POLO: REPORTING CHINA

The Venetian merchant Marco Polo claimed to have left Venice in 1271 and to have reached the Mongol Great Khan Khubilai's summer palace at Shangdu (Xanadu) in 1275. He stayed in the Mongol domains until 1292, when he was given the task of escorting a Mongol princess from China to Hormuz on the Persian Gulf. The accuracy of Polo's account has been challenged, but it certainly had a major impact on European knowledge about China and created a lasting impression of Chinese wealth. It also testified to the ability to travel vast distances overland. Polo believed that he had travelled 25,000 km (16,000 miles) from Venice to Beijing, instead of 11,000 km (7,000 miles); this helped create a false impression of the distance from Europe to China across the Atlantic that led Columbus to misunderstand what he would find when he sailed west.

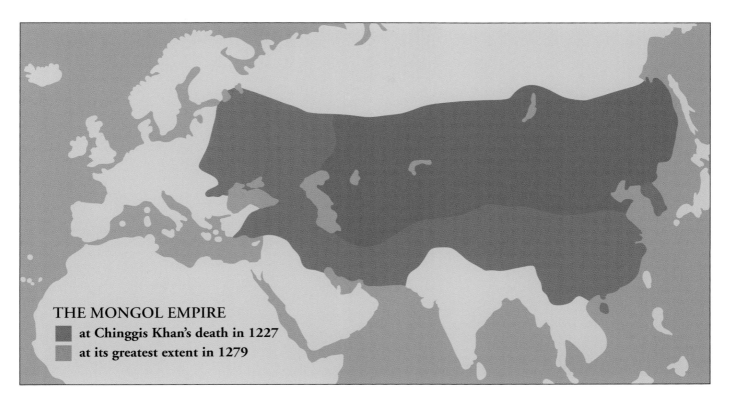

THE MONGOL EMPIRE
■ at Chinggis Khan's death in 1227
■ at its greatest extent in 1279

contact, the Mongols developed already existing links along the 'Silk Roads' which were particularly important to relations between China and Persia (Iran), and extended them to points further west, including on the Black Sea.

The Mongols did not create the bureaucratic mechanisms, governmental or intellectual, to take advantage of the diversity of the lands under their rule. There was neither an ecclesiastical and educational equivalent to the Christian churches, nor a bureaucratic and cultural analogue of the Confucianism of Chinese administration, whose respect for tradition and order immeasurably assisted the operation of Chinese governments from the Han onwards.

Ultimately, the Mongol empire did not last, and

Above: The Mongol Empire reached its greatest extent in 1279, before eventually suffering from internal divisions

Right: Detail from the *Catalan Atlas* (1375) showing the camel caravan of Marco Polo. The Mongols strengthened trade links along the Silk Roads, but did not establish strong bureaucratic institutions

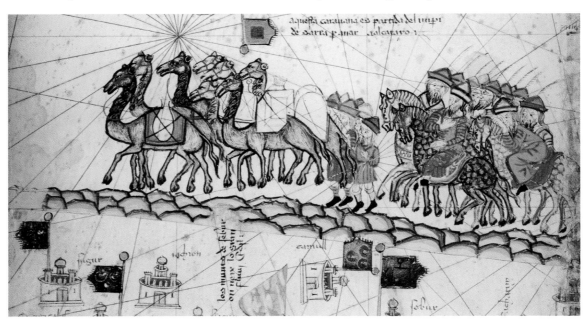

Above: Samarkand was the centre of Timur's empire, which expanded rapidly through Asia

its collapse hit opportunities to move goods and ideas across Eurasia. Rivalry from 1259 between the Mongol princes tore the inheritance into four empires, which in turn splintered further, just as Alexander the Great's empire had divided after his death in 323 BCE.

Subsequently, Timur the Lame (1336–1405; later called Tamerlane), modelled himself on the Mongols. Making Samarkand his capital, he conquered Central Asia, Iran, northern India and the Middle East, taking Herat (1381), Delhi (1398), Damascus (1401) and Baghdad (1401). At the time of his death, Timur was planning to invade China. When he faced resistance, Timur erected pyramids from the skulls of the slaughtered – possibly 70,000 people when he suppressed a rising at Isfahan (Persia) in 1387.

China, Europe and the states of South and South-western Asia had no answer to the power deployed by nomadic empires such as Timur's. It collapsed, however, after his death in 1405.

The end of the Mongol empire removed an obstacle to Western expansionism, but it did not remove the importance of links across Central Asia. Much of the region would remain independent of Western control or influence until the late 19th century when conquered by Russia.

Right: Timur the Lame, a descendant of Chinggis Khan, attained a terrifying reputation

Cities and Trade

Cities and the economics which depended on them suffered significant damage in the 'barbarian' invasions of the 5th and 6th centuries, but thereafter they revived, most notably in China. There, under the Tang (618–970), the capital Chang'an (modern Xi'an) had a population of about two million by the 8th century. The city's symmetrical layout indicated strong central government. The city was organized into specialized and orderly functional neighbourhoods, demarcated according to deeply-rooted Chinese ideas about the spiritual efficacy of spatial arrangements and alignments – ideas that were diffused to various degrees throughout East Asia. Chinese urbanization reached such a level under the Tang there were more than ten cities with populations of over 300,000, while, under the Song (960–1279), the trading entrepôt of Hangzhou had a million residents at a time when London had just 15,000, while the commercial wealth of 11th-century Kaifeng far outstripped that of any European city.

Asian urbanization was not confined to China. Angkor Wat, the capital of the Khmer empire of Cambodia, was founded in the 9th century and became a centre of Buddhist activity, with an impressive system of waterways that conserved and distributed the monsoon rains.

Trade was important to city development. Port cities developed to service trading routes between major economies, By around 1000, these included Aden for the Indian Ocean, Kulam Mali in southern India, and Kataha at the northern end of the Strait of Malacca, and Aden, Malacca and Brunei half a millennium later.

Important trading cities similarly developed in Europe, with Venice, Genoa and Pisa drawing on maritime strength and financial networks to dominate the Mediterranean, while in the Baltic the cities of the Hanseatic League, such as Lübeck became pre-eminent.

Above: Angkor Wat, the capital of the Khmer empire, was a centre of Buddhist activity

Medieval China

The Mongols under Khubilai (r. 1260–94), a talented grandson of Chinggis, were the first steppe peoples to conquer China south of the Yangtze, completing this difficult and lengthy process in 1279 with the overthrow of the Southern Song dynasty.

In the 14th century, Mongol rule in China was weakened by animosity between rulers and ruled; and the impact of natural disasters. Rebellions became acute from the early 1350s. The Red Turban army, a key insurgent force, captured the major city of Nanjing in 1356 and used the position to dominate the Yangtze valley. Zhu Yuanzhang, the Red Turban leader, moved north on Beijing, forcing the Mongol emperor to flee back to the steppe. Zhu then proclaimed himself emperor, founding the Ming dynasty, which lasted until 1644. The Ming subsequently completed the defeat of the Mongols in south-western China and eastern Mongolia.

China had a strict hierarchical order centred on the emperor, whose claim to universal kingship was an expression of sacred as well as secular aspirations and realities. The Chinese understood the interactions of heaven, earth and humanity in terms of a metaphysical order that drew on religious ideas central to Buddhism and Daoism, as well as on astrology and alchemy.

China was a major centre of technological development, including of printing and gunpowder (see page 88). Movable type was employed to create printed texts, which were widely available by the 11th and 12th centuries.

Left: Zhu Yuanzhang led the the Red Turban Rebellion against Mongol rule and established the Ming dynasty, proclaiming himself the Emperor Hongwu.

Above: Khubilai was the first Mongol to conquer the whole of China in 1279

Above: The mosque at Timbuktu was built in the 14th century and was typical of Islamic architecture in sub-Saharan Africa

African Empires of the Middle Ages

The Middle Ages saw significant political development in Africa, with urban growth acting as a prime motor for the spread of secular and spiritual authority. Egypt, which the Arabs had first conquered in 639, experienced particular growth and became an important possession of the Umayyad and Abbasid Caliphates. Under Islamic rule, the Mamluks, or slave soldiers, held an important military and political role there and developed into an influential warrior caste by the beginning of the second millennium CE. In 1250, the Mamluks rose up, overthrew the Ayyubid dynasty and before long extended their authority as far as Syria.

In the Sahel belt of West Africa and along the coast of East Africa, the spread of Islam and the growth of trade were linked to the expansion of cities, such as Jenne, Timbuktu and Gao on the River Niger, Kano in northern Nigeria, and Mogadishu, Malindi, Mombasa, Kilwa and Sofala on the Indian Ocean. These cities were important as transhipment points

Left: The Mamluks were slave soldiers who occupied increasingly powerful military and political positions. They established control over Egypt in 1250 after rebellion against the Ayyubid dynasty

linking different environments, such as the River Niger and the trans-Saharan caravan routes, or the Indian Ocean and the routes into the interior of East Africa, an important source of slaves. In the early 14th century, the gold-rich Emperor of Mali, Mansa Musa, undertook a famous pilgrimage to Mecca, in a journey that revealed to the world the wealth of West Africa and incited the interest of acquisitive rulers in North Africa.

In south-east Africa, the empire of Great Zimbabwe developed out of the gold and cattle trade, and its capital, also called Great Zimbabwe, built from the 11th to the 15th century, became a major city, with an impressive royal palace constructed in the 11th century. In much of Africa, however, and notably in southern Africa, hunter-gathering, nomadic herding, or farming remained the predominant form of society and these did not generate any significant state formation.

Labour shortages in Africa ensured that control over people was as significant as control over territory. This situation encouraged slavery, which was common within Africa and also fed by a long-established slave trade, that became particularly significant in the transport of slaves from sub-Saharan Africa to the Islamic world.

Above: Mansa Musa, the Emperor of Mali, was renowned for his wealth

Goods that changed the world – Gunpowder

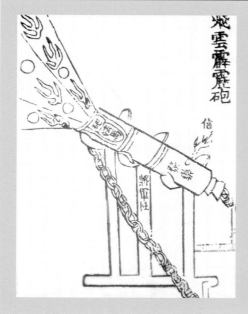

The formula for manufacturing effective gunpowder, a rapidly-burning mixture with a high propellant force, was discovered in China in the 9th century. It was then adapted for use in weaponry, firstly rockets and flamethrowers and then, around 1250, for cannon. Knowledge of gunpowder reached Europe around 1300 and before long hand-held gunpowder weaponry had appeared on battlefields. The range and killing power that these provided armies and the ability of artillery to destroy previously impregnable city walls had significant effects on the conduct of war.

Left: China discovered gunpowder in the 9th century. By the 14th century, metal cannons like the one pictured, were an important feature of Chinese warfare

American Empires before Columbus

Cultures and empires with a wide geographical range appeared in the Americas prior to the arrival of Spanish explorers from 1492. They were societies that lacked horses, printing and gunpowder, but in 1400 about 14 per cent of the world's population lived in the Americas.

In the 15th century, the Aztecs established an empire of city states in central Mexico, while, at a far greater range, the Peruvian-based Incas created one that spread to include much of modern Ecuador, Peru, Bolivia and northern Chile. In North America, the Mississippian culture had influence over much of the land east of the Rockies, while a series of agricultural cultures came to prominence in the south-west of the modern USA, and the Thule Inuit (Eskimo) dominated the Arctic regions. Agricultural settlements sprang up in the forested regions of Central and South America. Across the Americas ancestor cults were important and the range of ancient American art included rock art in caves, such as that produced by the Tainos in Puerto Rico.

The Incas were the most sophisticated of the imperial powers in the Americas, drawing on a system of forced labour to help create an

Left: The Inca *khipu* was a record created by making knots in cords and kept safe by specialists

Right: A sophisticated civilization developed along the shores of the Mississippi between 1000 and 1450

MISSISSIPPIAN CULTURE

In c.1000–c.1450, the Mississippi Valley became the centre of a diffuse culture with a series of chiefdoms and major centres, notably Cahokia and Moundville. Etowah, a 22-hectare (54-acre) site in Georgia, had a large encircling site protecting the town. The culture declined before the arrival of the Spaniards in the 16th century. Drought may have played a role in the collapse of the Mississippian, as it did earlier with cultures in the American south-west.

Left: The origins of Tenochtitlan, the Aztec capital, represented in the *Codex Mendoza*

extensive road network throughout the empire which they conquered in the 15th century. Their ruler was believed to be descended from the Sun. The Incas created records in the form of knotted cords called *khipus* which were stored in archives overseen by specialists. Many of the archives were situated inside accessible tombs, linking record-keeping to longevity and the sacred.

In the Aztec empire, which expanded from its base in the Valley of Mexico after 1427, authority was also sacred. Huitzilopochtli, the God of War, was their patron deity and human sacrifice played an important part in Aztec culture. Like the Incas, the Aztecs were highly militaristic, although they also made adroit use of alliances to cement their rule.

THE MAYA

Much about Maya civilization (at its height *c*.290–900) is obscure, but they established city-states in the jungles of Guatemala and the Yucatan peninsula, whose architecture, especially their stepped pyramids, such as Itza, are still impressive. Although they lacked wheels, pack animals and metal tools, the Maya traded extensively by land and sea, including in salt, obsidian, precious stones, gold and copper, a commerce which brought them power and wealth. They also developed a hieroglyphic writing system and a sophisticated calendar based on astronomical observations. The use of laser-technology to scan the region has revised upwards the scale and population density of Maya civilization, from five million people to fifteen. They also revealed a network of causeways between Maya cities in northern Guatemala, suggesting a significant level of trade. The causes of the Maya decline are unclear, but may have been due to the spread of arid conditions, which made the large population unsupportable.

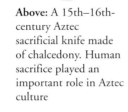

Above: A 15th–16th-century Aztec sacrificial knife made of chalcedony. Human sacrifice played an important role in Aztec culture

Left: The stepped pyramids of Chichen Itza reflected the power of the Mayan city-states during the Classic period, but the reasons for their decline remain mysterious

Science

The Middle Ages saw considerable intellectual, scientific and technological achievements across much of the world. The modern notion of separate categories for religion, culture and intellectual thought and pursuits is not appropriate during this period. Theology, for example, was called the 'Queen of Sciences' in Europe. Much of the discussion in 13th- and 14th-century Europe of the relationship between appearance and reality was framed in terms of philosophical and religious visions bound up in such questions as the validity of Christian visions and the nature of Biblical explanation. Only a few scholars such as Roger Bacon (c.1214–92), an English friar who was aware of intellectual developments in the Arab world, emphasized facts, experimentation and useful knowledge, in his attempt to understand better the workings of a cosmos created by a Christian God.

The period from the 11th to 13th centuries saw the appearance of universities in Europe, notably Paris, Bologna, Naples and Oxford, which became major centres of European thought. There commentators were influenced by the thought of Thomas Aquinas (1225–74), who had synthesized pre-existing philosophical doctrines taught in the Schools (proto-universities) with the works of Aristotle, translated from Arabic versions available in Spain and Sicily or directly from the Greek. Aquinas created a systematic rationalization of the content, methods and organization of existing knowledge.

Across the world, technical limitations restricted the capacity for scientific development, but it still occurred in places. This was notably so with a greater use of wind and water power than in the Classical period, the development in the use of blast furnaces for iron production and the invention of printing in China.

Right: Roger Bacon (c.1214–1292) took a scientific approach to understanding the cosmos

KNOWLEDGE IN THE ISLAMIC WORLD

The vast extent of the Islamic world allowed it to take advantage of information, ideas, and methods which flooded back from distant lands through conquest, trade and travel. Muslim-ruled territories stretched from India and Central Asia to north-west Africa and Spain. Caravan routes linked the Orient to the Middle East via Central Asia, and also crossed the Sahara, while Arab traders, benefiting from their astronomical knowledge, sailed the Indian Ocean and the Mediterranean. Taking advantage of monsoon winds, Arab traders sailed eastwards in the Indian Ocean and, in the late 8th century, began voyaging to Guangzhou (Canton). Mapping developed in the Islamic World and in this the legacy of Greek thought could be drawn on, notably in Egypt. The recursive or scholastic method of argument, first developed by Buddhist scholars and crucial to what would later be termed scientific method, was adopted by Islam alongside the madrasa (school or college) which originated in the Buddhist viharā.

The Islamic World was not culturally monolithic, and tensions between settled practices and more puritanical revivalist movements created sharp divisions. There was an astonishing range in belief and practice. The cosmopolitan interactions of major urban centres under Islamic rule, such as Alexandria and Samarkand, were very different to more closed regions where fundamentalist tendencies thrived. Instances of the latter include the Moroccan based Almoravid dynasty (1040–1147) and, even more, their Almohad successors (1121–1269). Almohad beliefs, such as asserting the unity of God and attacking those who looked to other traditions, had profound consequences, such as the orthodox interpretation of the Koran which forbade the representation of the human body. The Almohads abandoned the traditional Muslim willingness to allow non-Muslims to practise their religion in return for submission and payment. Instead they forced Jews and Christians to convert to Islam.

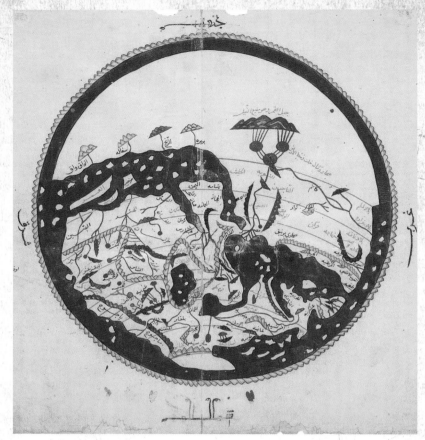

Above: Al-Idrisi's map, created in 1154 for Roger II of Sicily, was remarkably accurate and reflected the exchange of ideas and information occurring across the Islamic world

Left: The madrasas were centres of Islamic learning which used the scholastic method to advance knowledge

The Facts of Life

The Medieval World presented individuals with a hostile and unpredictable environment, with forces that could be neither prevented nor propitiated, and where the efforts of years were swept away in an instant by famine or plague. The line between independence and calamity, between being poor and falling into pauperdom, could be crossed easily, fast and frequently. Beset by such calamity and risk, many turned to religious solutions.

Sanitation and diet were major problems for the bulk of the population. Their housing conditions caused a high incidence of respiratory infections. Overcrowding, inadequate bathing facilities and the continual wearing of the same clothes led to louse infestation. This was just one of a range of assaults, including bed-bugs, fleas and tapeworms, to which

medieval people were subject, whatever their wealth.

Washing in clean water was not a widespread habit in the Middle Ages, and the proximity of animals and dunghills to human settlement also spread disease. The lack of clean drinking water became pressing, especially in coastal regions and lowland areas without deep wells, and manure often contaminated the water supply. Typhus, a deadly disease, was one result.

Poor nutrition greatly contributed to the spread of infectious diseases by lowering resistance. Malnutrition also limited sexual desire and activity, hindered successful pregnancy and increased infant mortality. Problems of food shortage and cost ensured that the bulk of the population lacked a balanced diet, even when they had enough food. This was a particular problem for the urban poor, who found

Above: This illustration from the *Nuremburg Chronicle* (1493) presented a romanticised vision of urban life in the Middle Ages

Above: Acquiring enough food to survive in the middle ages required hard labour while disease represented a constant threat to the peasantry

fruit and vegetables, let alone meat and fish, expensive, and who were also frequently ill-clad and shod as they lacked clothes and shoes. The diet of the peasantry was monotonous: they consumed little meat or fish and often ate a gruel or soup composed of vegetables.

Working conditions were poor: exposure to hazardous substances, such as lead and mercury, was commonplace, while construction work in particular was very dangerous. Millers worked in dusty and noisy circumstances, frequently suffered from lice and often developed asthma, hernias and chronic back problems.

There were some attempts to improve public health. Religious and civic institutions, such as hospitals, were created to quarantine infected populations and, when possible, provide relief to patients. In Venice, much money was spent on curing the sick, and for the defence of the city and the Adriatic coastal ports as a whole from disease. Measures were taken not only to prevent infections arriving by ship, but also to improve general hygiene.

In the early 15th century, the University of Padua in Italy became a centre for the study of medicine and anatomy, partly in order to solve the problem posed by infectious diseases. The spread of printing made it easier to communicate new medical information through the wider dissemination of printed text. Yet, traditional remedies such as folk cures and spiritual intervention also remained significant. In the *Chiesa di Sant' Agostino* (Church of St Augustine) in San Gimignano in Italy, Benozzo Gozzoli painted a fresco showing San Sebastian intervening to protect the city against the 1464 plague epidemic. Such beliefs remained important, and a major part of the ritual of particular communities and of their sense of identity.

Feudalism

The dominant system of political control and social organization over much of 11th-century Western Europe was feudalism. Its essential characteristic was a personal relationship between lord and vassal, cemented in an age of homage. Vassals received land in return for providing military service, usually in the form of knights (heavy armoured cavalry). The state in the modern sense – an agreed territory with sovereign powers and with a precise relationship with citizens – did not exist. Instead, there was a series of individual rulers each effectively sovereign within his own lands, though each in turn nominally owed allegiance to a king or another ruler. The roles of land ownership and military service continued to be important in political organization for the following centuries until industrialization, urbanization, conscription and nationalism fundamentally changed the situation in the 19th century.

Right: The relationship between lord and vassal was at the heart of feudalism as those lower in the social structure offered their loyalty and military service to their lords in return for their protection

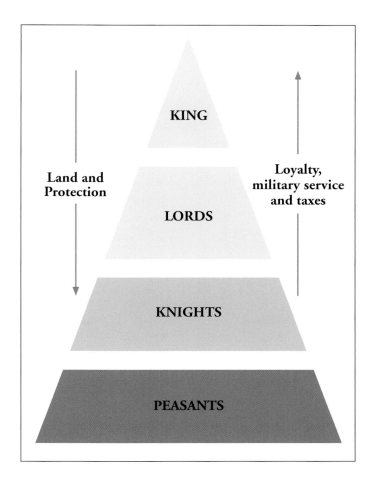

KING

Land and Protection

Loyalty, military service and taxes

LORDS

KNIGHTS

PEASANTS

CASTLES

Early castles were generally simple affairs of earth and timber construction, although they still required many man-days to construct. Timber-built forms were often of either motte (a mound of earth)-and-bailey or ringwork (enclosure) type. With time, major castles, such as the Tower of London and Krak des Chevaliers, were fortified in stone, which was resistant to fire and whose walls were harder for attackers to breach.

Left: The Krak des Chevaliers in Syria, built by the Knights Hospitaller 1142 on the site of an older Arabic fortress, was a monumental fortification

The Spread of the Market Economy

Medieval Europe experienced an increase in trade, which was linked to a monetarization of other aspects of life, especially in labour and rents, which required the production of large amounts of coinage. New financial instruments were devised to ease credit and borrowing, including bills of exchange, which acted as a means of merchants receiving guarantees of payment in one country which could be exchanged for cash in another, and also allowed them to unlock the value of future working capital.

The rise of trade and money affected social assumptions and practices. Markets for the trade of goods, services and land developed, with the coastal regions of the Indian Ocean, which provided a way to link East and South-east Asia to South and South-west Asia and on to East Africa, providing an area of particularly strong growth in trade.

Below: The *Fra Mauro* map from 1459 drew on new of discoveries in Asia, including those by Marco Polo

The Black Death and Society

Trade routes carried goods, but they also acted as conduits for the transmission of disease. A terrible outbreak of plague, the Black Death reflected the extent of biological exchanges by the 14th century. The plague probably originated in the Yunnan region of China, and then swept throughout China and westward along the Silk Roads to the Middle East and Europe. The disease was spread by infected fleas which lived on black rats and by fleas and lice carried by humans. In 1345–46, during the siege of the well-fortified Genoese-ruled trading city of Kaffa (modern Theodosia) in Crimea, the Mongols used trebuchets to fire corpses into the city, spreading the plague. Fleeing Genoese brought the disease back to Europe.

The plague caused a serious decline in world population, which fell and remained relatively depressed until the 16th century. Conditions were aggravated by a persistent turndown in the climate known as the Little Ice Age. Up to a third of the population of Europe died, leading to labour shortages. In Eastern Europe, this encouraged the spread of serfdom, a system of forced labour based on hereditary bondage to the land. This provided the mass labour force necessary for agriculture, and was intended to ensure a fixed labour force at a time when, in a largely pre-monetary and low-efficiency agrarian economy, there were few alternatives to remedy labour shortages. The legal essence of serfdom was a form of personal service to a lord in exchange for the right to cultivate the soil, a form of unequal contract that was not present for slavery, but which rendered the system compatible with Christian teachings.

In Western Europe, labour shortages provided

Above: The Black Death devastated Europe as approximately one third of the population died

Left: The Peasant's Revolt of 1381 in England reflected the increasing autonomy of the peasantry after the Black Death

Below: Belief in spiritual intervention remained important in medieval life. The fresco at San Sebastian was painted in 1464 to protect against the plague

the peasantry with opportunities to move away from the constraints of serfdom. The attempt in England to maintain labour discipline produced a reaction in the shape of the Peasant's Revolt of 1381 (although the revolt ultimately failed). There were more general strains in rural society, and the spread of a commercialism linked to greater agricultural production for market that led to an increased shift from food production to sheep-rearing. This focused not on meat, but on the production of wool that could be used in the cloth industry which developed in northern Italy, Belgium – notably the cities of Bruges and Ghent – and, eventually, England.

The crisis of later medieval Europe also affected the Church. Disputes over papal elections and power led to the transfer of the papacy from Rome to Avignon (1305–77) and the Great Schism (1378–1417) in Western Christendom between areas owing allegiance to rival popes in Rome and Avignon, events which challenged patterns of authority and obedience, contributing to a sense of fragmentation.

Australasian Thought

In Australia, which remained isolated from Eurasian developments in trade, technology and religious beliefs, aboriginal pictures depict ancestral stories and traditional relationships with the environment, although the symbolism is often difficult to interpret. This art appeared in many different media, including decorated tumuli, bark paintings and drawings, and rock paintings and engravings. The nature of aboriginal society and material culture encouraged variety in expression. Representations were made by, and for, local people and therefore could draw heavily on local meanings. Australian rock paintings and engravings were identified with mythic beings

particular to specific rocks. These rocks created a sense that the landscape possessed a sacred quality that spanned the generations. Rock formations and water holes were seen as both physical and supernatural entities, and were given a dynamic character by the idea that 'Dreamings' (ancestral beings) had travelled along paths between them. Time, past and present, was brought together.

In New Zealand, a strong Maori tradition of storytelling was also based on an understanding of geography and landscapes. Names commemorated events such as journeys and related to an oral world of stories which was the major way of recording, analysing and communicating information. Maori mythology focused on the demigod Māui, under whom the islands of New Zealand allegedly originated. The landing places of the original settlers' canoes were of more particular note, as genealogies were traced back to those who came in them. The assertion of a relationship to Māui was also important, as part of a process in which tribal success over other tribes involved conflict between gods, leading to the spiritual union of conquerors with the land they had conquered.

Polynesian Travellers

To the north of New Zealand, the ancestors of the Polynesian culture of the southern Pacific had reached the Fiji-Samoa region by about 1000 BCE. From *c*.200 BCE, Polynesian colonists using twin-hulled canoes settled all the islands of the Pacific, reaching Easter Island in about 300, the Hawaiian Islands by about 400, and New Zealand by about 1200. These were formidable achievements. The Polynesian sailors employed the star compass for direction-finding, and could read the changes in swell patterns caused by islands. They also used charts made of sticks (notably the midribs of coconut fronds) and shells.

Left: Australian rock paintings were closely linked to particular rock formations

RENAISSANCE AND ENLIGHTENMENT
1500–1750

The 15th to 18th centuries are known as the early-modern period. International voyages of exploration, the Renaissance, and the Reformation, led to a world in which Western European powers reached every inhabited continent by 1800, but was wracked by nearly constant warfare at home. Elsewhere, the Mughals in India and the Manchu in China established states that covered immense territories, while in the Americas the great empires fell to the combined onslaught of foreign arms and diseases.

Exploring the Oceans

Chinese ships visited the eastern Indian Ocean during the Western Han dynasty (206 BCE–25 CE). By the 11th century they were making the round trip across the South China Sea to South-east Asia frequently, and nautical mapping originated in China at the latest in the 13th.

Below: The Chinese junks that made up Zheng He's fleet were much larger than European ships of the same period

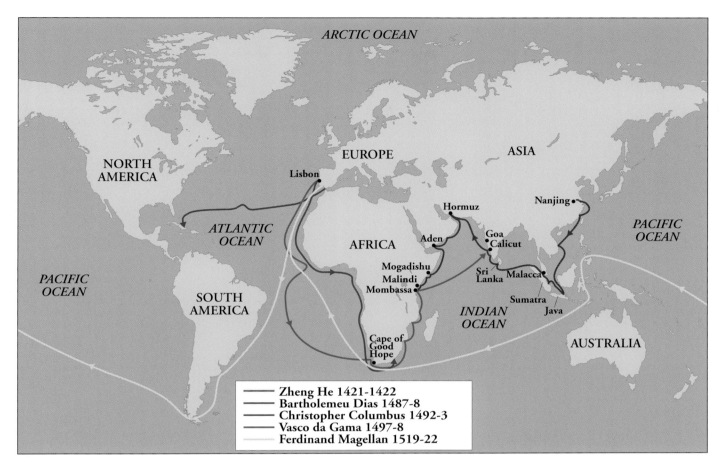

ARCTIC OCEAN

NORTH
AMERICA

EUROPE

ASIA

Lisbon

Nanjing

Hormuz

ATLANTIC
OCEAN

PACIFIC
OCEAN

AFRICA

Goa
Calicut

Aden

PACIFIC
OCEAN

Mogadishu
Malindi
Mombassa

Sri
Lanka

Malacca

SOUTH
AMERICA

Sumatra

INDIAN
OCEAN

Java

AUSTRALIA

Cape of
Good
Hope

——	Zheng He 1421-1422
——	Bartholemeu Dias 1487-8
——	Christopher Columbus 1492-3
——	Vasco da Gama 1497-8
——	Ferdinand Magellan 1519-22

Above: By the end of the 15th century, advances in naval technology allowed intrepid explorers to venture further afield than ever before

Right: Admiral Zheng He led great Chinese treasure fleets in voyages of exploration and diplomacy across the Indian Ocean between 1405 and 1433

In the early 15th century, Zheng He led a major series of voyages to explore the Indian Ocean. In their scale and conception these were like modern space programmes, with prestige, curiosity and technological achievements pursued alongside more specific military and political benefits. The voyages were intended to extend the range of the tributary system that was so important to China's view of its global position. Aside from sailing along the northern coasts of the Indian Ocean, Zheng went as far as the coast of East Africa.

The voyages were heavily dependent on political priorities rather than the pursuit of trade. A shift in China's strategic culture to concentrate on the land-based challenge of the Mongols, together with political changes within China and growing demographic and fiscal problems, led the Ming to order an end to the voyages in the 1430s. They were never to be resumed and Chinese maps and books showed only a limited knowledge of the trans-oceanic world.

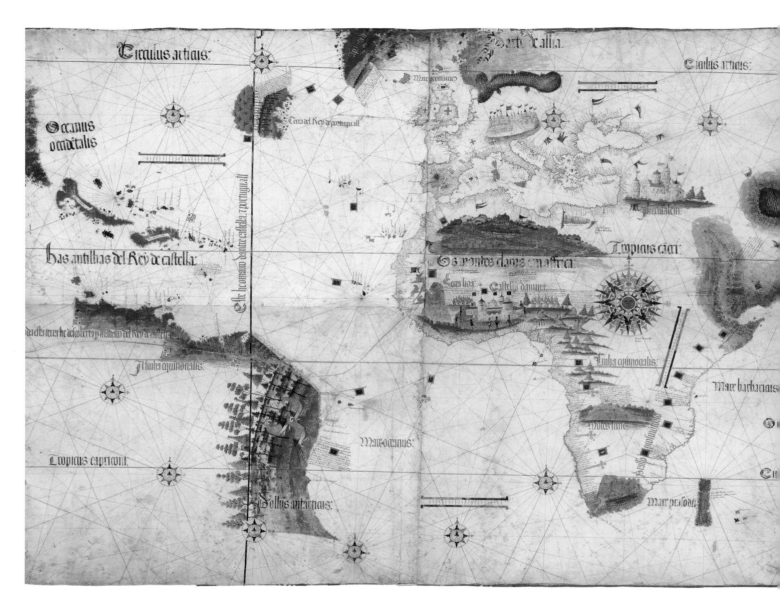

Above: The *Cantino Planisphere* showed the Portuguese discoveries in the Atlantic and Indian Oceans

Left: Christopher Columbus discovered the Americas in his quest to find a new route to Asia

Political factors were also important in the voyages of exploration undertaken by Portugal and then Spain in the 15th century. Their motivation was not simply the location of valuable goods, principally gold, but also as part of an intense rivalry with Islam. By sailing west in 1492 to discover a route to Asia, Christopher Columbus hoped to raise money to retake the Holy Land. Instead, he found the West Indies.

Bartholemeu Dias rounded the Cape of Good Hope in 1488 on behalf of Portugal, following a new route into the Indian Ocean which avoided that via Muslim-controlled Egypt and the Red Sea. A fellow navigator, Vasco da Gama, reached Calicut in 1498 at the end of the first all-sea journey from Europe to

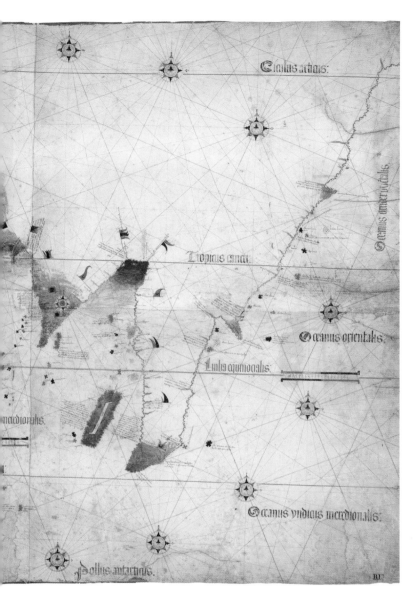

India. With their heavier cannon, his ships overcame resistance from Indian ships.

The Portuguese rapidly continued on from the Indian Ocean to China and Japan, establishing en route a series of bases, such as Malacca, conquered in 1511, that became the key points in a new naval-commercial empire, headquartered at Goa in India. The Portuguese also established trading bases at Macao in China and Nagasaki in Japan.

The first circumnavigation of the world, in 1519–22, begun by Ferdinand Magellan, was also the first

Right: In 1498 Vasco da Gama became the first European explorer to reach India by sailing around the Cape of Good Hope

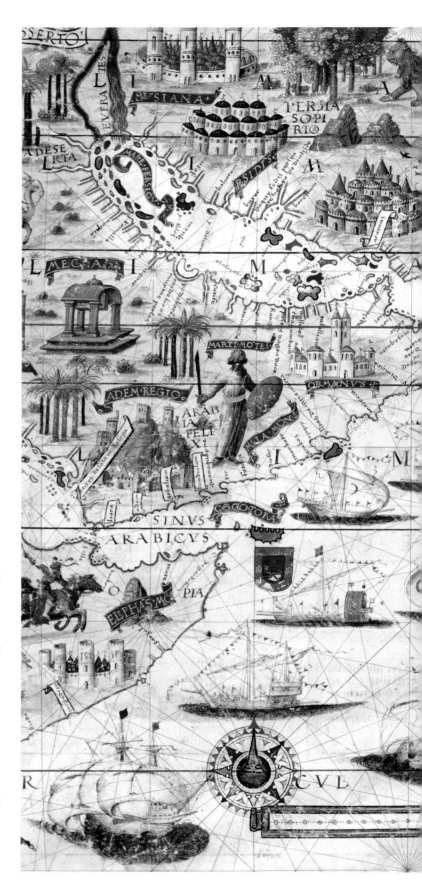

recorded rounding of the southern point of South America and the first recorded crossing of the Pacific, although Polynesian travellers had previously made long voyages across the ocean. Europeans were increasingly able to grasp the size and shape of the world, overthrowing the authority of Classical maps and geographers, and dealing a major blow to tradition as a source of information.

Western Europe's projection of its power also ensured that – once it had overcome the indigenous empires there – it was able to exploit the bullion resources of the New World, helping to increase liquidity and to finance trade with Asia. Although Spain profited greatly from this, with silver from Mexico and the 'silver mountain' at Potosi in Bolivia both coming from mines within the Spanish empire, those who traded with Spain, especially France and England, reaped much of the benefit. This enabled them to underwrite negative trade balances with Asia and to import goods from there.

Above: The New World provided a bounty of silver bullion for the Spanish. It facilitated trade with Asia and the Spanish Real, or piece of eight, became the currency of choice throughout the Americas

Left: Long ocean voyages were made possible by advances in shipbuilding technology

Right: The *Miller Atlas* demonstrated Europeans' improved understanding of the size and shape of the world they lived in

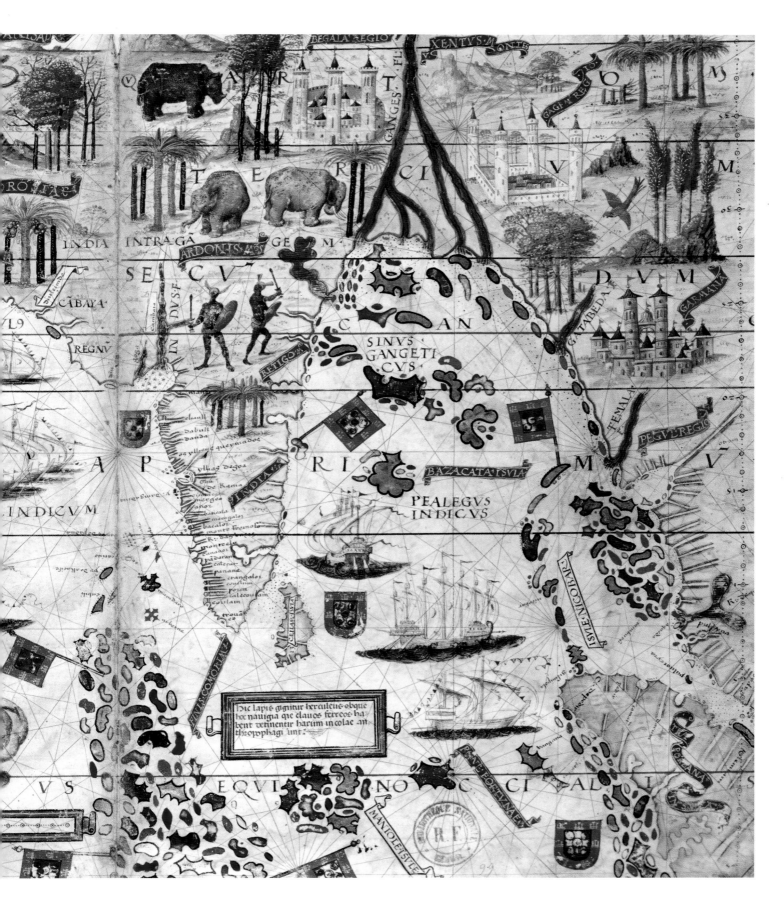

How we travelled – The Sea

Above: From the late 15th century, European ships grew larger and sturdier compared to their Indian Ocean counterparts

Large wooden ships, whether driven by sails, muscle-power (for galleys), or both (for galleys were equipped with masts and sails), were the single most costly, powerful and technologically advanced system of the period. The construction of large ships was the major industrial activity of the period. Carvel building (the edge-joining of hull planks over frames), a technique which spread from the late 15th century, contributed significantly to the development of stronger hulls in European ships compared to their Indian Ocean counterparts and allowed the carrying of heavier guns.

Developments in rigging permitted greater speed, improved manoeuvrability and a better ability to sail close to the wind. The number of masts rose, increasing the range of choices for rigging, and providing a crucial margin of safety in the event of damage to one mast. The use by Westerners of the compass for navigation had begun in the 12th century.

Mathematics was employed to produce maps for the great age of European exploration, notably with the use of the Mercator projection produced in 1569. Printing also became widespread, not only in producing maps but also in systematizing and disseminating knowledge and techniques, as with navigational treatises such as Edward Wright's *Certain Errors in Navigation* (1599) and Thomas Addison's *Arithmetical Navigation* (1625).

PIRACY

Piracy occurred wherever states were weak, as in the waters off South-east Asia. Pirates in effect taxed local trade, but they also profited from the growth of long-distance trade. To deal with their exactions, states had to deploy warships and also attack pirate bases on land. The most important maritime power, Britain, did this effectively: it operated against pirates in the 18th century in the Caribbean, in the 1750s, in Indian waters against Maratha pirates, and in the 19th century in those off South-east and East Asia, notably off northern Borneo. Prominent pirates, such as 'Blackbeard', Edward Teach, an English pirate who had blockaded Charleston and was killed in 1718, became romanticized figures.

Above: Pirates established themselves along trade routes across the world. In the Mediterranean, the Barbary pirates continued their war with European navies

Conquest of the Americas

Spain's conquest of the Aztecs of Mexico in 1519–21 and the Incas of Peru in 1531–35, transformed the New World, even though the Spanish never devoted the level of resources there that they used to protect their interests in Europe. Spanish conquest was not solely a matter of initial military success. In overthrowing the Aztecs, the Spanish superiority in battle, which owed much to steel helmets and swords, promised those who allied with them a good chance of victory, but the availability and willingness of local peoples, such as the Tlaxcaltecs, to co-operate with the Spanish reflected the nature of Aztec rule, and in particular the Aztec failure to assimilate subject peoples.

Below: Hernan Cortés, with a force of just 500 soldiers and the aid of local allies, defeated the far more numerous Aztec forces

In an echo of the clashes in the first century BCE between Iron Age peoples, neither Incas nor Aztecs had firearms or horses. Their societies were reliant on wood and stone, not iron and steel. Slings, wooden clubs and obsidian knives were no match for the Spaniards' firearms. Hernan Cortés had only about 500 Spanish soldiers, 14 small cannon and 16 horses when he landed at Vera Cruz in Mexico in 1519. Francisco Pizarro had just 168 Europeans, four cannon and 67 horses when he attacked the Incas.

The diseases the Spaniards brought with them were also crucial, notably smallpox, to which the inhabitants of the Americas had not been exposed and thus had no immunity. Smallpox decimated the population of the Caribbean as well as the Aztecs, killing up to half of the latter. The herding together of enslaved peoples, such as the Arawaks brought from the Bahamas to work the gold mines of Hispaniola, exacerbated the impact of disease.

Leadership weaknesses played an important role in the Aztec defeat. Montezuma, the panicky Aztec leader, was fascinated by Cortés, worried that

Above: Francisco Pizarro arrived at a time of turmoil among the Inca, allowing his force of 168 conquistadores to conquer a vast empire

Below: Atahualpa, one of the claimants to the Inca throne, was captured by the Spaniards and used to defeat his half-brother Huascar

he might be a god or an envoy from a powerful potentate, and unwilling to act decisively against him. In Aztec culture there was a strong overlap between humans and gods. Cortés reached the Aztec capital, Tenochtitlán, in central Mexico, without having to fight his way there from the coast. Montezuma was killed in a subsequent dispute in 1520, and his energetic brother, Cuitlahuac, who replaced him, died the same year from smallpox.

At the time the Spanish arrived in Peru, the Inca empire was affected by a disputed succession between Atahualpa and his half-brother, Huascar, which weakened it and affected how the faction reacted to the Spanish. Once captured by the Spaniards, Atahualpa was used against Huascar, before being killed.

Spanish conquest was followed by the arrival of colonists and their livestock, by Christian missionaries and the destruction of rival religious rituals, by the introduction of administrative and land-holding structures, and by a degree of Spanish acceptance of local elites and local material cultures, as well as of local adaptation to the Spaniards. Thus, after a period of highly-brutal destructiveness, some native religious

Above: Huascar succeeded Huayna Capac as Inca Emperor but his short reign was troubled by succession disputes and Spanish invasion

Left: Spanish missionaries were determined to establish Christianity in the New World

Above: Tupac Amaru, who reigned 1571–2, was the last Inca monarch, the son of Manco Inca. Manco Inca had led a major rebellion against Spanish rule in Peru in 1536, raising a force of 200,000 warriors and setting up a rebel state that survived until 1572

cults were given a place within Christianity.

In the Americas, native societies were typecast as harsh, primitive and uncivilized, and this encouraged not only total war and cruelty on the part of the conquerors, as in Mexico, but also a determination to extinguish the distinctive features of their society. There was a destruction of native religious sites and an extirpation of practices deemed unacceptable. While Christian worship in Spanish America might contain elements of compromise, there was no compromise about Christianity being the sole accepted religion.

Religion was the cause of tensions across much of Eurasia, although conquests by the Ottomans, Mughals or Manchus, did not lead to the end of other religious practices. In the Americas, the Spaniards and their descendants never outnumbered the indigenous or mixed population. As a result, although the Spaniards made unremitting war on the pagan deities, and used their control over native labour to lessen the position of the indigenous nobility, they left large tracts of land in the hands of co-operative natives. A similar pattern occurred during the Mughal conquest of northern India.

The Spanish regarded proselytism as a sign of superiority, a justification for conquest, and as a way to secure control. The outcome was an assault on native culture far greater than that seen for example in India, and a disruption of native society that contributed, alongside disease, to its breakdown. The result was a pattern of total conquest that drew its inspiration from the *Reconquista* (see page 81).

The harshness of Spanish rule was strengthened by key aspects of Western history and public culture in the 16th century. The assault on Christian territories by a revived Islam in the shape of the Ottoman empire (which involved the enslavement of Christians), and the increase in religious violence within Christendom due to the Reformation, deeply marked contemporary Spanish attitudes.

Discontent with the local power had led to the stunningly rapid collapse of the Aztec and Inca empires, but the Spanish found that consolidating their rule did not come easily. In Peru, a major rebellion broke out soon after the conquest was complete. Manco Inca, the younger brother of Huascar and intended as a Spanish puppet, escaped

Above: The expedition of Hernando de Soto into the Mississippi region of 1539–1542 brought devastating diseases to the local population

from Pizarro's custody and gathered an army of 200,00 warriors in 1536. Forced into the jungles of Vilcabamba, the rebellious state lived on until the death of Tupac Amaru, Manco's descendant, in 1572.

Elsewhere in North and South America, the Spanish faced opposition from local tribes. There was considerable variety in environment, economic development, social patterns and political organization. Some tribes were sophisticated, such as the emerald-mining Musica of the highland interior of Colombia, whom the Spanish conquered in a rapacious expedition of 1536. Yet, combined with difficult terrain, native opposition could pose formidable difficulties.

The scope and nature of the Spanish empire reflected the strength of local resistance. Where they had no local support, for example in central Chile, the Spaniards faced grave difficulties and were forced back from the southern Central Valley in 1598–1604: thereafter, the river Bió Bió was a frontier beyond which the Araucanians enjoyed independence. In northern Mexico, the nomadic warriors of the Gran Chichimeca used their archery to deadly effect in terrain that was often difficult for the Spanish cavalry. The Spaniards, in turn, raised allied native forces, so that the conflict became another version of the long-standing struggle between nomadic and sedentary peoples. The natives captured Spanish horses and used them to enhance their mobility. In the event, the Spaniards ultimately abandoned their aggressive policies, including slave-raiding, and switched to bribing their opponents with gifts, combined with Christian missionary activity, to lessen tensions. A 'middle ground' developed where colonizers and colonized interacted on the frontier and compromise rather than conquest was the rule. In northern Mexico, the alteration in Spanish policy provided an opportunity to increase settlements and establish forts.

Rumours of bullion encouraged Spanish expeditions north from Mexico into the American interior, such as that of Francisco Vásquez de Coronado into what is now New Mexico, and thence into the Great Plains in 1540. The rumours proved false. There were certainly no benefits to match those found in Mexico. There was no follow-up to the expedition of Hernando do Soto which brutally pillaged the Lower Mississippi and nearby lands between 1539 and 1542. In 1541, he won a battle with the Choctaw at Mobile (Selma, Alabama), whose lack of horses meant that the Spanish cavalry easily dominated the open ground. After Soto's death, de Moscoso pressed on in 1542–43 into what is now eastern Texas.

Recovery from the epidemics which expeditions such as this brought was made more difficult by colonial policies and practices. The requirements for large work-forces of plantation agriculture and mining, which became the predominant forms of economic activity, made the problem worse. The brutal solution was to engage in large-scale raiding outside Spanish-controlled areas, and the Spanish

Left: The *encomienda* system, which allocated land and native families to Spanish colonists, was criticized for its brutality by Spain's political opponents.

took large numbers of slaves in the sixteenth century among natives in Honduras and Nicaragua.

The sale of slaves destabilized native society by encouraging conflict between tribes in order to seize people for slavery. Royal legislation did affect control over native labour within the area of Spanish control, as it sought to address clerical pressure to treat the natives as subjects ready for conversion to Christianity, rather than as slaves. Native slavery was formally abolished in the *Leyes Nuevas* of 1542, but the legislation caused a rebellion among the Spaniards in Peru and was frequently ignored by local officials and landowners. Furthermore, systems of tied labour, especially the *encomienda* (by which land and native families were allocated to colonists), and forced migration, notably the *repartimiento*, under which a part of the male population had to work away from home, represented *de facto* slavery.

Although native slaves remained important in certain frontier regions, such as northern Mexico, cost and opportunity dictated their general replacement by slaves purchased in West Africa and shipped across the Atlantic. At first, Africans were shipped into Spanish America via Spain, but, from 1518, *asientos*, or licences, were granted allowing their direct movement. The expense of shipping meant that African slaves were initially more expensive than native slaves, and so they were often used as house slaves, a form of high-value slavery that indicated their cost.

By the mid-16th century, Africa was becoming more important as a source of slaves, in part because of the belief that Africans possessed greater physical strength than natives. The numbers of African slaves transported to the Americas increased greatly over the following century, but they remained more expensive than native labour which could be controlled by making service an element of debt repayment.

Spanish power expanded outside the Americas, as they established a base on the island of Cebu in the Philippines in 1565, followed by one at Manila. The island chain was then named after Philip II of Spain (r. 1556–98), who thereby became the ruler of the first empire on which the sun never set.

SHAKESPEARE AND THE AMERICAS

The English, too, were founding colonies. One major development in the lifetime of William Shakespeare's (1564–1616) was the establishment of English settlements in the New World, notably in Virginia, named after Elizabeth I, in 1607. Both Virginia and Bermuda have been presented as the inspiration for the play The Tempest *(first produced at the royal Court in 1611). Shakespeare captured the sense of spreading knowledge when, in* Twelfth Night *(1602), he has Maria say of the duped Malvolio 'he does smile his face into more lines than is in the new map with the augmentation [addition] of the Indies.' In* Henry VIII, *Shakespeare also commented on the fascination in London with the arrival of Native Americans: 'have we some strange Indian with the great tool [penis] come to court, the women so besiege us?' He presents popular curiosity in England as focused on novelty. In* The Tempest, *Trinculo sees the displaying to the public of Caliban, an inhabitant of the island, to the public as likely to earn money in England:*

*'not a holiday fool there but would give a piece of silver: there would this monster make a man; any strange beast there makes a man. When they will not give a doit [lift a finger] to relieve a lame beggar, they will lay out ten to see a dead Indian.' (*The Tempest *Act II, scene ii).*

Above: The new discoveries of the age made their way into Shakespeare's plays

Goods that changed the world – Sugar

For a culture short of sweeteners, sugar proved addictive, but the cultivation of sugar cane was an arduous task best suited to the heat and moisture of the Tropics. It became a leading factor in promoting the slave trade thanks to the establishment of plantation slavery on the Atlantic island of Madeira where Portuguese settlement began in 1424. From there, the slave-sugar economy spread to Brazil with the establishment of a Portuguese colony there, which had 192 sugar mills in around 1600, and then in the West Indies. On Jamaica, which the English had seized from Spain, there were 246 sugar plantations in 1684.

The slaves came mainly from West Africa where a large, well-established trade already supplied slaves to the Islamic world. The slave trade from Africa transformed the demographics, economics, society and politics of the eastern seaboard of the New World. About 12.5 million slaves were embarked from Africa to the Americas, although deaths in passage reduced the numbers who arrived to about 10.7 million. They were employed for a variety of tasks after their arrival, but principally in work on the plantations. Conditions for them were generally harsh

Sugar was the key source of profit from plantations, but plantation goods included tobacco, coffee and chocolate. Demand for sugar, as the sweetener of choice replacing honey, interacted with rapidly rising supply, leading to more investment and a fall in price in the 17th century. The addition of sugar to drinks increased their popularity by making them easier on the European palate: chocolate was altered by sugar, creating a sweet rather than

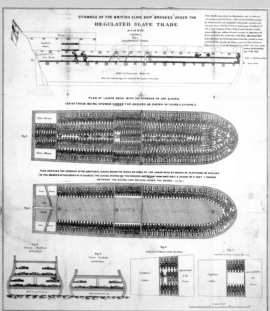

Above: The sugar economy that emerged in the 17th century required immense amounts of labour for challenging and dangerous work. Sugar and slavery went hand in hand

Left: More than 12.5 million slaves were packed onto ships to endure the terrible conditions of the middle passage from Africa to the New World

a bitter drink, which made it more popular in Europe and encouraged the growth in the import of its main ingredient, cacao. As the consumption of caffeine drinks, including tea from China, rose, so did demand for sugar. Teapots became an increasingly common item among household goods. Sugar's popularity was also attested by its addition to jam, cakes, biscuits and medicine.

The Ottoman Empire

While Europeans were establishing maritime empires, land-based empires were expanding in the non-European world. The Ottomans, a Muslim Turkic people and dynasty, established a frontier principality in Anatolia in the late 13th century and then enlarged it through incessant warfare with Byzantium, which had been greatly weakened by the crusaders' seizure of Constantinople during the Fourth Crusade in 1204.

Having gained a foothold in Europe at Gallipoli in 1354, the Ottomans conquered the Balkans in the 14th and 15th centuries, notably as a result of victory over the Serbs at Kosovo in 1389. The Ottomans benefited not only from the weakness of Byzantium but also from that of the Christian states that

Below: The fall of Constantinople to the Ottoman Turks marked a massive shift in power in the Mediterranean

challenged it. An invasion by Timur in 1402 briefly halted Ottoman expansion, but it resumed soon after, and Sultan Mehmed II took Constantinople in 1453.

The Ottomans combined the classic fluidity of Asian light cavalry tactics with an effective use of infantry, adapted to the possibilities offered by gunpowder. By the early 16th century, the Ottomans had successfully made the transition from tribal people to imperial power. In 1514, the Ottoman Sultan Selim I 'the Grim' (r. 1512–20) defeated the Safavids (who had recently conquered Persia), and then in 1516–17 overcame the Mamluks, seizing Syria, Lebanon, Israel, Palestine and Egypt. From Egypt, the Ottomans extended their power along the coast of North Africa and down the Red Sea to Aden.

Selim's son, Suleiman the Magnificent (r. 1520–66),

focused on Europe in the 1520s, capturing Belgrade (1521) and Rhodes (1522), defeating the Hungarians (1526) and unsuccessfully besieging Vienna (1529). Suleiman's subsequent choice to devote his attention to fighting the Safavids, from whom he conquered Iraq, eased the pressure on Christian Europe. Moreover, Christendom proved able to defend some of its key positions from Ottoman attack, notably Malta in 1565.

The Ottomans also developed a major naval capability based on the port-capital Constantinople. Ottoman naval power reached to the Indian Ocean and the Persian Gulf, but lacked the global range of the Atlantic powers. The most famous naval battle, that of Lepanto in 1571, was a crushing defeat for the Ottomans by a Spanish-Venetian fleet, but it did

not indicate any marked deficiencies in their naval technology. The Ottoman system partly rested on slavery to man their galleys and in producing the Janissaries, elite infantry.

In the 17th century, the Ottomans were unable to sustain their position. A second siege of Vienna in 1683 ended in a heavy defeat, after which they were driven from Hungary. A new war in 1717 ended with the loss of Belgrade, although the Ottomans recovered it in 1739 and continued to display considerable resilience, defeating Peter the Great of Russia at the River Pruth in 1711 and regaining southern Greece from Venice in 1715. Nevertheless, Russian pressure proved inexorable from the late 1730s and between then and 1812, Russia conquered the northern shores of the Black Sea and advanced south of the Danube.

Above: The Siege of Vienna in 1529 marked the furthest extent of Ottoman forces into Europe

Right: Suleiman I turned the power of his armed forces towards Europe

Africa

In Africa, the European colonial impact on Africa was limited in the 16th, 17th and 18th centuries. Portugal, the most active European power, suffered a heavy defeat in Morocco in 1578, failed to sustain an inland advance in Mozambique, and found expansion in Angola difficult. Instead, it was Muslim pressure that was most apparent. In 1591 a Moroccan force sent across the Sahara destroyed the Songhay empire of the Niger valley at Tondibi. Further east, the Ottomans supported attempts by the Muslim sultanate of Adal to conquer the Christian kingdom of Ethiopia. However, Serse-Dingil, who ruled Ethiopia from 1562, expanded his kingdom by defeating Adal and the Ottomans.

Sub-Saharan Africa experienced frequent conflict, in wars that produced slaves for the victors. Fighting was often linked to serious droughts and famine, although the introduction of maize, manioc and peanuts from the Americas helped support population numbers in Africa, just as the potato was to do in Europe. In Africa, the seizure of people for slavery was seen as a way to weaken rivals, while the availability of large numbers of slaves helped lower their price, which meant that their purchase by Europeans became more efficient as a way of addressing economic needs for labour in the New World. The nature of African agriculture lowered the cost of slaves further, with the widespread use of the hoe for cultivation, an inefficient practice that

Left: This warrior figure from the Niger valley dates to the 16th century and reflects the spread of bronze working in the region

Above: The Portuguese suffered a major defeat in Morocco at the Battle of Alcácer Quibir in 1578

limited the value of labour, ensuring that the benefit gained was not great.

In the 17th century, African warfare experienced a transformation, as firepower increasingly became preponderant over hand-to-hand combat, and armies grew larger. The European advantage in obtaining slaves came to rest not on greater military strength, but on their superior purchasing power derived from the prosperity of the plantation economies in the Americas and the integrated nature of the Atlantic economy.

THE RENAISSANCE

For centuries, learning and culture in Western Christendom had been largely confined to the monasteries, and mostly concerned itself with theological issues. Much intellectual effort centred around matters of religious doctrine, while painting, architecture and music were also largely in the service of the Church. The Renaissance, a movement of artistic and literary renewal which got underway in northern and central Italy in the 15th century, did not wholly change this situation, but it did encourage an engagement with lay issues and the concerns of lay patrons. The improving financial conditions of the middling orders, notably in the Italian cities, from the

Below: From the 14th century onwards, Italian scholars drew on the work of Petrarch and developed the doctrine of humanism that looked to Ancient Greek and Roman literature for inspiration

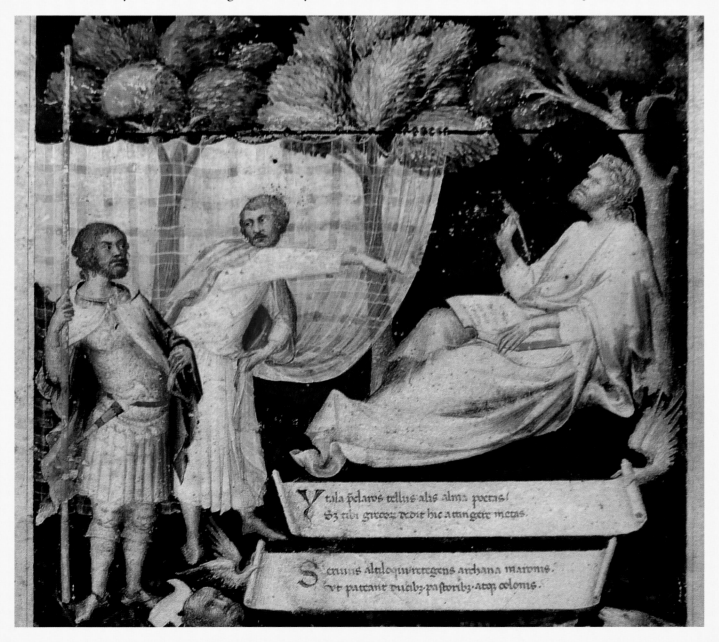

13th century, allowed wealthy citizens to seek a better education for their children, particularly their sons.

Far more than art was at stake. From the 14th century, a group of Italian scholars, inspired by the poet Petrarch, proposed a new educational syllabus, based on Classical literature, which they called *studia humanitatis*. Theology played no part, although the Humanists (as these scholars became known) did not go so far as to reject Christian doctrine. Instead, they shifted the emphasis from debating how a person should serve God to asking how the virtuous man should act.

The Renaissance also saw an upsurge in artistic activity, whose key figures were the Italian artists Raphael, Michelangelo and Leonardo da Vinci. They built on the achievements of a much broader Italian group which had made technical advances, such as in the understanding and presentation of perspective, and in the depiction of the human body. Notable in this regard were the sculptures of Donatello, including his *St George* (*c.*1416–17) and his *David* (*c.*1440–50), both held in Florence's Bargello museum.

The very diversity of Italy may have helped produce the variety and energy of the Renaissance. Cities such as Venice, Rome and Florence became centres of cultural creativity. Florence was at the forefront of this activity in the 15th century (*Quattrocento*), a position it lost to Rome and Venice in the 16th century (*Cinquecento*), notably with the paintings of Raphael and Michelangelo in the former, and of Giorgione, Titian and Tintoretto in the latter. The Florentine historian Francesco Guicciardini (1483–1540) discussed the idea that Italy's territorial divisions resulted in a diversity and competition that led to virtuosity. The divisions that allowed independence, for at least some cities, also provided opportunities for a distinctively Italian urban culture.

Renaissance thought represented both an attempt to understand new (and revived) information, much of it derived from rediscovered Greek and Roman works, and a drive to systematize it in order to provide a natural philosophy that could be used

Above: Sculptures like Michelangelo's *David* were iconic creations of the Renaissance

to comprehend and expound knowledge. The Renaissance advanced an ideal of good government, although a more ruthless pragmatism was also present, most obviously in the Florentine Niccolò Machiavelli, whose *Il Principe* (*The Prince*, 1532) provided a guide to winning power that was in part bitter, ironic and perceptive. Old and new ideas co-existed and interacted within Renaissance thought, such as in the interplay between science and astrology, where much attention was devoted to the cycles of the Heavens and their alleged impact on human life.

The Renaissance sought to rationalize the world, harmonizing the study of the natural world and Christian devotion to bring peace and fulfil divine goals. It linked intellectual speculation with religion,

and also with alchemy and magic. Harmony, the counterpoint of order, was believed to be inherently a good, as well as being a means to achieve good. Art was very much part of the process. Greater precision in representation was part of the process of showing God's work and the human sphere. Art and science combined in achieving this objective, as the understanding and use of perspective depended in turn on advances in mathematical knowledge.

Although it originated and flourished in Italy, the Renaissance also spread elsewhere. A Northern Renaissance took hold in major Belgian cities, especially Bruges and Ghent. Renaissance intellectuals also worked more widely, notably Leonardo da Vinci in France and the Dutch scholar Desiderius Erasmus (c.1466–1536) in Britain.

Above: Florence was the centre of intellectual and cultural creativity in the 15th century, only to be surpassed by Rome and Venice in the 16th

Right: Niccolò Machiavelli's political philosophy advocated ruthless pragmatism

Japan

Japan remained largely untouched by the expansion of the European maritime empires. Power in Japan was largely wielded by the *shogun*, the head of the government, as the emperor, whose court was in the city of Kyoto, was really a sacred figure with little secular authority. However, the *shogun*'s effective power was in turn limited by that of local warriors and rivalry between the military governors of the provinces. The Onin War of 1467–77, which arose from a succession dispute within the shogunal family, led to the age of *Sengoku* ('the country at war'). Warrior chieftains, known as *daimyo*, emerged, their position dependent on continual military success. Oda Nobunaga, a leading *daimyo*, achieved

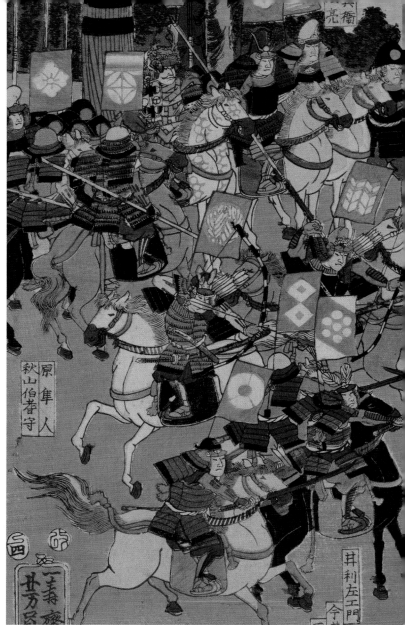

Above: Oda Nobunaga was a powerful *daimyo* and successful warrior but fell short of attaining the shogunate

dominance over most of the other warlords in the 1560s and 1570s, but was forced to commit suicide by a rival general in 1582. One of Nobunaga's protégés, Toyotomi Hideyoshi, defeated his principal opponents in 1582–85, conquered the island of Kyushu in 1587–8 and defeated the Hojo, the last clan to resist him, in 1590. Japan was largely united by the close of 1591.

Hideyoshi squandered his strength by an ultimately unsuccessful attempt to conquer Korea and take over China. Failures in Korea in 1592–93 and 1597–98, where China intervened against him, and Hideyoshi's death in 1598, led to the rise of Tokugawa Ieyasu, another *daimyo*. He overcame most of his opponents in 1600, finally defeating Hideyoshi's son, Hideyori, in 1614–15.

Above: The period 1467–1603 was known as *Sengoku*, the 'Age of the Country at War'

The Tokugawa Shogunate which Ieyasu established lasted until 1868. It was a long period of external peace in which Japan did not seek foreign conquests, or even the extension of Japanese control in the northern island of Hokkaido against the native Ainu people.

As with China, Japanese culture placed an emphasis on the purity of those who lived in the core areas of the state. Those who lived further away were considered impure, which lessened the possibility of learning from them and the value of any effort to do so. After the Chinese refusal in the 1590s to accept any equality of status, Japan saved face by restricting its diplomatic links largely to Korea and the conquered kingdom of Ryukyu.

Limited numbers of European merchants had traded with Japan, but the Portuguese were expelled in 1639 after the suppression of a rebellion by Christian converts and links with the Dutch were greatly reduced in 1641, when the *shogun* Tokugawa Iemitsu restricted the Dutch to an island in Nagasaki harbour. However, by the 18th century a significant increase in publishing and intellectual activity had occurred, with political economists who sought information about China focusing on ideas of national benefit. At the same time, social tension rose, in large part due to the pressure exerted by a growing population on limited resources, notably land. Alongside calls for reform, there was a degree of pessimism about how to deal with these problems.

Manchu Conquest of China

Nothing in the European world, and nothing else in Eurasia, compared to the scale and drama of the overthrow of Ming China, which brought down an empire established in the late 1360s. The Ming were replaced by the Manchu, descendants of the Jurchen Jin who had controlled northern China from 1126 until their overthrow by the Mongols in 1234.

From their base in the mountains of south-eastern Manchuria, the Jurchens expanded in the early 17th century under Nurhaci (1559–1626) to dominate the lands to the north of the Great Wall. Like the Mongol leader Chinggis Khan, Nurhaci employed organizational methods to overcome the reluctance of

the tribes to act together and also to bring cohesion to cavalry warfare.

Nurhaci repeatedly attacked China from 1618, but he also emulated the political techniques and administrative structures of imperial China, a process that increased the Manchu appeal to dissident and defeated Chinese. Authority was focused on loyalty to the ruler and not on the ethnic group of invaders.

Late Ming China suffered from a lack of unity, particularly after 1582 with a succession of weak emperors, increasingly arbitrary central government, oppressive taxation and the rise of ambitious, independent figures in the provinces. Li Zicheng, one of these regional warlords, ultimately toppled the incompetent Chongzhen emperor (r. 1628–44) who committed suicide when Beijing fell. Li proclaimed the Shun dynasty, but his army was poorly disciplined, and he lacked legitimacy, the support of powerful allies or an administrative apparatus. Key Ming commanders, notably Wu Sangui, preferred to turn instead to the Manchu and Li was defeated in 1644. The Manchu then used supportive Chinese units to help in the rapid conquest of central and southern China, capturing Nanjing in 1645.

The Manchu conquest involved redefinitions of cultural loyalty in which distinctions between Chinese and 'barbarian' became less apparent and definitions less rigid. The Manchu state owed its lasting success in large part to its ability to draw on and adapt to different traditions; as Spain had done to a degree in Central and South America, and Britain was to do in India. Manchu expansion continued under the emperors, with the conquest of Taiwan, Tibet and Xinjiang and much of Turkestan in the period 1680–1760, representing a marked extension of control over peoples who were not ethnic Chinese.

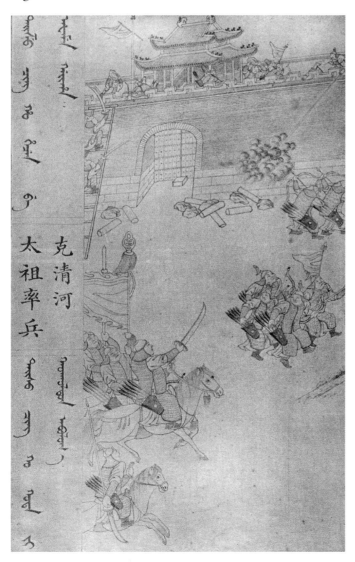

Left: Manchu forces based in the north-east repeatedly attacked China from 1618 and replaced the Ming dynasty in 1644

Cities – An Asian-dominated Hierarchy

During the early modern period, the world's major cities were situated in Asia, where two-thirds of the world's population also lived. There were significant changes in the urban hierarchy in Asia, in which both economic and political factors played a role. In north India, Agra was founded in 1505 as the capital of the Lodi sultanate, so beginning its development into a major centre. Beijing and Nanjing remained key governmental centres in China, while in Japan Kyoto was challenged by the rise of Edo (Tokyo).

Above: The city of Edo (Tokyo) challenged the old capital of Kyoto for dominance in Japan

However, it was those cities that directed the expanding Europe-based maritime empires that were of growing global importance, first Lisbon and Seville and, later, Amsterdam and London. There were also new cities in the European empires that became the centres of government and commerce: Havana and Panama were both founded by Spain in 1519; Quebec (1608), New Amsterdam (1626, later New York), and Cape Town (1652) were established by France, the Dutch and the British respectively.

Despite the powerful desire of many cities to run their own affairs as independent entities, territorial states were effective providers of protection to urban areas. Many states developed as combinations of the landed power of rulers and rural elites married with the financial resources and mercantile interests of urban elites. This process, common in Western Europe, was less so elsewhere due to the greater social, ethnic and religious differences between rural and urban elites.

Asian cities remained dominant in the 18th century, but European centres began to challenge them. Of the 19 cities in the world believed to have had a population of over 300,000 in 1800, five were in Europe: London (in 3rd position), Constantinople (Istanbul, 8th), Paris (9th), Naples (14th), and St Petersburg (17th). London was becoming the world city, the centre of trading companies such as the East India and Hudson Bay that reached across the globe. Rebuilt after the Great Fire of 1666, London greatly impressed contemporaries as the city of the new. In some regions, though, cities were less important: sub-Saharan Africa had few of them, and Australasia none at all.

Mughal India

Early Modern India was dominated by the Mughal empire. Founded as a result of the overthrow of the Lodi sultanate of Delhi in 1526, it was initially based in northern India, but expanded greatly under Akbar (r. 1556–1605) and, even more, under Aurangzeb (r. 1658–1707). Although the Mughals conquered central India, Aurangzeb faced growing resistance from the Hindu Marathas based in the Western Ghats and was unable, despite major efforts, to crush them.

Despite the Mughal establishment of observatories, notably five at Jaipur between 1722 and 1739, they did not create a scientific infrastructure similar to the Western one. The strong and continuing Mughal loyalty to their Central Asian legacy affected the ability of the Mughal emperors to respond to the intellectual, cultural and economic challenges of India. Nevertheless, there were significant advances in Indian science and technology, major efforts to understand the natural world and considerable interest in Western scientific knowledge, which served as the basis for the strong Indian contribution to the subsequent science of British India.

The Maratha Confederacy was established in the Deccan Plateau in 1674. After Aurangzeb's death, the Mughals suffered from Maratha expansionism and the increasing independence of its governors. Invasions of northern India by Nadir Shah of Persia in 1739 and by the Afghans in 1761 further weakened the Mughals. In 1803, the British occupied Delhi and in 1857 deposed the last Mughal emperor.

Right: Under Aurangzeb, the Mughal empire expanded to encompass most of the Indian subcontinent, but was unable to overcome the resistance of the Marathas in the Western Ghats

The Reformation

Europe, although economically expansive overseas, suffered considerable instability at home. Deep unease at the corruption of the Catholic Church was harnessed by the German monk Martin Luther, who in 1517 publicized his grievances by fixing his *95 Theses* to the church door in Wittenberg. The Reformation, the movement that Luther sparked, swiftly moved from being a potential force for revival within Roman Catholicism and, instead, took new form in the different religious systems of Protestantism, especially Lutheranism and Calvinism. Rejecting the authority of the Pope, Protestants sought validation from the Bible rather than the Church. This led them to emphasize the importance of the people being able to read the Bible (and so to promote literacy), and to favour its publication in the vernacular (the native language), rather than in Latin. The new technology of printing was critical to the success of the Reformation: printers were able to produce copies of Luther's sermons more speedily than the Church could destroy them.

The Reformation shattered important traditional patterns of faith, as with the ending of masses for the dead and the attack on sacred places, saints and miracles. Protestants argued that miracles had occurred in biblical times (confirming the divine origin of the Bible), but they claimed that they had ceased thereafter, and that assertions to the contrary by the Catholic Church were a form of false information.

Protestant churches became the established (state) church in Scandinavia, Scotland, England, the Netherlands and

Left: The printing press was essential to the spread of the Reformation. Bibles in the vernacular could soon be found across Europe

Below: Martin Luther attacked the corruption of the Catholic Church and began the Protestant Reformation when he nailed his 95 theses to a church door in Wittenberg

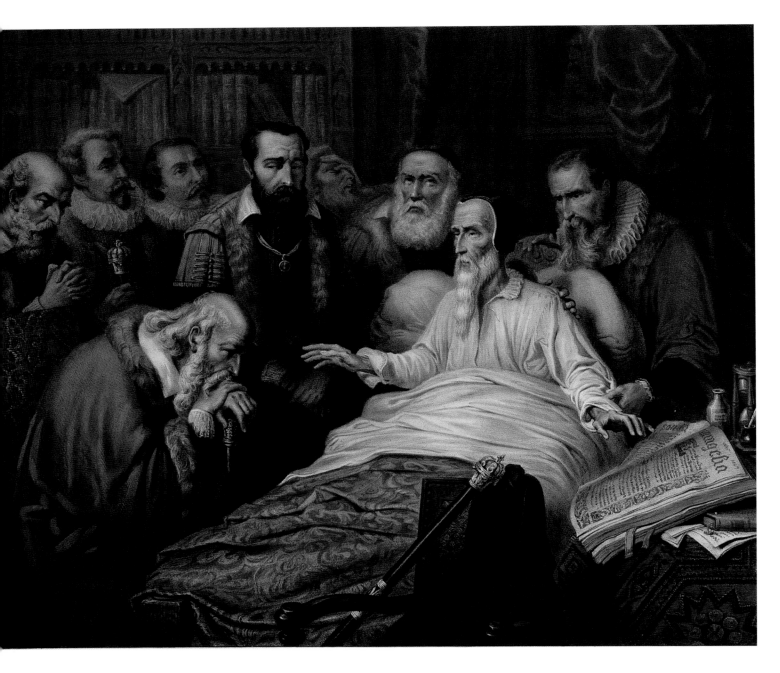

Above: John Calvin preached a different variant of the Reformation to Luther which held sway in Scotland, Geneva, the Netherlands and parts of Germany

much of Switzerland and Germany. The Church of England was the distinctive national church there. Scotland, Geneva, the Netherlands and parts of Germany followed Calvinism, while Lutheranism became the main form of Protestantism in Scandinavia and north Germany.

The Catholic Church reacted to the advances of Protestantism by launching its own movement for renewal, the Counter-Reformation, that began in the mid-16th century. Between 1545 and 1563, the Council of Trent reaffirmed the key doctrines of the church. New religious orders were established, reforms were made to eliminate the worst abuses, such as simony (the selling of church offices), that had plagued the medieval institution. Over the period 1614–48, the renewed Catholicism defeated Protestantism in what became Austria, the Czech Republic, Hungary, Slovakia, Belgium, France, Poland and much of Germany.

European Warfare

In Europe, as elsewhere, notably India and Japan, war was a major feature of the 16th century. The frequency of conflict reflected the extent to which the ability of European states to finance military activity increased in the late 15th and early 16th centuries, with their greater political consolidation, administrative development and economic growth as populations recovered from the Black Death. Although the Protestant Reformation increased demographic divisions from the 1520s, challenging this consolidation, the population growth of the 16th century helped ensure that more resources could be tapped, both in manpower and finance.

The growing strength and sophistication of government were most apparent at sea, where fleets far larger and more powerful than those of the 15th century were created and maintained. Maritime capability and warfare required detailed planning, logistical support, political commitment, administrative competence, leadership and training, as well as an ability to overcome the challenges posed by technological innovation. Military and political factors combined to ensure that no one power was able to dominate Europe in the 16th, 17th and 18th centuries. Battles were usually won by experienced and motivated troops whose dispositions had been well arranged, as with the Swedish victory over Austrian forces at Breitenfeld (1631) during the Thirty Years' War (1618–48). If armies were evenly matched, battles tended to be inconclusive encounters or were determined by other factors, such as terrain, the availability and employment of reserves and the results of cavalry clashes on the flanks, which could leave the victorious cavalry free to attack the infantry in the flank or rear. Sieges were also a key factor in warfare, one in which investment in new fortifications was countered by the development of siege techniques, not least due to more powerful artillery.

The cost of armies and navies put pressure on the ability of states to sustain conflict. Many smaller states turned to mercenaries to match the demands for vast numbers of high quality soldiers. Fighting in the Swiss Guard, the German *Landsknechte* or the Scottish and Irish Gallowglass proved highly profitable careers in

Above: Muskets and pikes came to dominate the European battlefields of the 16th and 17th centuries

Right: Gustavus Adolphus' victory at the Battle of Breitenfeld in 1631 owed much to a disciplined and experienced army

EUROPEAN WARFARE 1560–1648

The 'Wars of Religion' in Europe in the 16th and early-17th century helped define the boundaries of Protestantism and Catholicism in Europe to the present. The conflicts also ensured that Spain would not be able to dominate Western Europe, while the Austrian Habsburgs were unable to crush opposition. As a consequence, Christian Europe remained 'multipolar.' Moreover, Spain's failure proved important to the development of Dutch and English maritime power and ambitions.

the war-obsessed world of 16th- and 17th-century Europe.

The demands of war and the growing military capability it required increasingly shaped the states which conducted it. Capitalism intersected with the state to enable governments to marshal the necessary resources, leading to the establishment of institutions such as the Bank of England, founded in 1694.

Above: Many states relied on mercenaries for their military needs. The German *Landsknechte* were a highly respected, and highly expensive, mercenary force

| 1550 | 1560 | 1570 | 1580 | 1590 | 1600 | 1610 |

1562–1598
French Wars of Religion

The struggle between Protestants and Catholics challenged and then overturned French stability, culminating in a total collapse in 1589. Foreign intervention complicated the stiuation. A precarious stability was regained in the late 1590s.

1585–1604
Anglo-Spanish War

English concern about the Spanish suppression of Dutch Protestantism led to the outbreak of full-scale war. It was also waged on the oceans with English attacks on Spanish trade and colonies. A Spanish attempt to invade England by means of the Armada failed totally in 1588.

1566–1648
The Eighty Years War

The Dutch provinces ruled by Philip II of Spain rejected his attempt to limit their liberties and this led to a long war in which Spain regained what became Belgium, but failed in what became the Netherlands. The former became Catholic, the latter Protestant.

| 1620 | 1630 | 1640 | 1650 | 1660 | 1670 | 1680 | 1690 | 1700 | 1710 | 1720 | 1730 | 1740 | 1750 | 1760 |

1688–1697

The Nine Years' War

The expansionism of Louis XIV of France was stopped in this conflict and in the subsequent War of the Spanish Succession (1701–14) by an alliance of Austria, Britain and the Dutch.

1740–1748

War of Austrian Succession

The rise of Prussian power was a key element in this conflict, as was the failure of the French-backed Jacobite rebellion to overturn the British system.

1756–1763

Seven Years' War

Britain emerged as the dominant power after conquering much of the French and part of the Spanish overseas empires. Naval power, amphibious capability and fiscal strength were key elements.

Absolute Monarchy

The wars of the period 1560–1660 were followed by a period of consolidation and relative internal stability, notably under Louis XIV of France (r. 1643–1715). Monarchs increasingly resisted constraints on their powers, claiming their power descended from God rather than up from the people. They maintained they should not be subject to the demands of their subjects and developed a system of government known as absolutism which became prevalent in the period.

Absolutist states were traditionally seen as powerful entities who monopolized power by the government and strictly followed the will of the ruler. In practice, the ruler's power was limited by hostility to government demands, the often tenuous control of the ruler over the bureaucracy and attitudes towards the proper extent of monarchical authority. In Europe, clear hostility to the idea of despotism, and conventions of acceptable royal behaviour, limited the possibilities for wielding power. Powerful advisers such as Cardinal Richelieu in France could also wield extraordinary influence, in part due to their ability to control access to the monarch.

Loyalty to a dynasty did not provide the ideological focus for unity that nationalism was to offer in the 19th century. Central governments were short of

Left: The impressive Palace at Versailles helped to mask the king's continued dependence on local institutions and the support of allies in court

Above: Louis XIV of France, the 'Sun King' was the epitome of absolute monarchy

resources, lacked relevant information and had poor communications. The best way to govern and address the problem of raising taxation was in co-operation with those who wielded social power and with local authorities. Behind the façade of absolutism, the imposing palaces imitating Louis XIV's Versailles, and the larger armies, governments were dependent on local allies and sought the co-operation of the influential. Even Louis XIV's officials had to co-operate with local institutions, while the reach of Prussian government did not extend to the estates of the aristocracy.

The Scientific Revolution

In attacking the role of the Catholic Church as a source and guarantor of truth, the Reformation opened the way to the Scientific Revolution of the 17th century by encouraging an emphasis on scientific research based on empirical perception and measurements. The state became more involved, as, for example, in England, with the foundation of the Royal Society in 1660.

The work of Isaac Newton (1642–1727) represented a major advance in Western thought. The laws on scientific reactions developed by Newton, Robert Boyle and others sought to establish clear causal relationships with universal applicability. The physical system was mathematized, permitting theoretical extrapolation from scientific observations. The stress on a mechanized cosmos reflected a general focus on regular and predictable processes and forces. It formed part of a revolution that helped ensure that in a world that was more and more understood in scientific terms, these terms were Western and linked to other aspects of Western Culture.

Technology opened a significant divide between the West and much of the rest of the world. The development of lenses was one exampleå. The use of glassmaking for lenses and equipment became more sophisticated in the West compared to China and the Islamic world. In the West, telescopes, microscopes and glass chemical apparatus that permitted the observation of reactions were all significant to experimentation. Galileo used the telescope to increase greatly the understanding of the solar system (discovering several new moons of Jupiter in 1610). The standardization of both equipment and measurement aided all areas of life, including science, administration and trade.

Left: Isaac Newton's discovery of gravity was part of a scientific revolution in 17th century Europe

Enlightenment

The Enlightenment was a highly diverse movement, part of a tendency in 18th-century Europe towards critical enquiry and the application of reason. Enlightenment thinkers believed it necessary to use reason, uninhibited by authority and tradition, in order to appreciate man, society and the universe, and so improve human circumstances. Some thinkers, such as Jean-Jacques Rousseau (1712–78), believed that existing authorities were an active restraint on the quest for reason and adopted critical views accordingly, but his views were untypical. Most Enlightenment figures were able to reconcile their universalist and subversive theories of reason with the particular circumstances of their countries and positions, and with the suppositions of traditional authorities. Challenges to Christian teaching were few.

The contradictions among Enlightenment figures ensured that there were pessimistic and optimistic strains, as well as humanitarian, liberal, moral and totalitarian dimensions. The crusading zeal of particular Enlightenment campaigns, for example against torture and against the Jesuits, was not matched by a consistent code, other than one expressed in generalities such as tolerance and reason.

Enlightenment thought affected policy. The so-called Enlightened Despots, such as Frederick the Great of Prussia (r. 1740–86), Catherine the Great of Russia (r. 1762–96), and Joseph II of Austria (r. 1780–90), sought to reform government and improve society as well as strengthen the state. The Enlightened Despots attacked clerical power and privileges, and backed religious toleration and legal reforms.

Left: The *Weimarer Musenhof*, featuring esteemed writers and thinkers such as Goethe and Schiller, was an example of the new approach to thought embodied by the Enlightenment

Right: Jean-Jacques Rousseau was one of the few Enlightenment thinkers who genuinely clashed with traditional authorities

Improving Communications

Even in Enlightenment Europe, with distance as the enemy and accurate news a luxury, society was at the mercy of rumour and speculation. Information could only be confirmed by waiting for subsequent messages. Uncertainty about the speed and even arrival of messages ensured that they were often sent simultaneously in multiple versions by separate routes. From India to Britain, routes ran via the Middle East, either up the Red Sea or the Persian Gulf, and then overland, and also by sea around the Cape of Good Hope. From Constantinople (Istanbul) to London, routes ran overland via Vienna and also by sea, up the Adriatic to Venice and then overland, or by the Mediterranean to Marseille and then overland, or by sea all the way.

In response to these limitations, postal courier systems developed in Europe from the 15th century. At first government-operated, they were opened up to the public, proving important to merchants and in the development of newspapers.

Road-building provided benefits, especially in Japan and France. Even so, speed was determined by animal endurance and muscle, and human porterage was crucial in many areas, including Japan, sub-Saharan Africa and South America. Rainfall affected roads, while both snow melt and heavy rains could make it impossible to pass rivers by fords or ferries. Rivers were also affected by drought, freezing and weirs, and mountain crossings by snow and ice.

There were significant improvements in transportation by sea, especially better rudders and, in the 18th century, an enhanced ability to calculate the position of ships thanks to the ability to measure longitude. Nevertheless, strong winds or the absence of wind, as well as ice, and poor charts, all affected sea travel.

The world before telegraphs, railways and steamships posed major challenges for the transmission of information. It is not surprising that details of the movements of letters and couriers, and of their all-too-frequent mishaps and related uncertainties, crop up regularly in the correspondence and diaries of the period.

Below: Extensive road-building occurred in Europe and Japan, allowing for faster travel and the development of postal systems

CHINA AND THE JESUITS

As societies expanded their activities across the world, issues of comprehension and questions of adaptability came to the fore. Cultures claiming to deploy universal truths had to decide how to respond when faced with different world views. In the 17th century, Jesuit missionaries sought to accommodate Christianity to Chinese customs, especially ancestor worship, in an attempt to create a dialogue with Chinese traditions and to show how the Christian message complemented the local culture. The scientific skills of the Jesuits were useful to the Chinese government which was increasingly aware – through the presence of Westerners on their coast and of Russia in Siberia to the north – of a shifting world order. The Jesuits provided information on cannon-casting, mapping and astronomy. The Qianlong Emperor (1735–96) favoured their presence on the Chinese Board of Astronomy in order to prevent partisan accounts of eclipses and other phenomena. However, the Jesuit willingness to accept Chinese rites led to papal condemnation. Most Chinese intellectuals were hostile to the Jesuits, and there was no equivalent in China to the sustained engagement with outside culture seen in Russia from the reign of Peter the Great (r. 1689–1725). China's quest to order and understand information continued to be pursued on its own terms.

Right: Matteo Ricci (1552–1610) was one of a number of Jesuit missionaries to China, who adapted their practices to local Chinese customs

The World Economy in the 18th Century

The bullion resources of the New World remained under European control. Alongside Spanish silver, Britain gained much of the commercial and financial benefit from the significant gold deposits found from the 1700s in the expanding Portuguese colony of Brazil, notably in Minas Gerais. Alongside commercial strength, political stability, and the continuity of a Parliament-funded national debt, this resource helped the British government to borrow at a low rate of interest. As a result of its exploitation of bullion resources, the West acquired an important comparative advantage. Asian powers might receive bullion for their products, such as the tea and ceramics imported by Westerners from China, but access to bullion supplies ensured that Westerners were able to insert themselves into the non-Western world and had the resources to hire local troops, as

Below: The Portuguese colony of Minas Gerais in the south-east of Brazil continued to expand throughout the 18th century

both the British and the French did in India.

The projection of its power overseas and the subsequent development of its capability on land enabled Western Europe to develop and exploit a hinterland in the Americas. This proved both larger and more economically useful than that of any non-European power, especially that of China in the expanses of Mongolia, Tibet, Xinjiang and the Amur Valley. The New World hinterland offered the West a host of advantages, including, by 1800, relatively low protection costs in the face of native peoples unable to threaten the core Western settlements in the Americas. There were also important economic benefits, not least rich soils that had not yet been denuded by intensive cultivation, were well-watered and in terrain that was not particularly mountainous (all advantages that the Chinese hinterland did not enjoy).

In North America, there were also fewer problems with disease than were encountered in tropical areas, for example by Europeans in the Caribbean and West Africa, and by the Chinese in Myanmar in the 1760s. Yellow fever and malaria were particular obstacles in the tropics, and made more so by a total failure to understand how they operated. In particular, the vectors of disease, their means of transmission, for example by mosquitoes for malaria, were unknown.

The trade in importing planation goods from the colonies that Western Europe could not produce – sugar, coffee, rice, cocoa, indigo and cotton – proved very profitable. It helped underscore the growth of Western-run transoceanic trading systems and of Western financial and mercantile capital and organization, including the flow of information about production and markets, and the accompanying understanding and control of risk. The predictability of international trade increased.

Although China's population rose greatly from about 150 million in 1650 to about 300 million in 1800, in part as a result of the introduction there of New World crops (sweet potatoes and

Above: China's population grew rapidly over the 18th century, partly due to the introduction of New World crops, but did not receive the same economic benefits from these as did the West

peanuts), there was no comparable economic benefit for China or other non-Western powers. Approaching the New World from the Atlantic, an ocean far smaller than the Pacific, was not an option for these powers, but there was no inherent reason why the heavily-populated regions of East and South Asia should not have sought colonial expansion elsewhere in Asia or further afield. Such expansion, however, was not in accord with the ruling groups, Ming, Manchu and Mughals, which focused insteads on the security considerations raised by invasion and the threat of attack from the Eurasian interior. The extent to which trans-oceanic maritime trade to East and South Asia was, in the main, conducted by Westerners also greatly affected the strength of the local maritime infrastructure.

Left: International trade became more predictable by the 18th century and Chinese porcelain could soon be found around the world

REVOLUTION AND NATIONALISM
1750–1914

The 19th century saw European countries and the United States becoming increasingly dominant on the world stage. European political power, economic activity and cultural spread encouraged Westerners to regard themselves as at the cutting-edge of civilization. The Western world changed dramatically between 1756 and 1830. Britain became the dominant imperial power, but European colonial control then collapsed over most of the Americas as a struggle for power, and of ideas, within that world completely reshaped it. Combined with the major economic changes known as the Industrial Revolution, this transformation of the Western world provided the background for the spread of Western control over most of the world by 1920, though there were important exceptions in Japan, Ethiopia and Thailand.

Right: Benjamin West's famous 1770 painting of the death of Benjamin Wolfe at Quebec in 1759 depicted one of many dramatic moments in the Seven Years' War

1750

1800

1789
French revolution
begins

1783
Independence of the future
United States recognized

1775
Revolution begins in
North America

1821
Bolivár secures Venezuelan
independence from Spain

1804
Revolution in Haiti ends with
independence from France

The Seven Years' War, 1756–63

A key element in the modernization of the world was provided by the British maritime and imperial dominance secured in a series of wars with France and its allies between 1756 and 1815. This dominance helped direct the pattern of developments in the 19th century, including securing the independence of Spanish America and underwriting free trade and a liberal economic order.

The Seven Years' War began as a result of fighting in 1754 in the interior of North America, where French and British expansionist projects clashed in the Ohio River Valley, and then became full-scale and was formally declared in 1756. Initially, France did well in North America, but in 1758–60 British forces conquered New France (Canada). A key element in North America was the determination of the British government to act there well before naval superiority was clearly achieved in 1759, an attitude which led to the adoption of an offensive strategy with the dispatch of major forces. Political attitudes were crucial, ensuring that British failures in North America in 1755–57 encouraged greater commitments rather than withdrawal. The British also conquered most of the French positions in the Caribbean as well as those in India and West Africa. Spain came into the war on France's side in 1762, but the British then captured the key Spanish overseas bases of Havana and Manila.

In Europe, British naval victories saw off a French invasion attempt in 1759, while Britain's ally Prussia held off a powerful coalition of Austria, France and Russia, thanks to the skilled generalship of Frederick the Great (r. 1740–86). The peace saw Britain acquire Canada, Florida and a number of Caribbean islands.

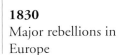

1850

1900

1830
Major rebellions in Europe

1851
Taiping Rebellion begins in China

1848
A new wave of rebellions in Europe

1857–59
Indian Mutiny

1861–65
The American Civil War

1868–69
Overthrow of the shogunate in Japan

The American War of Independence

The American War of Independence began in 1775 as a challenge to the authority of the British Parliament to lay down rules for its North American colonies, and notably to levy taxes. In 1776 it became a struggle for independence. By the end of March that year, all British troops had been driven out of the 13 colonies that had rebelled.

The British hit back with a formidable effort, as befitted the leading naval power in the world. They captured New York in 1776, Savannah in 1778, and Charleston in 1780. The war continued until 1783, and it was unclear what would happen. With the British victorious at Long Island (1776), Brandywine (1777) and Camden (1780), and the Americans at Saratoga (1777), neither side could knock out the other. The entry of the French on the side of the

Below: In 1776, the Thirteen Colonies signed the Declaration of Independence in protest against British taxation

rebels proved decisive, as the war became a worldwide one and France was soon joined by Spain. In the end, Britain, with part of its army defeated in North America at Yorktown in 1781 by an American-French force, faced a political crisis at home in 1782 and had to concede independence, but most of the British empire survived the struggle.

Independence was clearly linked to expansion, notably with the British cession of the 'Old Northwest' – Trans-Appalachia – to America in 1783, a cession that greatly increased the land mass offered by the 13 colonies. In fact, few Americans lived there.

Above: The British defeat at Yorktown was a turning point in the American War of Independence

Made without mention of, or the consent of, the Native population, this was followed by American claims, warfare, and settlement in the region. The Natives were seen as at an earlier stage of human development and as unable to share in the future of North America unless they became 'civilized' on American terms. Ambition and anxiety combined to drive forward American expansion, but attempts to conquer Canada failed, and it remained part of the British empire.

Revolutions in Science

Revolutions were not confined to the political sphere. In the late 18th century, great advances occurred in the field of chemistry. Chemistry was created as a separate science, with a language and methodology that sought to distinguish it from alchemy. The period saw the discovery of five gaseous elements and the intensive investigation of about a dozen gaseous compounds. Antoine Lavoisier (1743–94), the key figure, systematized the chemistry of gases by his formulation of the law of conservation of mass in 1789: the weight of all compounds obtained by chemical reaction is equal to that of the reacting substances. Henry Cavendish (1731–1810) defined hydrogen as a distinct substance in 1766, and in 1781 he was the first to determine the composition of water. In the 19th century, chemistry provided the development of dyes and a wide range of new products. Knowledge concerning electricity increased greatly, also, with Alessandro Volta inventing the battery of cells and the dry pile around 1800.

ROMANTICISM

The crucial cultural movement within Europe in the late 18th and early 19th centuries emphasized the individual and emotional responses, rather than an established set of artistic rules. In music (Beethoven), painting (Goya), poetry (Wordsworth), and the other arts, key figures sought to turn sensation and keen emotion into artistic form. This was an artistic equivalent of the political radicalism of the period, although not all artists were politically radical.

Left: Antoine Lavoisier was a leading figure in the emergence of chemistry as a separate subject

Above: New approaches emphasizing emotion and individualism took hold of the arts during the early 19th century

The Crisis of the 1790s

The Crisis of the 1790s saw conflict across the world, pitting a range of military systems against each other. The decade saw the outbreak of the French Revolutionary Wars; the successful rising against French rule in St Domingue, which led in 1804 to the independence of Haiti, the first black state in the Americas; the Russian suppression of Polish independence, the outbreak of the White Lotus rebellion in China; and the British conquest of Mysore. Even systems which seemed successful, such as the Marathas and that of Revolutionary and Napoleonic France would succumb by 1820. While the Chinese would understand by 1860 that their own system was in need of radical change, this was not so clear in 1800.

THE UNIFICATION OF HAWAII
Kamehameha, the unifier of the Hawaiian archipelago, based his power on the west coast of the island of Hawaii, a coast frequented by European ships, and he both acquired guns and cannon and used Europeans as cannoneers. Having won dominance of Hawaii in 1791, he conquered the islands of Maui and Oahu in 1795.

Left: Kamehameha I unified the Hawaiian archipelago and made use of European mercenaries and technology

Above: Toussaint L'Ouverture led a slave rebellion against French rule in St Domingue and established Haitian independence in 1804

Britain and Russia were clearly impressive powers by 1700 and, even more, by 1800. They and China were the key military successes of the eighteenth century.

In contrast to China and the Western states, the Turks and the Mughal and Safavid successor states in South Asia and Iran all lagged in creating the infrastructure of institutional politics and in establishing stable civil-military relations. The Turkish failure to maintain the strength of the system which had proved so successful during their phase of expansion was made clearer by the willingness of provincial governors to rebel.

The French Revolution and Napoleon

Rebellions in European states were far from rare, but the one which broke out in France in 1789 became increasingly radical as a result of the failure to establish trust between the opposing parties necessary

Above: Napoleon Bonaparte was an accomplished general who eventually overreached by invading Russia

to secure a settlement and because of the outbreak in 1792 of war with France's neighbours. France was declared a republic in 1792, King Louis XVI was executed in 1793 using the guillotine, and the new revolutionary authorities abolished Christianity as well as the feudal system.

The radical excesses of the Revolution reached their culmination in the Reign of Terror of 1793–4, but thereafter a reaction set in and Napoleon Bonaparte, a general who had made his name with victories over the Austrians in 1795–6, and with the invasion of Egypt in 1798, seized power in a coup in 1799. He became a major war leader, crucially defeating Austria in 1800 and again in 1805, and Prussia in 1806. His generalship was characterized by an embrace of mobility and by the concentration of force in the attack. His victories included Ulm (1805), Austerlitz (1805) and Jena (1806).

Within France, Napoleon directed a dictatorial war-state and sought to introduce reforms, including a Civil Law code. However, he overreached by attacking Spain in 1808 and Russia in 1812. The former became an intractable struggle, the latter swiftly proved a terrible disaster. Napoleon fought his way to Moscow, but Alexander I of Russia was unwilling to negotiate and the French army then disintegrated under attack by the cold and the Russians. In the aftermath, Napoleon's empire collapsed following defeat at the battle of Leipzig in 1813. An Allied coalition invaded France in 1814, and Napoleon was forced to abdicate. The French Bourbon monarchy was restored in the person of Louis XVIII.

Exiled on the island of Elba, Napoleon challenged the verdict in 1815. He easily regained control of France, but the European powers, whose representatives were meeting in the Congress of Vienna (1814–15), were not prepared to accept him back. Napoleon invaded Belgium, only to be totally defeated by the British (under the Duke of Wellington), Dutch and Prussian armies at Waterloo. Napoleon was then exiled to the distant, British-ruled island of St Helena, where he died in 1821.

Colonies of Settlement

Imperial powers not only seized territories. They also settled some with their own population, a process encouraged by the major increase in the world's population from the mid-18th century and by improvements in communications. This was not a new process: China had previously settled people in Xinkiang, Russia in Siberia, and the English in what became the United States. However, the process accelerated in the 19th century, thanks to the speed with which steamships could carry large numbers of people. This was true in particular of Britain, notably in Canada, Australia and New Zealand, and of France in Algeria.

The settlement colonies were treated very differently to the others. The British rapidly moved theirs toward self-government, a process symbolized by the Parliament building in Ottawa, Canada, which was modelled on London's new parliamentary buildings. The British eventually gave their settlement colonies dominion status, which meant that Australia, Canada, New Zealand and South

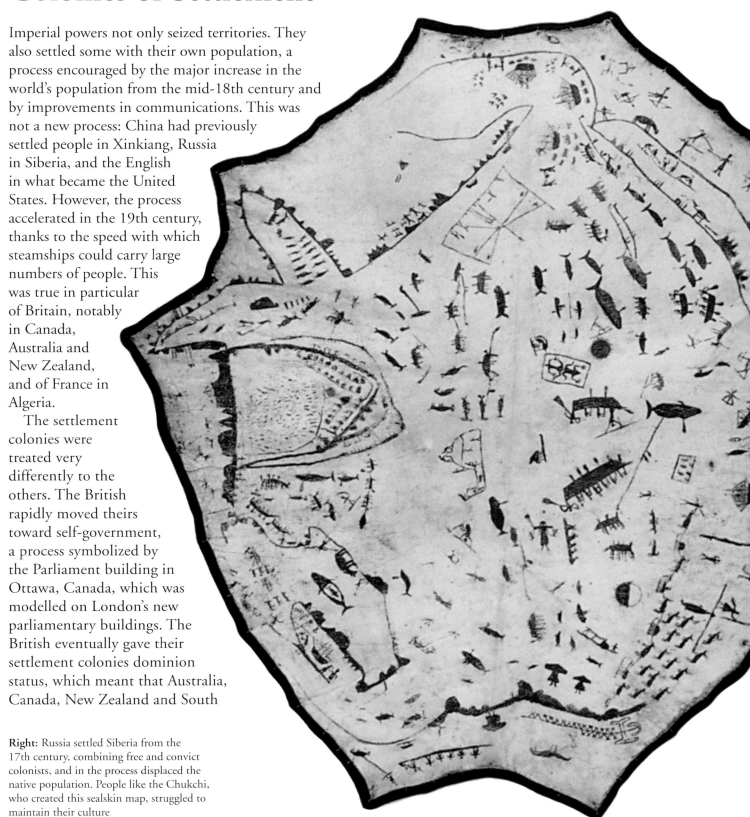

Right: Russia settled Siberia from the 17th century, combining free and convict colonists, and in the process displaced the native population. People like the Chukchi, who created this sealskin map, struggled to maintain their culture

Africa gained self-government. Algeria, in contrast, was to be treated as part of metropolitan France, with its own representation in the parliamentary assemblies in Paris.

The settlement colonies were most successful where the native population was small, as in Australia.

However, the basis for continued French rule in Algeria, and for South Africa as an independent, white-ruled, former British colony, were jeopardized from the 1950s by the degree to which the descendants of their European settler population were a minority.

CONVICT COLONIES

Britain initially founded settlements in Australia from 1788 as places to which convicts could be sent. This new use of the established pattern of convict labour was regarded as a way to develop colonies. The 19th-century sequel was the building of prisons in home-countries, such as the Russian convict colonies in Siberia.

Above: Some colonies began life as convict settlements, which employed their labour to establish the basic infrastructure of colonial life

The Fight for Freedom in Latin America

European power overseas was not always in the ascendant in the 19th century. In the late 1810s and early 1820s, Spanish and Portuguese power collapsed in Latin America. The disruption brought by Napoleon's invasion of Spain in 1808 challenged Spanish power. Attempts by Ferdinand VII of Spain from 1814 to re-establish his authority served to exacerbate the situation, leading to widespread conflict from Mexico to Chile. As in the War of American Independence, the revolutionary forces did not enjoy automatic success.

The international dimension of the conflict was crucial, just as it had been in North America. The British had long been interested in commercial penetration in Latin America and so supported its colonial independence from Spain. British volunteers and diplomatic and naval support played a role in dissuading the French from intervening on behalf of Spain. Once independent, there was no Spanish or Portuguese reconquest. Latin America developed close trading relations and became a prime area for British investment, particularly in building railways. Argentina became part of the British 'informal empire' until the British were supplanted by the Americans.

The wars led to the disruption of the bureaucratic colonial state, and the rise, instead, of *caudillos*: regional chieftains who used control over land and armed clients to build a form of power that was more personal than institutional. In Latin America, force came to be a common means for the pursuit of domestic power and was often the means by which governmental authority was transferred.

Right: Simón Bolívar led the rebellion against Spanish rule in South America

SIMÓN BOLÍVAR
The Spanish-American George Washington, Bolívar (1783–1830) played a key role in defeating Spain, notably in driving the Spaniards from Colombia (1819), Venezuela (1821), Ecuador (1822), Peru (1824) and Bolivia (1825). Persistence in the face of adversity helped him survive defeats in the 1810s. However, the 'Liberator' found it difficult to bring political stability to the newly independent countries and he died against a background of failure.

The End of Slavery in the New World

In 1800, there were major slave economies in the Americas, principally in Brazil, the Caribbean and the southern United States. In the early 19th century, abolitionism (ending slavery) became a significant cause, in large part due to Christian evangelicalism. This led to the ending of the slave trade by Britain in 1807, and then of slavery itself, first in the British colonies in 1833–8, in the French colonies in 1848, in the United States in 1865, and in Brazil, the leading slave state, in 1888. Ten times as many slaves had come to Rio de Janeiro than had entered all of the USA.

Former slave societies changed greatly. In the British West Indies, many ex-slaves left to seek land of their own, where they followed subsistence agriculture. This hit the productivity and profitability of the sugar estates, as free labour proved more expensive and less reliable than slaves. The former plantation economies suffered a drop in exports, rendering them less attractive to investment and less able to afford imports from Britain. Most former slaves did not experience any great change in their lives, and many remained dependent on their ex-masters or on new masters, and continued to be treated harshly. In addition, racism remained an issue, and in Brazil and Cuba pigmentocracies developed where those with a darker skin found themselves discriminated against.

Below: The end of slavery in the Caribbean brought numerous economic challenges. Conditions for freed slaves changed little, sparking the Morant Bay Rebellion in Jamaica in 1865

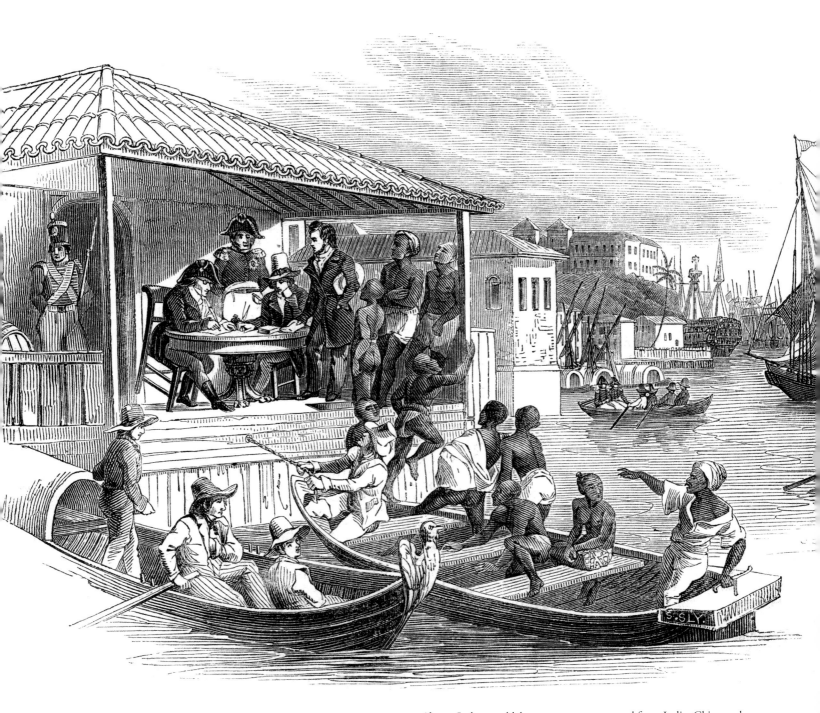

Above: Indentured labourers were transported from India, China and elsewhere to the British West Indies and the islands of the Pacific Ocean

INDENTURED LABOUR

The globalizing, expanding economy of the 19th century continued the practice of indentured labour, which had been extensively used in the 17th and 18th century to send white workers to North America. In return for their passage, they accepted hard terms of employment for a number of years. In the British world after the end of slavery, the main source labour was India which provided cheap indentured labour to the British West Indies, especially Trinidad,

British Guiana (now Guyana), South Africa, Fiji and other colonies. Similar systems were also employed elsewhere. In Cuba and Peru, indentured Chinese workers were treated harshly and found that, although 'free', they could not buy their way out of their contractual obligations. Critics claimed, often with reason, that indentured labour was another form of the slave trade.

The American Civil War, 1861–65

Slavery proved a defining issue for the United States. The election as President in 1860 of Abraham Lincoln, who wished to prevent the extension of slavery into new territories not yet accepted as states of the USA, led to the secession of the South and the formation of the Confederate States of America. Lincoln and the Republicans argued that the Union was essential to the survival of America and that the superiority of the federal government over the states was an essential component of the idea of the American Nation. However, the national parties were no longer effective and American mass democracy was faltering. Compromises on slavery which were being offered no longer seemed able to generate a consensus between North and South.

Fighting broke out in April 1861 when Southern forces shelled the federal garrison in Fort Sumter in Charleston harbour. Union hopes of a swift end to the war were thwarted by the resilience of the Southern defence. From 1863, when the Confederates were defeated at Gettysburg, their last major advance north, the possibility of victory for the South receded. Lincoln's victory in the 1864 election cemented the political

Left: A lithograph depicting the assault on Fort Sanders, 1863, one of the many bloody battles of the American Civil War

Right: Abraham Lincoln was elected as President in 1860, sparking the secession of the southern states of the Union and the beginning of the American Civil War

coherence of the North and left the South without viable options. Northern warships blockaded the South. By then, Northern forces had successfully advanced deep into the South, relying on General Sherman's march from Atlanta to the Atlantic, a strategy designed to stop Southern support for the war by crippling morale. By late 1864, the Union generals, particularly Sherman and Ulysses S. Grant, were closing on victory and in April and May 1865, the Southern armies capitulated.

When he surrendered in 1865, Robert E. Lee, the commander of the South's Army of Northern Virginia, told his men they had been defeated by superior resources. The Union certainly had the advantage in manpower, tax receipts, industrial and agricultural production, trade, railway mileage, shipping and bullion. Yet it was also important that Union forces had become more effective, due to the combination of experience and the application of organizational advantages in communications and logistics. The movement and supply of such numbers of men was unprecedented in North America. The maintenance of political determination was significant, as there had been many politicians willing to consider a partial accommodation of the Confederacy in order to end the war.

Above: The surrender of Robert E. Lee at Appomattox Court House in 1865 brought an end to the American Civil War as the other Southern armies surrendered soon after

Manifest Destiny: American Expansion

Confidence in the destiny of the United States encouraged Americans, hungry for land and mineral rights, to extend their power over the Native Americans. There were American defeats, notably of the rash and outnumbered George Custer by the Sioux at Little Big Horn in 1876, but, more commonly, it was the Native Americans who were crushed. The Native Americans were also hit hard by smallpox and by the drought that affected the bison on which they fed. The American government forces also destroyed crops and villages. The firepower and mobility of the regular American troops and their ability to stage winter campaigns were crucial to the US government victory.

The army forced the Natives onto reservations, often on bleak land, and also supported the economic integration of the West, by establishing settlements and encouraging the building of railways. In British-ruled Canada, there was not the same violence, in large part because the pace of settlement was less intense, while the government was more mindful of the Native population.

Meanwhile, economic growth was transforming the North American interior. Steel ploughs permitted the working of the tough soils of the midwest, and were also to be important on the Canadian prairie. Railways took grain and livestock to distant ports and cities.

THE LOUISIANA PURCHASE

In 1803, Napoleon sold the colony of Louisiana to the United States for $15 million in order both to stop it being a target for British attack and to gain money for operations in Europe. This brought America all or much of the future states of Montana, North and South Dakota, Minnesota, Wyoming, Colorado, Nebraska, Iowa, Kansas, Missouri, Oklahoma, Arkansas and Louisiana. In practice, most of the territory gained was under Native American control.

Above: The defeat of George Custer's forces at Little Big Horn in 1876 marked the last time the Native Americans successfully resisted the US

The Industrial Revolution

The 19th century saw a profound transformation in the industrial potential of advanced societies. The application of steam power drove changes in manufacturing and transport that combined to create a sense of progress which led to the period being titled the Industrial Revolution. Previously utopian ideas now appeared plausible. As industrialization gathered pace, so did the contrast between the industrialized regions and the rest of the world. Industrial workers enjoyed a purchasing power that increased their demand for manufactured goods as well as food. They lived in cities and these grew substantially in the 19th century. In Newcastle in Britain, a key centre of coal-based industry, the rise in population was from 28,294 in 1801 to 215,328 in 1901. Industrial growth initially focused on textiles and metal smelting, but then increasingly concentrated, in the later-19th century, on engineering, shipbuilding and chemicals. Industrialization produced more goods, encouraging the countries that did so, notably Britain, to support free trade. This opened foreign markets and their less-efficient producers could be driven from business.

Below: New factories, equipped with the latest technology, made Britain the 'workshop of the world', but dangerous working conditions, long hours and meagre rewards made life challenging for the labourers who worked in them

Goods that changed the world – Coal

A readily transportable and controllable fuel, coal provided a power source that was more effective in calorific value than its predecessors: wood and charcoal. Coal was the fuel used to drive steam engines, the icons of the new age. Thomas Jefferson, the future American president, toured the New Albion Mill, a steam-powered flour mill, when he visited London in 1786. Britain led the way in production and utilization. The annual average production of coal and lignite, in million metric tons, amounted to 18 for British in 1820–24, and two for France, German, Belgium and Russia, the other leading European industrial powers, combined; the comparable figures for 1855–59 were 68 and 32. William Cobbett wrote in 1830 about northern England that:

'All the way along, from Leeds to Sheffield, it is coal and iron, and iron and coal … Nothing can be conceived more grand or more terrific than the yellow waves of fire that incessantly issue from the top of these furnaces.'

Below: Coal became the essential fuel for the Industrial Revolution

Steam Power

Steam engines were potent symbols of a new world. With its plentiful coal supplies and entrepreneurship, Britain played the key role. The steam pump demonstrated by Thomas Savery in 1698 was of little practical importance, unlike the atmospheric engine introduced by Thomas Newcomen in 1712. James Watt (1736–1819) invented the separate steam condenser, which greatly increased the fuel efficiency of engines, and his first full-size steam engine was installed in 1776. In 1779, James Pickard, a Birmingham button-manufacturer, fitted a crank and flywheel to his Newcomen engine in order to use its steam power to drive a mill that could grind metals. This innovation greatly enlarged the market for steam engines which was exploited by Watt. His Wheal Virgin steam engine of 1790 could do the work of 953 horses.

Improved steam engines were used for mining and for driving machinery. By 1800, well over 2,000 had been built throughout Britain. Each represented a choice for change. Steam-powered boats, mills and other machines helped render uneconomic earlier techniques dependent on human, animal, water and wind power, or wood burning. This had major consequences for economic production, organization, the nature of work, and the sense that change could, and would, transform life. As a mobile source of energy, the steam engine enabled industry to move away from previous locations, especially the fast-flowing rivers important for water-driven mills. Industry was increasingly concentrated on coalfields.

Watt's STEAM ENGINE.

Plate CCCCLXXIX

Fig. 12.

Fig. 11.

Fig. 13.

Left: The steam engine designed by James Watt in 1776 was a technology that would transform all aspects of life

How we travelled – Railways

Steam technology and ironworking, both powered by coal, came to fruition with the development and spread of railways. They began in the 1820s as a way to move coal, with the first railway running from Stockton to Darlington in England. They changed the nature of trade, determined the fortunes of cities and governments and had a major impact on war. Unlike canals, railways moved both freight and passengers.

Railways were established across much of the world during the 19th century. Beginning in Europe, there were soon major rail projects in the United States, Latin America, and in European colonies such as India. Aside from laying the track, the rail industry involved the building of bridges and stations and the manufacture of locomotives. Railways spanned continents, with that across the United States followed by the Trans-Siberian. It became easier to move freight, which helped in the integration of economies and in the development

Above: Railways quickly spread across Europe and the Americas during the 19th century where they changed the fortunes of cities, trade, and even warfare

of comparative advantages.

Cities such as Chicago, Vancouver and Buenos Aires owed their growth, and their reshaping, to their ability to shape and profit from the new transport system. The railways stimulated suburbanization, enabling many of the newly wealthy middle classes to move into leafy, outlying suburbs. Districts were demolished and reconfigured to accommodate the lines, goods yards and centrally-located terminus buildings, while urban street layouts were greatly affected by the new focus on railway stations. Railways provided a new focus for the transport networks within cities, from cabs and buses to the revolutionary new form of mass-transport system: underground railways.

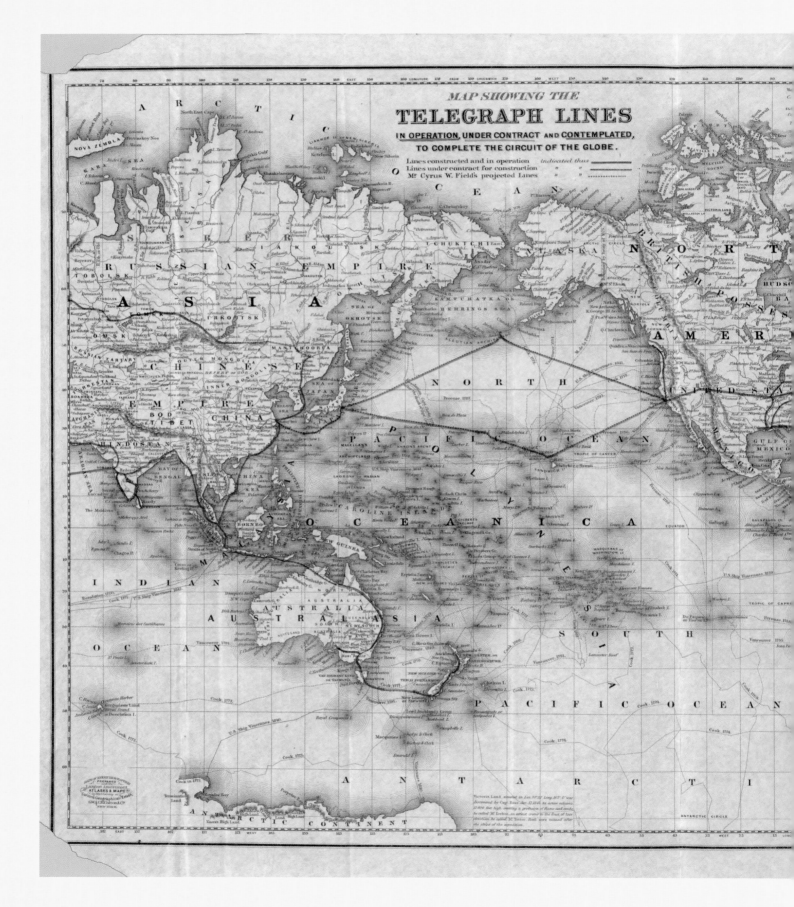

COMMUNICATIONS TECHNOLOGY

Samuel Morse (1791–1872), an American, developed a simple operator key and a code for use in transmitting signals using the new technology of the telegraph. This became Morse code. In 1838, he was able to transmit ten words a minute using his code of dots and dashes. In 1843, he persuaded Congress to finance a telegraph line from Washington to Baltimore. In Britain, the electric telegraph was initially used by private companies to transmit information about trains on the rapidly expanding rail network, but expanded greatly when opened up for public use. Economic and other news spread rapidly. However, despite recent claims suggesting that the emerging global system of telegraph cables operated like the modern Internet, there were significant problems for the former in reliability, the speed of transmission and the density of the network.

The growth of the postal system was linked to the spread of rail and steamship services and encouraged a reliance on, and demand for, rapid and inexpensive communication, that led to the development of the telegraph and then of the telephone. In 1840, the UK government replaced the earlier system of calculating the cost for each individual piece of post, and instead introduced a new, relatively inexpensive, uniform charging system, issuing to that end the Penny Black, the world's first postage stamp. The number of letters delivered in Britain and Ireland rose from 82.5 million in 1839 to 411 million in 1853. This helped

Left: The telegraph allowed rapid communication across continents

create a postal culture of speeded-up and reliable correspondence. The process was not restricted to Europe and the Imperial Indian Postal Service came to rival European systems. Compared to three billion items in 1876, 31 billion were posted in Europe in 1928, and the volume of telephone calls there did not exceed that of posted items until 1972. In the age of the Internet, the post can appear a restricted and anachronistic form of communication. In its early years, in contrast, it offered a reliable and consistent means, one that was not dependent on personal connections.

Left: Introduced in 1840, the Penny Black was the world's first postage stamp

Alexander Graham Bell (1847–1922) showed the possibilities of innovation in the rapidly developing technological culture of the West. He worked on the iron lung, the hydrofoil, the aeroplane aileron, and the photophone (which transmitted speech by means of light), as well as the telephone. In America, Bell created an integrated and standardized telephone system. In the 1890s, when his patent lapsed, other telephone companies moved into the American market, adopting electromechanical switchboards. By removing the need for operators, this made the service cheaper and encouraged popular uptake; as did the intimacy of voice communication and the ease of use compared to the telegraph. By 1912, there were seven million telephones in the USA.

Left: The telephone had been widely adopted in the United States by 1910

Nationalism

The 19th century saw a growth in national consciousness which led to nationalism, the subordination of other values to the idea of a distinct nation that occupied a particular area. Important ideological and intellectual changes were involved, while stronger states, improved communications, national systems of education, mass literacy, industrialization, urbanization, and democratization, were all crucial preconditions for nationalism.

Below: Nationalism led to the creation of new states in Italy (1860–1) and Germany (1866)

Nationalism had a symbolic aspect: a growing belief in concepts such as fatherland, motherland and homeland encouraged nationalism as did the decline in alternative allegiances, such as to the locality. Nationalism also provided a new basis for group dynamics, accommodating within itself developments such as the rise of the universal male franchise. Nationalism facilitated conscription in the military because conscription was legitimated by new revolutionary and nationalist ideologies. Indeed, part of its intention was to transform the old distinction between civilian and military into a common purpose. Nationalism led to state formation, notably transforming Italy (1860–61) and Germany (1866) into political units. In each case, the defeat of Austria, a multinational empire ruled by the Habsburg dynasty, was a key element. Italy was organised around the kingdom of Piedmont and Germany around that of Prussia, but they each had a new role as nation-states.

In general, the development of democratic ideals both helped nationalism and opposed imperial states. As a result, nationalism led to agitation for independence against imperial rule, especially in Poland and Finland against Russia, and in India and Ireland against Britain.

MAKING HISTORY OPERATIC

The great Italian composers of the period provided a heroic reading of the past. In Norma *(1831), Vincenzo Bellini (1801–35) drew a parallel between Gaul under Roman rule and Italy under that of Austria. Deeply committed to the* Risorgimento *(the unification of Italy), but mindful of Austrian censorship, Giuseppe Verdi (1813–1901) used distant and indirect references. In* Nabucco *(1842), the exiled Hebrew slaves in Mesopotamia (Iraq) are an allegory for oppressed Italians, while* La battaglia di Legnano *(1849) employed the defeat of the (German) Emperor Barbarossa by the Lombard League in 1176 as a present-day rallying call.* La Forza del Destino *(1862) showed the defeat at Velletri in 1744 of the Austrians by the Neapolitans. Verdi supported Garibaldi's expedition in 1860 and served in the Italian parliament.*

Other Italian operas confronted the present, notably the verismo *of the 1890s with its depiction of peasants, as in Pietro Mascagni's* Cavalleria Rusticana *(1890), and slum dwellers, as in Umberto Giordano's* Mala Vita *(1892). Set in Sicily and Naples respectively, these operas also offered a view of the 'Southern problem' for audiences elsewhere in Italy.*

Right: Giuseppe Verdi was an Italian nationalist but was subject to Austrian censorship, so he found ways to include subtle and indirect references in his music

The Raj

The assertion of national identities in Europe was not accompanied by increased European respect for that of peoples outside Europe. The fall of the Mughal Empire was accompanied by increased European expansion into India. Trading companies, such as the British East India Company and the Dutch *Verenigde Oost-Indische Compagnie* (VOC), sought to establish increasingly direct control over the subcontinent. Soon, however, the Dutch turned their attention to the Indonesian spice islands and left Britain a free hand in India. Robert Clive commanded the British forces at the Battle of Plassey (1757) which established East India Company rule over Bengal by defeating its Nawab. Victories over Mysore (1799) and the Marathas (1803) provided a crucial prelude to a major expansion in control over much of India, as well as to annexation of particular parts.

Above: At the Battle of Plassey (1757), Robert Clive established British rule over Bengal

Above: The Maharajah Duleep Singh entering the palace at Lahore in 1846, escorted by British troops

Unlike their rivals, the British were capable of conceiving and sustaining strategies and logistics that spanned all of India. Although they lost an entire Anglo-Indian division in a poorly-conducted winter-time evacuation of Afghanistan in 1842, they acquired the Maratha dominions in western India in 1818, Arakan and Tenasserim from Burma (Myanmar) in 1826, Mysore in 1831, Sind in 1843 and Punjab, after two bitter wars with the Sikhs, in 1849. Kashmir became a vassal state in 1848. The support of Indian troops played a key role in these British successes.

The Crown took over the government of India from the East India Company in 1858 and Queen Victoria was proclaimed Empress of India in 1877 at the Delhi Durbar.

Much of India remained under the rule of local princes as part of a multi-layered and generally successful search for support. At the same time, India became the most populous part of the British empire.

THE INDIAN MUTINY, 1857–59

The largest revolt against European rule during the century was serious because many Indian soldiers in British service mutinied. Their reluctance to serve abroad was a key issue, and the rising was triggered by the demand that the soldiers use a new cartridge for their new rifles which was allegedly greased (to keep the powder dry) in animal fat, a measure unacceptable for religious reasons to Muslims and Hindus. Thanks to the support of much of the Indian army and of the major princes, notably those of Hyderabad, Kashmir and Nepal, the British were able, amid tough fighting, to overcome the badly-led rebels. In Indian public history, the Mutiny is sometimes referred to as the first War of Indian Independence or simply as the Uprising.

Below: In 1857, a major rebellion occurred against British rule

Qing Decline

China, too, suffered a comparative economic and political decline in the 19th century. With a population of about 450 million in 1850, the country had failed to develop its industrial base, which had earlier been strong. In contrast, the West's ability to become central to global economic links, and to the process and profits of globalization, put non-Western powers at a disadvantage.

China became relatively weaker in the 19th century, in part due to internal division, but also thanks to the difficulty of adopting ideas and practices of industrial transformation and strong government comparable to those seen in the West. The Opium Wars (1839–42, 1856–60) were a depressing revelation to Chinese officials of their strength in comparison to the Western powers.

Left: Commissioner Lin Zexu wrote a patronizing letter to Queen Victoria demanding the end of the opium trade

Above: The Opium War of 1839–1842 was the first time a Western European state had waged war on China

By the late 1830s, opium was increasingly regarded as a scourge on Chinese society, with increasing numbers of addicts. To the dismay of British merchants, Commissioner Lin Zexu recommended a prohibition on the drug. The profit from opium was central to the financial system of the tea trade in Asia and the conflict escalated quickly as neither side took a diplomatic approach. Lin wrote a patronizing memorandum to Queen Victoria to protest against the opium trade in which he described the British people as 'barbarians'. When no change was forthcoming, the Chinese authorities expelled British merchants from Guangzhou and seized their opium.

Ceding to pressure from the public, the British blockaded major Chinese positions, focusing in 1842

on the Yangtze, where they proceeded up the river to Nanjing. China gave way. British successes led China to cede Hong Kong by the Treaty of Nanjing (1842). The treaty enforced lower tariffs on British goods at the expense of China's right to regulate its economy and society, granted compensation for the opium destroyed in 1839, and opened five ports to British trade. This was the first time a Western European state had waged war on China, yielding the first European victory over the Chinese, and one achieved in China itself.

The second war arose when Britain sought to open all of China to British trade. The acting consul in Canton, Henry Parkes, and the prime minister, Viscount Palmerston, actively sought conflict. The arrest in Guangzhou of the *Arrow*, a Hong Kong cargo ship with a Chinese crew that was said to be flying the British flag, provided the perfect excuse. In 1856, the British bombarded Guangzhou. Anglo-French forces

Cities of Empire

It was under the impact of Western rule or influence that non-Western cities acquired many of the features of their counterparts, such as railway stations, boulevards, telegraph buildings and major hotels. The Western imperial powers both remodelled existing cities to reflect their own priorities and developed new cities that would one day play important roles in a new world coming into being. In 1819, the British established Singapore as a deep-water harbour. By 1860 its population was 80,000.

Kuala Lumpur (Malaysia) was transformed from a shantytown for tin-miners into a city of 40,000 by 1900, with grand buildings on the pattern of British India, where, in the case of Calcutta, the second largest city of the British empire, there were a series of official buildings in the governmental quarter, such as the High Court (1872). Seized by Britain in 1841, Hong Kong developed into a leading port and city. Government House was finished in 1855, and the Hong Kong and Shanghai Bank, established in 1864, played a key role in financing trade.

Above: The city of Kuala Lumpur was filed with impressive British colonial buildings by 1900

occupied the city on 1 January 1858, and attention then shifted to north China, focusing on the forts at Dagu near Tianjin. After failing to do so in 1859, an Anglo-French expedition seized the forts and Tianjin in 1860. They then defeated a Chinese army outside Beijing and entered the city, a major blow to Chinese prestige. The imperial Summer Palaces were destroyed as a reprisal for previous Chinese atrocities. The Convention of Beijing of 1860 which ended the war added Kowloon to Hong Kong, Britain and France received an indemnity, freedom of religion was established in China, and China was further opened to foreign trade, including in opium.

Like other European imperial powers, the British sought to impose their definitions and their rules, as well as their interests. In turn, the defeat and humiliation of China hit the prestige of the Qing system and led to attempts at reform, beginning with the Self-Strengthening Movement (see page 174).

The principal cause of weakness in the 1850s and 1860s was the Taiping Rebellion. Even prior to the European pressure from the 1830s, there were signs of major difficulties in Chinese government, including widespread corruption, losses of tax revenue, the destructive role of the tax farmers, and the insufficient control of the central authorities over its provincial viceroys. The costly White Lotus rebellion of 1796–1805 had exposed many faults in administration, while China faced difficult regional challenges on the north-west and south-west frontiers. The efforts devoted to these campaigns, which ended in 1873, accentuated the landward interests of the Manchu elite and distracted attention from coastal and maritime concerns.

THE TAIPING REBELLION

The Taiping Rebellion of 1851–66, the large-scale revivalist movement of the Heavenly Kingdom of Peace, aimed at the overthrow of the ruling Qing dynasty. It was the most destructive of all civil wars, with a death toll of 20–30 million; indeed its death toll far exceeded that of the American Civil War of 1861–65. It remains one of the least known major wars. Ideological conviction was an important tool during the rebellion in battle and on campaign. It helped lead troops to cross the killing-ground, and encouraged persistence in the face of inadequate logistics. It made the Taiping reckless of their lives and thus formidable in battle, although their seriously divided leadership was badly flawed. Taiping armaments were antiquated, relying heavily on spearmen, halberdiers and matchlock muskets. Although the Taiping took the major city of Nanjing in 1853, they were eventually defeated in 1866.

Below: The Taiping Rebellion (1851–1866) was the most destructive civil war in history with an estimated 20–30 million casualties

Right: The Meiji Emperor oversaw a period of rapid modernization in Japan

Meiji Restoration

Japan was confronted with Western development and power, too, when four American naval warships under Commodore Matthew Perry entered Tokyo Bay in 1853 to enforce American demands to open up Japan to trade. His steamships were a new threat and, under renewed naval pressure in 1854, Japan accepted American demands. Other powers followed the American lead.

The resulting pressure for change led to a civil war in 1868–69 that displaced the Tokugawa shogunate and restored the power of the emperor. The new system in turn saw off a rebellion in 1877. The Meiji ('Enlighted Rule') Emperor (r. 1867–1912) oversaw a period of rapid governmental change and economic transformation, which included the promulgation of an ideology of modernization. Japan was divided into

prefectures, a centralized bureaucracy created, and new industries introduced, including shipbuilding. The number of steamships rose from 26 in 1873 to 1,514 in 1913. A rail system was constructed. To strengthen its view of national identity, the government also established a dominant national dialect called 'standard language'.

The new state actively pursued territorial expansion, in particular seeking to profit from the weakness of China, which had traditionally overawed Japan culturally. Japan defeated China in 1894–95, a conflict followed by the Japanese annexation of Formosa (Taiwan), while victory over Russia in 1904–05 led to the annexation of Korea and the spread of Japanese power in northern China. The last was a dramatic demonstration of European weakness.

The Scramble for Africa

In Africa, the European presence was for long largely restricted to the coastal fringes. However, in the first half of the 19th century, Europeans moved into the interior in some areas, such as the Senegal Valley and South Africa. This process was dramatically accelerated from the early 1880s after an agreement on Africa made by the European powers at the Congress of Berlin (1884–85) encouraged them to pursue their political and economic competition through the conquest of African territory and raw material sources.

The conquerors benefited greatly from local assistance, from hiring soldiers to exploiting local political rivalries. The Europeans could provide an alternative to threatening African rulers, a situation that aided both the British and the French in West Africa, and the British in southern Africa.

The effort involved in imperialism reflected the extent to which European governments could tap the economic growth of the Western-dominated world economy, as well as greater governmental, political and public interest in distant imperial expansion than had been the case in the early 19th century. In part, this effort and interest was a product of a grandiose assertion of national prestige, of political and economic competition between Western states, and of optimism about national expansion and racial roles.

KING LEOPOLD'S PRIVATE KINGDOM – THE CONGO

An adroit political manoeuvrer, Leopold II, king of Belgium (r. 1865–1909) benefited in 1885 from the competition between the greater European powers in Africa to become ruler of the Congo Free State. The large territory in central Africa was brutally exploited as Leopold sought

to raise money by the exploitation of natural resources, notably rubber and minerals. International outrage grew as the abuses in the colony came to light, and led to the territory being transferred to the Belgian state in 1908.

Left: King Leopold II of Belgium treated the Congo as a private fiefdom. Evidence of the abuses taking place there led to international outrage

Above: The Berlin Conference of 1884 divided Africa between the European powers and began the so-called 'Scramble for Africa'

The Challenge of the West

Western strength and imperialism led to a variety of responses. There were attempts to understand Western methods. The Iwakura embassy sent by Japan to the USA and Europe in 1871–73 provided important information on economic matters that contributed to Japanese modernization. Western society was also praised, as in *Conditions in the West* (1866) and *Outline of a Theory of Civilization* (1875) by Fukuzawa Yukichi, for rewarding intellectual and social mobility.

In China, the Self-Strengthening Movement from the 1860s attempted to acquire an understanding of Western proficiency, which led to the acquisition of technology and the search for information that would help modernization.

There was also opposition to Western materialism, individualism and its mistaken claims to cultural and intellectual superiority. In India, scientists were keen to detach science from an imperial context and to present, instead, their work in terms of Indian traditions and values. Hindu and Muslim revivalism was linked to the rejuvenation of indigenous medicine, and nationalists demanded public-health policies more favourable to the native population.

Left: Prince Iwakura of Japan led a mission to the USA and Europe in 1871–3 to learn more about Western economics

MAPPING SOCIETY

In the West, too, there were voices which called for social reform. In the middle of the 19th century, there was increasing concern about living and working conditions within major cities. Social reformers and campaigners argued that extreme poverty, overcrowding and insanitary conditions, which could cause epidemics that affected rich and poor alike, should be eradicated in civilized society. The scientific collection of data, and the development of thematic mapping to illustrate a range of issues, contributed to a revolution in political, medical and social attitudes. Charles Booth's *Inquiry into Life and Labour in London* (1886–1903) produced colour-coded maps of London by social class. He was very critical of the 'Lowest class … vicious, semi-criminal…. Their life is the life of savages, with vicissitudes of extreme hardship and their only luxury is drink.'

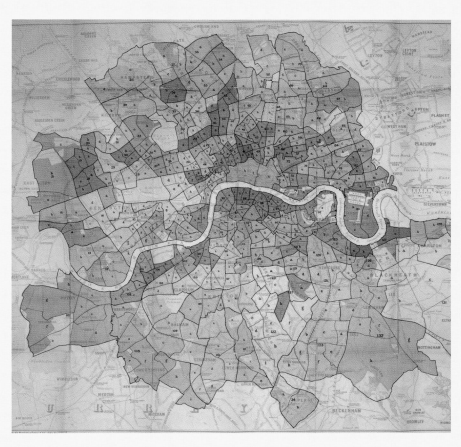

Above: Charles Booth created colour-coded maps of London that mapped the location and extent of poverty in the capital

Above: Charles Darwin's journey on HMS *Beagle* inspired his famous work, *The Origin of Species*

CHARTING THE OCEANS

The exploration of the oceans was a key theme that brought together the search for information, its accumulation, depiction and use. Britain's global commitments and opportunities, naval and commercial, made it both easier and more necessary for it to acquire and use the information. Used in war, charts also helped in understanding the opportunities offered by the ocean. Charting also contributed to the development of evolutionary theory. Charles Darwin found his voyage of 1831–36 as naturalist on HMS Beagle *a formative experience, notably his journey to the Galapagos archipelago in the Pacific. In 1859, he published* The Origin of Species by Means of Natural Selection, *a work that very much did not agree with the* Book of Genesis.

THE WORLD AT WAR
1914–1945

Wars totally remoulded the world between 1914 and 1945, shattering empires, overturning ideologies and transforming social practices and cultural understandings. Tens of millions died and the legacy of the period still rests heavy on the public history of the countries whose societies experienced so much suffering.

Above: States invested heavily in their navies in the early 20th century and feared falling behind their rivals

Turn of the Century

International competition became more acute in the early 20th century. A policy of watchful prudence, resting on support for an international order based on a mutual acceptance of great power interests, was replaced by a more volatile search for national advantage, particularly by Germany. Rival alliance systems developed and committed the powers to the interests of their allies. A sense of anxiety based on the belief that the present situation was unstable was accentuated by concerns about the consequences of industrial society, urban living and democratic populism.

States invested heavily in their militaries. On land and at sea, powers sought to integrate new weapons, as well as improved weaponry, such as new artillery, and organizational means and systems, into their militaries, their manoeuvres and their plans.

The range of conflicts which resulted in the 1910s included the Chinese revolution of 1911, the Mexican revolution after a coup in 1913, and American interventions in Nicaragua, Haiti, the Dominican Republic and Mexico.

World War I

CAUSES

The outbreak of World War I was to a great extent shaped by the perception of its participants regarding regional political and diplomatic developments. The Germans were concerned about growing Russian military preparedness on their eastern frontier, including railway construction that would speed mobilization, and came to believe in the inevitability

of war, which fuelled a desire to begin it at the most opportune moment. They also looked back with pride and confidence to successful recent wars.

Austria-Hungary, Germany's main ally, saw its strategic and political situation apparently worsening, and was worried about Russian-supported Serbian assertiveness and its challenge to the stability of Austria's Balkan possessions. There was a growing frustration amongst the Austrian leadership at not being able to shape their own destiny. War with Serbia appeared the answer.

On 28 June 1914, the Austrian heir, Archduke Franz Ferdinand, and his wife Sophie, were assassinated while visiting Sarajevo, the capital

Above: The assassination of the Archduke Franz Ferdinand was the spark that began World War I

of Bosnia, by Gavrilo Princip, a Bosnian Serb. He belonged to the Black Hand, a secret Serbian nationalist organization pledged to the overthrow of Habsburg control in South Slav territories (which included Serbia, as well as Bosnia). When the news reached Vienna, there was shock and the sense that action was needed. The assassinations provided the excuse to take care of the Serbian threat.

Confident that German backing would deter Russia, Austria sought a limited war with Serbia.

Ein Vierverband, doch nicht von Englands Gnaden,
Kein heimlich Machwerk brit'scher Mühlerei;
Ein freier Bund von Waffenkameraden
Zu brechen Englands Völkertyrannei.

Above: The Central Powers of Germany and Austria saw the crisis as the perfect opportunity to advance their ambitions and were later joined by Turkey and Bulgaria

Germany decided to act because no other crisis was as likely to produce a constellation of circumstances guaranteeing the commitment of Austria and the support of the German public. Seeking to knock out France and then turn on its ally Russia, Germany attacked via neutral Belgium in August 1914, which led Britain, one of the guarantors of Belgian neutrality, to enter the war.

Military considerations, and the army leaderships themselves, pushed governments to act. The German war-plan required that hostilities rapidly follow mobilization. World War I was intended by each of its participants as a short and manageable, albeit costly, international war between regular forces.

The war was the result not so much as a failure of statecraft as a breakdown of deterrence. Pressure from the military was highly significant. The decision-makers had lost the sense of the fragility of peace and order. The politicians used the threat of war to put the other side at a disadvantage and, in doing so, they miscalculated. Everyone made mistakes. Austria wanted war (albeit only a Balkan one); Germany was criminally negligent and, through fumbling, created a situation in which she could not rein in Vienna or retreat in the face of Franco-Russian opposition; France was rigid; and Russian policy was incompetent. Britain's guarantee of Belgium ensured that her inherent geopolitical logic left her with no choice but to enter the war.

In 1914, the British sought to rely on the traditional means of addressing an international crisis, that of the Concert of Europe, a system which had kept the peace since the Congress of Vienna (1814–15) at the end of the Napoleonic Wars. This, indeed, had succeeded in the case of the First Balkan War (1912–13) between Ottoman Turkey and a coalition of Balkan powers in preventing a wider war. In 1914, however, Austria and Germany were unwilling to do so. The German preference was to some extent associated with the political and cultural bellicosity

Above: Britain believed that the Concert of Europe could prevent war, as it had done at the London Conference of 1912–13 in dealing with the First Balkan War

Right: President Poincaré of France, King George V of the United Kingdom and Tsar Nicholas II of Russia made up the Triple Entente

that was so strong in Germany, in particular in the early 1910s. A fervent national patriotism was linked to a strong fear of falling behind and a sense that the opportunity that existed to attack might not continue.

Germany subordinated political to military considerations in bringing Britain and the United States into the war against her respectively in 1914 and 1917. In each case, although the policies were justified on military grounds – advancing more easily via Belgium and trying to knock out British trade by submarine attack respectively – these were serious strategic mistakes that contributed greatly to eventual German failure.

The dominant image for that cataclysmic conflict, that of the apparent bloody stasis and senseless slaughter of trench warfare, is endlessly repeated and became the leitmotiv of public commemoration.

The situation was in fact far more complex.

Perceptions of tactical stalemate, operational failure, lack of strategy and indecisive conflict are all not well-founded if the war as a whole is considered. From the perspectives of Eastern Europe, the Balkans, the Middle East and Germany's overseas colonies, the war saw much movement. Serbia and Romania were in effect forced to drop out of the war in 1915 and 1916 respectively, while, in 1917, Russia was knocked out, and Italy nearly was. In 1918, Bulgaria, Turkey, Austria and Germany were all defeated to the point of surrender.

The Western Front was not truly static, despite

appearances. The Allies worked out how to direct unprecedented firepower with effect and broke out into and through German trench systems and made fresh advances. In 1918, it proved possible for the Allies to coincide and sustain attacks along a broad front to prevent the German sealing of any breakthrough by means of concentrating reserves.

The Allies overcame problems that had confronted perceptive commentators in the pre-war decades as well as longer-lasting command issues, notably that of the combination of firepower and mobility. Technology played a role with the use of effective aerial reconnaissance to map opposing trench systems and direct artillery fire. The net effect was a conflict

Left: Nationalist uprisings, like the Easter Rising of 1916, focused on the capitals

Above: The failure of the intial German attack led to the development of trench warfare along the Western front

that was able to deliver a decisive military and political result.

The campaigns of movement outside the Western Front were more consistent with conflicts elsewhere, while capital cities were the crucial settings for the Irish rising in 1916, the Bolshevik takeover of Russia in 1917, and the nationalist movements in the Austro-Hungarian empire at the close of the war.

The German campaign had failed in 1914 even before the Allied counterattack in the Battle of the Marne and the subsequent stabilization of the Western Front along what became the trench lines. Britain's entry into the war promised that what was already, due to Russian involvement, a two-front war would become a longer and more difficult struggle. It was a stark contrast to 1864–71, when Prussia-Germany had not faced such a two-front war in its conflicts with France.

By late 1914, the carefully-prepared German pre-war strategic planning appeared precarious and over-optimistic. A dangerous over-confidence was apparent at every level. Germany had envisaged a repeat of the Franco-Prussian War, with France collapsing, having suffered similar command failures to those in 1870. Nothing played out according to the script, as their opponents proved to be tougher to break than anticipated, leading to exhaustion and very

Above: High casualties and terrifying injuries were a constant theme of World War I

Below: The ability to redeploy troops by rail was essential to France's ability to resist German attacks

high casualties. Austria failed badly in an attempt to conquer Serbia, whose army was less well resourced, but much better commanded, and Austria also found itself under heavy pressure by Russia.

The 1914 campaign showed, moreover, that German war-making, with its emphasis on surprise, speed and overwhelming and dynamic force at the chosen point of contact, was not effective against a French defence that retained the capacity to use reserves by redeploying troops by rail. The Germans also underrated the potential use of fortifications as a base of manoeuvre. All senior German commanders appear to have been convinced that entrenched camps need only be bypassed after being screened. This neglect of the ability of French troops to attack out of their defences contributed to the German failure of 1914 when the French Sixth Army attacked out of Paris, halting the German advance and initiating the

Battle of the Marne.

The manoeuvre stage of the war in the West, with its emphasis on a strategy of envelopment in order to secure total victory, and on a battle of annihilation, had ended by October 1914. Generals were to try repeatedly throughout the war to re-create this flexibility, and to reopen a war of movement by breaking through their opponents' frontline, but the goal proved elusive. Instead, a front line, the Western Front, soon crystallized into a complex series of trench systems.

Only in 1918, after four years of grinding conflict, was there a conclusive breakthrough. By then, the Germans were living off the substance of their military machinery and failed to display the resolve and persistence demonstrated (at very heavy cost) by the French. In the final attacks, the British focused on improving artillery firepower and accuracy,

Above: Trench warfare was the dominant mode of conflict on the Western Front, but there were periods of movement and encirclement, too

OFFENSIVES OF THE WESTERN FRONT

Two major and unsuccessful offensives on the Western Front, the German attack on French-held Verdun, and the British offensive on the Somme, served for many to demonstrate the failure and futility of war. Casualties were very high – about 700,000 men in the Verdun campaign and over a million on the Somme – and there was scant gain of territory in fighting that became heavily attritional. However, *the campaigns also demonstrated results: the French thwarted the Germans at Verdun, while, as a result of the Somme, the initiative on the Western Front was wrested from the Germans and they did not mount a major attack there in 1917.*

Below: The Battle of the Somme, July–November 1916, had vast casualties for the participants

so dominating the battlefield and applying firepower more effectively than in earlier offensives.

The unexpectedly early end of the war left the consequences of the development of certain new forms of weaponry unclear, and in particular that of the tank, a technology which Britain and France led. Indeed, tanks, essentially a tool for operating on the frontline, were more suited in 1918 for assisting in transforming static warfare into mobile warfare, rather than for conducting the latter itself. In providing moving firepower, tanks helped overcome the problems that trenches posed to attackers. Tanks provided more accurate tactical fire which allowed the better exploitation of massed bombardments that generally preceded offensives on the Western Front. In practice, however, durability, firepower, protection, speed, range, mobility, command and control, and reliability were all major problems with tanks in 1918, problems which the rapid development by the Germans of anti-tank techniques and weaponry accentuated. As a consequence, tanks were most successful as part of a combined-arms force, and when moving to support infantry.

THE EASTERN FRONTS

The less concentrated area of operations in Eastern Europe ensured that the force-to-space ratio was lower than in Western Europe. As a result, it was easier to break through opposing lines and advance rapidly, as the Germans demonstrated at Russian expense in 1915. The conquests of Serbia in 1915 and Romania in 1916 by Austria, Bulgaria and Germany demonstrated the ability of contemporary armies to achieve decisive victories in certain circumstances. The Allies also rapidly overran all the German colonies, bar German East Africa. The Turks proved a more formidable foe. The Gallipoli offensive, an attempted knock-out blow at the Turkish centre, failed in 1915, and the initial British advance into Mesopotamia (now Iraq) was unsuccessful. It was not until 1918 that Turkish resistance was overcome.

Above: Tanks offered the promise of immense firepower, but issues with their durability and speed, combined with the development of anti-tank weapons, limited their effectiveness

Below: The Gallipoli campaign (1915–1916) failed to knock out the Ottoman Empire from the war and was a failure for the Allied forces

The Russian Revolution

Repeated defeats at the hands of Germany in World War I and the serious social and economic strains on Russia of the war provided the Bolsheviks (better known as Communists), a radical revolutionary movement, with an opportunity to seize power in October 1917. Tsar Nicholas II had already been overthrown earlier in the year, but the republic that replaced him had continued with the unsuccessful and unpopular war. Vladimir Ilyich Lenin (1870–1924), the Bolshevik leader, had hoped that the spread of revolution to Germany would make negotiations unnecessary, but continued German advances forced him to cede territory as the cost of peace in 1918. The Communists then overcame counter-revolutionaries in a bitter civil war between 1918 and 1920, as well as trying to hold together the territorial span of the old Russian empire.

The Communists leader, first Lenin and then Joseph Stalin, took key sectors the Russian economy into state ownership, forced the country into industrialization and displaced the Orthodox Church. The secret police, which Lenin and Stalin both supported, were a crucial prop to the Revolutionary government. Terror and government-tolerated famine killed at least 11 million in Stalin's 'peacetime' years, warped the lives of the remainder of the population and made casualties of faith, hope and truth. A paranoid figure who feared the betrayal of the Revolution, Stalin directed his terror at government officials, the army, wealthy peasants who were unlikely to welcome the collectivization of land and intellectuals who protested against the brutality of the regime.

Below: The strains of the war led to revolution in October 1917, in which the Bolsheviks ultimately seized power

Above: The influenza epidemic of 1918–19 killed between 50 and 100 million people

The Spanish Flu

Conflict and famine took a terrible toll, but the global influenza epidemic of 1918–19 killed more people than World War I. The number who died was at least 50 million, mostly in Asia, with the percentage of deaths reaching as high as about six per cent of the Indian population. Groups who were particularly affected were the very young, young, fit 20–40 year olds, pregnant women and the very old. Birds were the source of the pandemic, but railways and steamers speeded its spread. There was no effective treatment, and the structure of the flu virus was not determined until 1943 when effective electronic microscopes became available. Virology itself was largely not understood until 1931 and vaccination against influenza only began in 1936. In contrast to the Spanish Flu, so-named because many prominent Spaniards suffered from it in May 1918, only about a million died worldwide from the 1957 Asian Flu and the 1968–69 Hong Kong Flu pandemic, indicating the success of vaccination programmes.

The Interwar Period, 1919-38

The overthrow of the old orders in the 1910s, in China, Mexico, Turkey, Russia, Austria and Germany, the last four as a direct result of World War I, as well as a more general challenge to established and conservative practices and values, encouraged cultural and social change in the 1920s and 1930s. This was true of such varied phenomena as the growing emancipation of women, the energy of the young, consumerism, the impact of Hollywood, the jazz age, cultural Modernism and new ideas in psychology.

These developments overlapped. The cinema revolved around sexuality and presented women who were not defined by matrimony and motherhood, a changed viewpoint that was increasingly prominent in the West. Female readers were of growing importance for the publishing industry. There was a widespread willingness in both books and cinema to present women as more independent emotionally and, often, more engaged in gainful employment than had been the case prior to World War I. A reaction against realistic representational culture, Modernism challenged traditional forms and preferred an experimental moulding of form in order to shake the reader, viewer or listener from established patterns of response. It drew inspiration from the new social sciences, such as the works of Sigmund Freud and Sir James Frazer, and their challenge to established assumptions.

In literature, Modernism's distinctive characteristics included the use of the stream of consciousness technique and a fascination with myth, both characteristics of the novel *Ulysses* (1922) by the Irish writer James Joyce. Free verse was employed to throw together very different voices and fractured ideas, as in the influential poem *The Waste Land* (1922) by T.S. Eliot. The novels of Virginia Woolf displayed an experimental and fluid structure and a lyrical use of language. Woolf rejected what she presented as 'materialist' writing and, instead, sought a new aesthetic sensibility. In her essay 'Mr Bennett and Mrs Brown' (1924), she distinguished between what she considered the false 'realism' of surface description and a 'modernism' that searched for true realism. In

Above: Modernist writers like James Joyce reacted against realistic literature and experimented with forms and language to create something new

music, the Austrian composer Arnold Schoenberg offered atonal and serial compositions. In painting, Cubism, Expressionism, Vorticism, Surrealism and Dadaism all reacted against Realism.

At the same time, much of the public preferred conventional approaches. For example, the 'middle' and 'low-brow' writers despised by the Modernists enjoyed greater sales in Britain. They benefited from the rising disposable income of the 1920s, from the ready availability of inexpensive books, and from increased leisure. Works by painters such as the Spanish Surrealist Salvador Dali and his compatriot Pablo Picasso had only a limited appeal for contemporaries. The new music with greatest public appeal was jazz.

SALVADOR DALI (1904–89): THE ARTIST AS ICONOCLAST

Born in Catalonia to a comfortable family, Dali studied art in Madrid, where he experimented with Cubism, and then became a Surrealist working in Paris. He refused to commit himself during the Spanish Civil War, and spent the troubled years of mid-century in safe New York, returning to Spain in 1948. His willingness to live there during the Franco years displeased those who stayed in exile, as did his praise for the dictator. Increased Catholic devotion was another difference. In 1982, Dali was made a marquis by King Juan Carlos. The Teatre-Museu Dali *in his birthplace, Figueres, is a surrealist fantasy house in a one-time theatre.*

Left: The Chrysler Building, completed in Manhattan, was an iconic piece of Art Deco architecture

Above: Salvador Dali was a surrealist artist who supported Franco

A combination of styles that enjoyed great popularity in the 1920s, Art Deco was launched in France before World War I, but became more significant thereafter as a visual display of modernity and a means to combat traditional notions. An international style that lent itself to a variety of forms and materials, Art Deco became particularly associated with American skyscrapers, notably the Chrysler Building in Manhattan, which was completed in 1930.

Women and the Vote

The early-20th century saw important political reforms, particularly in the widening of the franchise. Successive extensions of the right to vote in the 19th century were restricted to men; New Zealand, in 1893, was the first country to give women universal suffrage. Even in countries that counted themselves as progressive, modern standards of equality were a long way from being achieved. The notion of 'separate spheres' was well-established and women's special role was defined as that of home and family.

The world wars led to a large increase in the number of women entering the labour force, which in turn had an impact on encouraging moves to extend the right to vote to them. Britain gave women the vote in 1918 and the USA in 1920. However, the election of women to national assemblies, and their appointment to senior government positions, was uncommon before the second half of the 20th century.

Left: The suffragette movement in Britain sought to obtain women's right to vote in the early 20th century

China: Birth of the Republic

East Asia experienced major political changes in the early 20th century. Sapped by its inadequate response to pressures for change, the Qing (Manchu) dynasty fell relatively easily in 1911–12, rather as the Soviet Union was to do in 1991. An uprising by reformist army officers in Wuchang on 10 October 1911 led to demands elsewhere in China for change. In the face of the widespread revolt, and the declaration of a republican constitution by Sun Yat-Sen, the last emperor abdicated on 12 February 1912. A general, Yuan Shikai, seized power as president, and refused

THE MAY FOURTH MOVEMENT
China's vulnerability provided Japan with the opportunity to increase its power in Chinese coastal areas, notably in Shandong. Japan's claims led to a nationalist upsurge in Shanghai in 1919, the May Fourth Movement. This was significant in encouraging the rejection of foreign influence as well as in building up pressure for modernization, notably among the educated urban young.

to accept the republican constitution despite the elections of 1913 showing support for its exponents. Yuan sought to become Emperor, only to die in 1916. China then fragmented into regional power zones.

WARLORDS OF CHINA

Longstanding regionalism as well as developments prior to the rebellion of 1911–12 meant that regional military units had gained considerable autonomy. The death of Yuan Shikai in 1916 and subsequent rivalries among the now leaderless northern generals, combined with their patronage links to provincial commanders, led to full-scale civil war in 1920. The leading generals used territorial bases to contend for power over all of China. Their conflicts provided the Guomindang with an opportunity to gain the initiative from 1926. Because they lost, the warlord-generals are treated as anachronisms. As Kemal Atatürk in Turkey and Ibn Saud in Arabia show, success can provide a very different gloss.

Above: The general Yuan Shikai seized power in 1912 but was unwilling to accept the republican constitution

Left: Sun Yat-sen led the nascent Chinese nationalist movement and founded the Guomindang party, who established a republic in the city of Guangzhou

THE GUOMINDANG

Led by Sun Yat-sen, the Guomindang had struggled to establish a nationalist republic in Guangzhou (Canton). Soviet support, intended to help limit British influence in China, crucially helped in the development of a more effective Guomindang army. Sun died in 1925, leaving no agreed successor. His military aide, Jiang Jieshi, used the army to take over the Guomindang government, and commanded the Northern Expedition, a drive north against independent warlords in 1926-8 which captured Wuhan (1926), Shanghai (1927), Nanjing (1927) and Beijing (1928). Jiang sought to follow Sun's policy of modernization through centralization.

Cinema

Among the new forces which came to shape society in the 20th century were the film and television industries, and no other country matched the USA for their growth and impact. They spread potent images of American society and material culture, like the use of the motorcar, and influenced style and consumption around the world, such as in women smoking in public. This was true of all types of film. American cartoon characters such as Mickey Mouse, devised by Walt Disney in 1928, Donald Duck and Popeye were recognizable around the world. Other cultures, notably the Soviet Union, produced film and television but with less impact outside their boundaries. From the 1970s, the most active alternative to the USA in the film industry was India. Bollywood, the Indian film capital in and near Mumbai, was consciously named as an alternative to Hollywood and, by the late 1990s, produced more than 800 films a year.

Right: American cartoon characters like Mickey Mouse became recognizable around the world

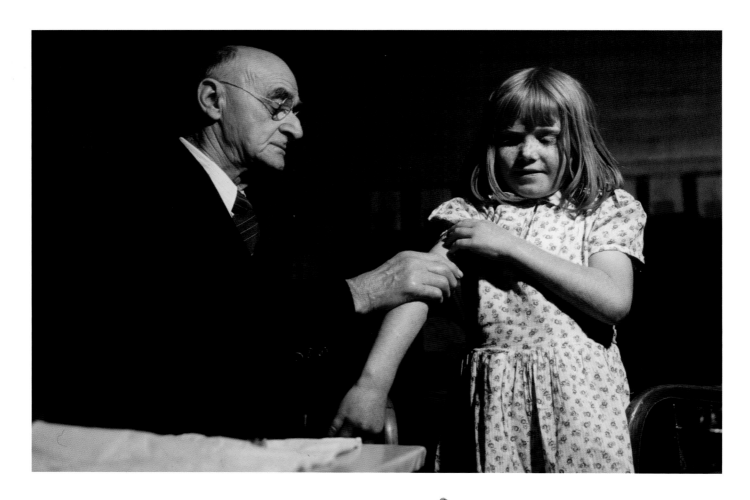

The Battle Against Disease

The pace and impact of medical changes was greater in the 20th century than ever before. Indeed, as general medical knowledge increased enormously, the ability to identify and treat disease increased exponentially. These improvements touched the lives of billions and altered the condition of the world's population. Previously it took new discoveries and their dissemination to overcome fatal illnesses or debilitating diseases and conditions. The impact of diabetes was greatly lessened by the discovery of insulin in 1922. In the 1920s and 1930s, other advances included the use of gamma globulin against measles, the first sulphonamide drugs (as important in veterinary medicine as human), and improved blood transfusion techniques. In 1928, Alexander Fleming accidentally discovered penicillin, a mould that could destroy bacteria. Its isolation and production as a drug led to the antibiotics revolution that began in the 1940s and that transformed the treatment of diseases such as gonorrhoea.

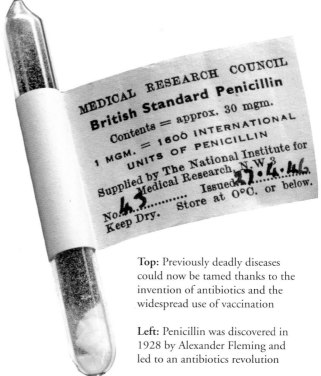

Top: Previously deadly diseases could now be tamed thanks to the invention of antibiotics and the widespread use of vaccination

Left: Penicillin was discovered in 1928 by Alexander Fleming and led to an antibiotics revolution

How we travelled – Air

Manned heavier-than-air flight, first officially achieved by the American Wright brothers in 1903, was rapidly followed by the development of the military and commercial possibilities of air power, and by its technological range. World War I greatly accelerated changes in air capacity. The use of aircraft for combat led to considerable investment in their development, and to a marked rise in the specifications of machines, for example their speed and manoeuvrability. Air power exemplified the growing role of scientific research in military capability: wind tunnels were constructed for the purpose of research. Strutless wings and all-metal aircraft were developed. Engine power increased and size fell. The speed and rate of climb of aircraft rose. In 1919, a converted British bomber was the first aircraft to cross the Atlantic non-stop.

Air services developed rapidly in the 1920s and 1930s, notably in the United States, with the network of routes and the number of airports and aircraft expanding. Journey times progressively shortened, but the range of most aircraft was such that frequent refuelling was necessary. It was not until 1939 that a passenger aircraft was introduced that was able to fly the Atlantic non-stop. Nevertheless, by then, aircraft had clearly established their superiority to the earlier technology of gas-filled airships. Imperial powers established networks to link their possessions. British aircraft flew to Australia, Hong Kong and South Africa. The French and Belgians also developed air systems to link and support their empires. In an effort to build-up political influence, Germany fostered air services to Latin America, where they competed with those of the United States.

Below: The first passenger aircraft able to cross the Atlantic were not introduced until 1939

The Great Depression

The economic and industrial progress of the United States faltered in the 1920s, when the seriously overheating American economy collapsed as a result of the October 1929 Wall Street Crash, the bursting of a speculative boom in share prices in New York. This deflating of an asset price bubble became far more serious as the inexperienced central bank cut the money supply, which greatly affected liquidity. The tightening of the financial reins, including the calling in of overseas loans, caused global financial crisis. The Kreditanstalt bank in Vienna collapsed in 1931, leading to a major run, first on the German banks and then elsewhere.

Then, in 1930, the Hawley-Smoot Act increased American tariffs and depressed demand for imports. Other nations followed suit, leading to a worldwide protectionism that dramatically cut world trade by 1932. Already hit hard by World War I and the Russian Revolution, free trade, which had been revived after the war, disappeared.

As export industries were hit, unemployment rose substantially across the industrial world. In the USA, the national unemployment rate rose to nearly 24 per cent in 1932, by when manufacturing was at only 40 per cent of capacity. As the industrial world's imports of raw materials, such as minerals, declined, commodity producers were hit, bringing serious economic and political problems throughout the developing world, for example in Latin America and Australasia. In addition, these producers were now less able to finance imports from the industrial world.

The Depression destroyed the liberal economic order, and led to a collapse of confidence in capitalist structures. As a result, governments increasingly thought in national (rather than international) economic terms, and state intervention in the economy increased.

Food

In the late-19th century, transoceanic products, transported in refrigerated ships, had a major impact on Western Europe. Meals heavy in carbohydrate predominated in most homes and restaurants, and there was little fresh fruit. There was a high consumption of sugar in hot drinks, desserts and confectionary. Dairy products were important, and butter and lard were widely used for cooking. The poor ate much cold food – bread, cheese and cold meat – and potatoes were very important in their diet. Traditional dishes retained great popularity and there was only limited interest in alternatives. The disruptions of the two World Wars and the protectionism of the 1930s increased the emphasis on local foodstuffs.

The Rise of Extremism

Anger after World War I, notably with the terms of the Versailles peace agreement of 1919, combined with serious economic strains, helped enable authoritarian figures to seize power in an increasingly volatile political and ideological situation. Benito Mussolini did so in Italy in 1922 and Adolf Hitler in Germany in 1933. Hitler benefited from the appeal of his nationalist and racist populism, from German anger with defeat in World War I, and from right-wing concern about Communism, sentiments which enabled him to destabilize the democratic system in Germany. Once he gained power, Hitler transformed Germany into a dictatorship, combining, in 1934, the office of president with that of chancellor, which he already held.

Above: Adolf Hitler rode a wave of anger at the Versailles peace agreement and the economic strains of the 1930s to power

WORLD WAR II

1931 18 September 1931 - The Japanese invade Manchuria and set up a puppet state called 'Manchukuo'

1936 18 July 1936 - The Spanish Civil War begins

1937 7 July 1937 - The Marco Polo Bridge Incident begins the Sino-Japanese War

12 March - The *Anschluss* unites Germany and Austria

1938 30 September 1938 - The Munich Conference results in the Sudetenland being conceded to Germany

1939 15 March 1939 - Germany occupies Czechoslovakia

1 September 1939 - Germany invades Poland

3 September 1939 - Britain and France declare war on Germany

1940 9 April 1940 - Germany begins Operation Weserübung, the conquest of Denmark and Norway

10 May 1940 - Germany invades Belgium, the Netherlands, and Luxembourg, and bypasses the Maginot line in its invasion of France

22 June 1940 - France surrenders to Germany

1941 22 June 1941 - Germany launches operation Barbarossa, the invasion of the Soviet Union

7 December 1941 - Japanese attack on Pearl Harbor brings the USA into the war

1942 4 June 1942 - Battle of Midway

1 – 27 July 1942 - First Battle of El Alamein

23 August 1942 – 2 February 1943 - Battle of Stalingrad

23 October – 4 November 1942 - Second Battle of El Alamein

1943 5 July–23 August 1943 - Battle of Kursk

9 July 1943 - Allies invade Sicily

1944 6 June 1944 - D-Day – Allied Forces invade Normandy

22 June – 19 August 1944 - Operation Bagration – the Red Army advances into Eastern Europe

17 October 1944 - US forces invade the Philippines

1945 8 May 1945 - Germany surrenders

6–9 August 1945 - The atomic bomb is dropped on Hiroshima and Nagasaki

15 August 1945 - Japan surrenders

The dictators acted as war-leaders in peacetime. The systems they created lacked effective institutional and political restraints on their power and ideas, or the facility to offer any reasonable range of policy options. In Germany, Hitler monopolized control and direction of foreign and military policy, his long-term views interacting with the short-term opportunities and anxieties presented by international developments. His ideology was that of continual conflict against opponents, both domestic and international. Opposed to Communists, Socialists, homosexuals or anyone of an independent disposition, and manically obsessed by anti-Semitism, Hitler's hysterical politics depended on an atmosphere of emergency.

THE SPANISH CIVIL WAR

With the Spanish Civil War, the rise of extremism led to a full-scale civil war. A group of senior army officers, who called themselves the Nationalists, sought to seize power in 1936. They were opposed to the modernizing policies of the left-leaning

Above: The Spanish Civil War (1936–1939) is often seen as a harbinger of World War II

Republican government, and also concerned about the possibility of a Communist seizure of power via the *Frente Popular* (Popular Front) after the narrow left-wing electoral victory by the Popular Front in the hard-fought elections of February 1936. The army's attitude to politics explains its rebellion. Claiming that the government had lost control (which in practice was due to right-wing as well as left-wing violence), they were really against the Republic itself, and, with it, democracy and freedoms. The Nationalists, however, achieved only partial success in 1936, which led to a bitter civil war that only ended on 28 March 1939 when they seized Madrid.

The Spanish Civil War is commonly seen as a harbinger of World War II, with an emphasis on ideological divisions. Indeed, the Nationalists, who stressed religious themes, depicted the Republicans as servants of the Antichrist. Yet this ideological angle was scarcely new. It had played a role in Spanish domestic conflict throughout the 19th century.

The Sino-Japanese War

Nationalism flourished in Japan in the 1930s, where many in the army believed in the idea of war as 'the father of creativity.' In 1931, Japan invaded Manchuria, China's industrial heartland. China was seen as a base for the resources, such as coal, iron and land, necessary for Japan to confront the Soviet Union and the USA, and Japan presented itself as a new imperial power pursuing its place in the sun. Civilian views had become less significant, where a sense of mission was strong among the military. Japan's government outlined a New Order for East Asia, aimed at ending Western imperialism and Communism.

In 1937, this prospectus broadened into a full-scale attack on China, designed to force the Chinese to act as a junior partner to Japan. Jiang, however, was ready to fight back in order to assert Chinese sovereignty. In 1937, Japan overran Beijing and Shanghai, going on to make further gains in 1938, including Guangzhou and Wuhan, although, crucially, without ending resistance or winning sufficient Chinese support.

Below: The Sino-Japanese War began in July 1937. Japan initially made rapid gains in China, taking Beijing and Shanghai by the end of the year

THE RAPE OF NANJING

The Guomindang capital, Nanjing, fell to Japan on 13 December 1937. The subsequent slaughter of civilians which was a deliberate step to crush resistance, made a compromise peace unlikely. The massacre of large numbers, including the use of people for bayonet practice, as well as mass rape, was the culmination of barbarous conduct during the Japanese advance up the Yangtze. This brutality did not break Chinese morale, but testified to an emerging immoral and callous attitude within the Japanese military. Recent attempts to minimize the severity of the massacre do not command confidence. It remains today a major aspect of China's presentation to the world of its history, especially in terms of an historic need to resist outside pressure.

World War II

INITIAL GERMAN SUCCESSES

World War II is an umbrella term for a number of closely-related struggles that each had their own cause, course and consequence. Seen from the perspective of Italy or Iran, Japan or Jamaica, it can look very different. A war that began in 1939 over Hitler's attack on Poland, and the decision by Britain and France to intervene in support of the Poles, came to involve much of the world in two major alliances (the Axis, led by Germany, and the Allies, uniting the forces of Britain, France and other powers, to be joined in 1941 by the Soviet Union and the USA). This reflected the range of interests involved, the failure of the system of international adjudication and peace-making (whether by means of the League of Nations established after World War I, or by negotiations between a few powers, as at Munich in 1938), and the vortex-like nature of war.

In particular, the outbreak of hostilities led to a heightened pace of fear and opportunity. The unwillingness of the Germans to try to translate initial victories into a widely accepted peace ensured that the cessation of offensive operations with the

Below: Germany invaded Poland in September 1939, which drew Britain and France into war

THE *BLITZKRIEG*

Myths about the effectiveness of the German Blitzkrieg (lightning war) served German objectives at the time, yet also contributed to the misleading post-war assumption that the Germans were the most impressive military, but had eventually lost because of greater Allied resources. In fact, the effectiveness of the Blitzkrieg, and the importance of tanks and air-support, has been exaggerated. It represented more of an improvization than the fruition of a coherent doctrine. Much of the German army remained unmechanized and horses still played a major role in German logistics. The German achievements in 1940 owed more to German fighting quality and poor French strategy than to mechanization.

Below: Air-support and tanks played an important role in the *Blitzkrieg* strategy, but the majority of German forces remained unmechanized

rapid conquest of Poland did not end the conflict.

Hitler rapidly conquered Denmark and Norway in April 1940, and then planned an attack on France, which was successfully launched the following month. At the same time, German forces seized Belgium and the Netherlands, and British forces were driven from the Continent in defeat, although most were successfully withdrawn in an evacuation operation from Dunkirk. German success led Mussolini to bring Italy into the war on Hitler's side and he went on to attack Greece unsuccessfully. In early 1941, Germany pressed on to secure the alliance of Romania and Bulgaria and to invade Yugoslavia and Greece successfully.

OPERATION BARBAROSSA

In June 1941, Hitler's over-confidence and contempt for all other political systems, his belief that Germany had to conquer the Soviet Union in order to fulfil its destiny and obtain *lebensraum* (living room) for German settlers, combined with his concern about Stalin's intentions, led him to mount Operation Barbarossa. This attack on the Soviet Union was based on confidence that the Soviet system would collapse rapidly. Hitler was happy to believe totally misleading intelligence assessments of the size and mobilization potential of the Red Army. His refusal to accept what others might consider objective diplomatic and strategic considerations ensured that the local wars he had won so far were transformed into a world war he could not win. There was no adequate strategy for converting battlefield triumphs, which were many in the early months of the year, into Soviet collapse or surrender. The resilience and fighting quality of the Red Army proved a surprise, while

German campaigning, although causing heavy Soviet casualties, was seriously mishandled at the operational level, as it failed to settle on a consistent and viable course of action. In particular, there was the unsettled question of whether the Germans should focus on destroying the Soviet army or on capturing territory and, if the latter, what came first.

The Germans failed to take Moscow or Leningrad, the Soviet regime did not collapse and the Germans became stuck in an attritional struggle they could not win and that used up much of the army. Fresh offensives in 1942 and 1943 also failed with heavy losses, at Stalingrad and Kursk respectively. An entire German army was surrounded and forced to surrender at Stalingrad. After Kursk, in the summer of 1943, the Germans did not mount any more offensives on the Eastern Front. Instead, they were heavily defeated in successive Soviet campaigns, notably Operation Bagration in the summer of 1944 which led the Soviets, having defeated Army Group Centre, to advance to near Warsaw. In that year, other Soviet forces advanced into the Balkans, forcing Romania and Bulgaria to abandon their German ally and leading the Germans to evacuate Greece.

THE WAR IN THE ATLANTIC

As in World War I, Germany sought to knock out Britain, not only by destroying its continental alliance system but also by naval action. Attacks by surface warships played a role in this, but Germany was outnumbered in these. Instead, the Germans focused on submarine attacks that were designed to starve Britain into submission. The conquests of Norway and France in 1940 gave Germany submarine bases on to the open ocean.

Britain suffered heavy losses, but the Germans ultimately failed and clearly so in 1943. In part

Below: The Battle of Stalingrad led to great losses on both sides and marked a turning point of the war on the Eastern Front

this was due to the development and adoption of effective anti-submarine techniques, but the German declaration of war on the United States in December 1941 helped swing the naval balance in the Atlantic. The mid-Atlantic Gap where Allied long-distance planes could not carry out anti-submarine operations closed after the neutral Portuguese allowed the use of bases on the Azores in 1943.

Victory in the Battle of the Atlantic made it possible for the Allies to build up their strength in Britain in preparation for the invasion of France in 1944. The Allies' victories in the war in the sea and the air were an important prelude to the total defeat of Germany on land.

D-DAY AND THE FALL OF GERMANY

The defeats inflicted on Germany in 1944, both by the Western Allies and by the Soviet Union, ensured that the war was approaching its end by the close of the year. 1943 had already seen the defeat of

Above: The development anti-submarine techniques and the involvement of the USA in the war ensured Allied success in the Battle of the Atlantic

German and Italian forces in North Africa and the Allied invasion of Italy, leading to the overthrow of Mussolini. Operation Overlord, the invasion of Normandy on D-Day, 6 June 1944, was the largest amphibious operation in history, and proved a success. It was clear that Germany could not win, but Hitler refused to accept the logic of the situation. He decided to fight on to the very end. An attempt in July 1944 by members of the army leadership to use a bomb to assassinate Hitler failed.

The Allies continued heavy bombing attacks until the end of the war. The bombing both hit German industrial production and also demonstrated to the German civilian population that continued resistance would be damaging.

In 1945, the Allies successfully invaded Germany, with Soviet forces capturing Berlin, amid whose ruins

Hitler committed suicide, while Anglo-American forces fought their way across the River Rhine and defeated the Germans in northern Italy. On 7 May 1945, Germany surrendered unconditionally, and was then divided into occupation zones by the Allies.

THE WAR IN THE PACIFIC

The collapse of France and Netherlands under German attack in 1940, and the weakening position of Britain, already vulnerable in the Pacific, created an apparent power vacuum in East and South-east Asia, encouraging Japanese ambitions southwards, while leaving Japan's principal opponents in the region as the USA (which protested against Japanese moves into French Indochina, particularly Vietnam).

On 7 December 1941, Japan launched a devastating air attack on Pearl Harbor, the base of the American Pacific fleet, without any prior declaration of war. In the winter of 1941–2, the Japanese overran the Philippines, Malaysia, the Dutch East Indies (modern Indonesia), and Burma (Myanmar). The initial Japanese ability to mount successful attacks and to gain great swathes of territory in the face of weak and poorly-led opponents did not deter the Americans from the long-term effort of driving them back. America was not interested in a compromise peace and Japan therefore lacked a realistic war plan to consolidate its victories.

Right: The Normandy Landings on 6 June 1944 were the largest amphibious military operation in history

Below: The surprise attack on Pearl Harbor by the Japanese brought America into the war

In the summer of 1942, the American navy blocked the Japanese fleet in the Pacific, inflicting a heavy defeat at Midway in which four Japanese aircraft carriers, the new currency of naval power, were sunk. In 1943, American amphibious operations supported by carriers drove back the Japanese in the south-west and central Pacific, while US forces invaded the Philippines in late 1944. The Japanese navy was crushed. The use of atom bombs on Hiroshima and Nagasaki by the USA in August 1945 was seen as necessary in order to overcome Japan's suicidal determination to fight on and the inevitable losses which would be incurred by an invasion of Japan itself. The atom bombings were followed by a swift and unconditional Japanese surrender.

THE HOLOCAUST

Hitler's hatred of Jews led to a campaign to wipe out all Jews and their culture. Murderous mistreatment of Jews began before the outbreak of the World War II, and Jewish communities in Germany were progressively deprived of their legal rights, notably by the Nuremberg Laws of 1935. The situation became much more violent after the Germans invaded the Soviet Union in 1941. Large numbers of Jews were slaughtered by advancing German forces. Within German-controlled Europe, Jews were moved to concentration camps which began large-scale killing from 1941, often involving the use of gas. About six million Jews were murdered in total, with the largest number, about 1.5 million, being killed in Auschwitz. The slaughter was accompanied by degradation and humiliation. The old and children were generally murdered at once, and the rest were largely worked to death. The Germans went on killing Jews until the end of the war, which indicated the centrality of race conflict to Nazi policy. Much of the German public was aware of the brutal mistreatment of Jews.

THE 'ARSENAL OF DEMOCRACY': THE AMERICAN HOME FRONT

Already responsible for 31.4 per cent of world manufacturing in 1938 (compared to 12.7 for Germany, 10.7 for Britain, and 9.0 for the Soviet Union), the USA was the key to the out-production of the Axis by the Allies. The absence of a need to

Above: The war required a vast increase in arms production

defend America's industrial capacity from air attack was a contributory factor to the country's ability to focus so many resources on the manufacture of goods for overseas military operations. America employed the techniques of mass production developed in peacetime, notably of motorcars, producing 297,000 aircraft and 86,000 tanks during the war and out-producing its opponents in many other weapons and weapon-systems, such as aircraft carriers.

The war economy brought great benefits to the United Sates. Company profits rose, workers enjoyed full employment and rising real wages, funding consumption and the government from a growing tax base. The only leader of a major state to face an election during the war, Franklin Delano Roosevelt, who had already won elections in 1932, 1936 and 1940, was easily re-elected president in 1944. The strength of the American economy in resources and organizational capacity was shown in its ability to establish a programme to produce nuclear bombs, which no other power succeeded in doing.

Goods that changed the world – Oil

Coal remained very important as an energy source in the 20th century, but oil became much more so, notably because it was necessary for vehicles, including tanks. The dominance of the USA was in part linked to its central role in the growth of the oil industry, first as a major source of production and refining and, secondly, because American oil companies, notably Esso, played a crucial role in the development of oil resources elsewhere, particularly in Saudi Arabia, and also in controlling the oil trade. America's opponents in World War II – Germany, Japan and Italy – lacked such resources and their quest for oil shaped strategic decisions, as when Germany tried (unsuccessfully) to advance to Baku on the Caspian Sea in 1942 and devoted much effort in 1943–44 to protecting the Romanian oilfields at Ploesti, the only ones in Europe, from Allied air attack. Conversely, one reason why the Soviet Union, despite its economic inefficiencies, was able to mount a sustained challenge to the USA in the Cold War was because it was one of the world's biggest producers of oil and natural gas.

By 1998, excluding wood and dung, oil provided about 40 per cent of the world's energy consumption, compared to 26 per cent for coal and 24 per cent for natural gas. Nuclear power and hydro-electric power were far less significant. Important developments in engineering and information technology aided the exploitation of oil resources.

It became feasible to drill to greater depths and the understanding of oil fields grew. The political significance of the Middle East increased because of its importance to oil production. The enhanced strategic important of oil-producing countries such as Saudi Arabia, the leading producers, and Iraq led to the need by outside powers to seek allies there and encouraged interventions such as the 2003 US invasion of Iraq. However, unlike coal in 19th-century Britain, oil has not produced an industrial revolution in producing areas, and there has been no creation of jobs sufficient to cope with the rapidly rising population.

Below: The Germans went to great lengths to protect the Ploesti oilfields in Romania, but were unable to stop this raid by the US Air Force in 1943

KEY BATTLES: MIDWAY

The Japanese navy suffered a heavy defeat by the Americans at Midway on 4 June, 1942 with the loss of four Japanese aircraft carriers to American carrier-based air attack. The Japanese defeat owed much to American command quality, to the American ability to seize advantage of unexpected opportunities and to the more general resilience of American naval capability. Midway demonstrated that battles at sea would now be dominated by air power rather than exchanges between battleships.

Above: The Americans won a great naval victory at the Battle of Midway, sinking four Japanese aircraft carriers

HOME FRONTS AND PROPAGANDA

Concern about civilian morale in a long war led, in many countries, to a social politics that put a greater emphasis on social welfare, as well as to systematic attempts to report on the public. Propaganda reflected the sense, even among the totalitarian powers, that popular support had to be wooed. it was an aspect of a re-education of the public that ranged from eating habits (so as to make rationing work) to political goals. Hitler saw propaganda as a way not only of maintaining resolve, but also of waging war with Germany's enemies.

Left: German air attacks on London from 1940, first by aircraft and then by missiles, had a devastating effect

Right: Germany used propaganda both to maintain the morale of its own people and to wage war with its enemies

THE MODERN WORLD
1945–Present

Alongside international and ideological division, warfare, and the threat of a nuclear conflict leading to the destruction of much of the species, a high rate of change took place, affecting humanity as a whole. Population growth, technological development and urbanization were key elements in the drive towards change.

The Cold War

Below: At the Yalta Conference in 1945 Churchill, Roosevelt and Stalin met to discuss the shape of the world after the end of the war

Wartime alliances frequently do not survive peace. The ideological division between the Western powers and Soviet Union was too much to overcome. Indeed, by 1944 differences about the fate of Eastern Europe were readily apparent, especially over Poland, which Stalin was determined to dominate.

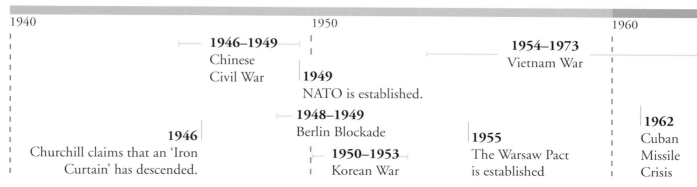

1940

1950

1960

1946–1949
Chinese
Civil War

1949
NATO is established.

1948–1949
Berlin Blockade

1954–1973
Vietnam War

1946
Churchill claims that an 'Iron
Curtain' has descended.

1950–1953
Korean War

1955
The Warsaw Pact
is established

1962
Cuban
Missile
Crisis

COLD WAR MILITARY ALLIANCES

- Founding members of the North Atlantic Alliance (NATO) 1949
- Entry: Greece and Turkey 1952, West Germany 1955, Spain 1982
- Founding members of the Warsaw Pact 1955
- Entry: East Germany 1956
- Withdrawal: Albania 1968

Right: Two military alliances faced off in Europe – NATO in the West and the Warsaw Pact in the East

Iceland

Sweden   Finland

Norway

Denmark

Ireland   Netherlands

United Kingdom   East Germany   Poland   Soviet Union

West Germany   Czechoslovakia

Belgium   Luxembourg   Switzerland   Austria   Hungary   Romania

France   Liecht.   Yugosalvia   Bulgaria

Andorra   Italy

Portugal   Greece   Turkey

Spain   Albania

Morocco   Algeria   Tunisia   Cyprus

The Cold War which emerged from these differences was not a formal or frontal conflict, but a period of hostility lasting until 1989 that involved a protracted arms race, as well as numerous proxy conflicts in which the major powers intervened in other struggles. The latter sustained attitudes of animosity, exacerbated fears and contributed to a high level of military preparedness. A potent feeling of uncertainty on both sides, of the fragility of military strength, international links, political orders and ideological convictions, encouraged a strong sense of threat, and fuelled an incessant and expensive

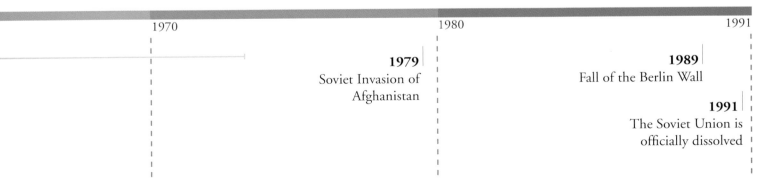

1970   1980   1991

1979
Soviet Invasion of Afghanistan

1989
Fall of the Berlin Wall

1991
The Soviet Union is officially dissolved

arms race that was to be central to the Cold War. Indeed, the arms race was the Cold War. Both sides claimed to be strong, but declared that they required an extra edge to be secure. Only the Mutually Assured Destruction (MAD) threatened by massive nuclear stockpiles eventually brought a measure of stability.

The Soviet Union initially lacked the atom bomb, but its army was well placed to overrun Western Europe and could only have been stopped by the West's desperate use of nuclear weapons. The American offer of Marshall Aid, a programme of economic assistance to help recovery after World War II, was accepted by many Western European nations, but rejected by the Soviet Union as a form of economic imperialism, and this created a new boundary line between the areas in Western Europe that received such aid and those in Eastern Europe that did not. The Soviet abandonment of co-operation over occupied Germany and the imposition of one-party Communist governments in Eastern Europe, notably in Czechoslovakia, led to pressure for a Western response. Soviet actions appeared to vindicate Churchill's 1946 claim that an 'Iron Curtain' was descending from the Baltic to the Adriatic. In 1949, the foundation of the North Atlantic Treaty Organization (NATO) created a security framework for Western Europe. The USA abandoned its tradition of isolationism, played a crucial role in the formation of the new alliance and was anchored to the defence of Western Europe. In turn, in 1955, the Soviet Union organized the Warsaw Pact, its own military alliance, in Eastern Europe.

Left: In 1968 Soviet forces invaded Czechoslovakia when the 'Prague Spring' threatened liberalization

THE EUROPEAN UNION

The establishment in 1958 of the European Economic Community was part of a process in which the political structures of Western Europe were transformed after World War II. A reaction against nationalism was important to European integration. West German willingness to accept the concessions France required helped lead the latter to back the scheme.

With time, the EEC expanded geographically and became more ambitious, with the Treaty of European Union signed at Maastricht in 1992 creating the European Union, the new term an indication of the new prospectus. Moreover, the Euro, a common currency for most of the EU, was launched as a trading currency in 1999. In addition, more states joined the EU, which proved a way to consolidate post-Communist Eastern Europe in the new order.

THE KOREAN AND VIETNAM WARS

The total Communist victory over the Nationalists in the Chinese Civil War (1946–49) heightened American concern to stop further Communist advances. In 1950, an American-led alliance intervened in 1950 under the auspices of the United Nations to prevent Communist North Korea from conquering South Korea, resulting in the Korean War (1950–53). Having driven back the North Koreans, the Allies invaded the North, only to be pushed back when the Chinese intervened. The conflict settled down into an impasse. An armistice was finally negotiated only after the Americans threatened the use of nuclear weaponry.

In turn, the Americans intervened in the early 1960s in South Vietnam to thwart a Communist rebellion by the Viet Cong, who were supported by Communist North Vietnam. Able to stop, but not to defeat, their opponents, and facing mounting domestic criticism, the Americans withdrew in 1973. South Vietnam fell to Communist attack in 1975. The conflict had also destabilized neighbouring Cambodia and Laos, where American-led and Communist forces competed for control. All these conflict stoked Cold War tensions, with both the Soviet Union and China backing North Vietnam, while Australia, New Zealand and South Korea sent troops to help the Americans.

Below: Mounting casualties in the Vietnam War led to intense criticism by the American people

OXIDIZER TRAILERS

2 MISSILE TRANSPORTERS

OXIDIZER TRAILER

6 MISSILE TRANSPORTERS

PROB IRBM PROPELLANT TRAILERS

ERECTOR

3 MISSILE TRANSPORTERS

Right:
A reconnaissance photo shows the locations of the Soviet missiles at Mariel Naval Port in Cuba, 8 November 1962

THE CUBAN MISSILE CRISIS, 1962

The nuclear competition between the superpowers became more urgent in the 1950s, first with the development and deployment of hydrogen bombs, far more dangerous than their nuclear predecessors, and then with the advent of intercontinental rocketry. In 1957, the Soviet Union launched *Sputnik I*, the first satellite, into orbit, making the USA vulnerable to missile attack.

In the early 1960s, mutual anxieties about achieving an edge in the growing nuclear arms race encouraged John F. Kennedy (US President 1961–63) to aim for a strategic superiority over the Soviet Union, and Nikita Khrushchev (First Secretary of the Soviet Communist Party, 1953–64) to decide in 1962 to deploy missiles in Cuba, where the anti-American Fidel Castro had

recently seized power and survived an American-backed attempt in 1961 to overthrow him, in the controversial Bay of Pigs episode. Soviet missiles so close to its shores would pose a serious threat to the United States.

In response to this deployment, the Americans considered an attack on Cuba, and imposed an air and naval quarantine to prevent the shipping of further Soviet supplies. Kennedy also threatened a full retaliatory nuclear strike. In complicated bargaining, the Soviets agreed to remove the missiles, but the gap between decision, use and strike by nuclear weaponry had been shown to be perilously small. For the first time, the world had for a while teetered on the edge of a nuclear holocaust.

REAGAN

After a measure of *détente* or peaceful co-existence in the mid-1970s, the Cold War heated-up in the late 1970s with conflicts between American and Soviet protégés in Angola and Somalia/Ethiopia, and then in response to the Soviet invasion of Afghanistan in 1979. Under Ronald Reagan (US President 1981–89), there was a marked intensification of the American commitment to fighting the Cold War. The United States armed anti-Communist forces in Afghanistan, Central America, and sub-Saharan Africa, and there was a major build-up in the American military. The resilience of the American economy, combined with the ability of the Reagan government in the 1980s to use the state's capacity to raise money in the bond market, helped the US government mobilize American resources for a military build-up that the Soviets, lacking the money against which to raise credit, could not match. The Americans were greatly helped by a strategic alignment with China against the Soviet Union. As a result, the costs to them of waging the Cold War fell. The Soviet Union had, too, to be mindful of the opposition of China which, indeed, fought Vietnam, a Soviet protégé. While the Soviet Union's economy stagnated, the USA experienced significant economic growth and no recurrence of the 'stagflation' of the 1970s, a combination of stagnation and inflation which had led to a sense of uncertainty and malaise. The American economy, more focused on the skills and investment required for increasingly complex manufacturing processes than on the raw materials needed for basic processes, was better adapted for growth. Capital invested per worker remained high, and the openness of the American internal economy and market, accentuated by deregulation, encouraged the speedy diffusion of most efficient economic practices and of capital flow to whatever seemed profitable.

THE FALL OF SOVIET COMMUNISM

The collapse of the Soviet Union and of its area of control in Eastern Europe was unexpected. Mikhail Gorbachev, who became Soviet leader in 1985,

Left: Ronald Reagan intensified American competition with the Soviet Union

Above: Soviet troops cross the border into Afghanistan in 1979

Below: The fall of the Berlin Wall symbolized the collapse of the Soviet bloc

sought to modernize Communism by introducing reforms, rather than to overthrow it. The centralized command economics of the Soviet Union were experiencing serious problems by the mid-1980s, and earlier attempts to reform them proved flawed. Economic difficulties limited the funds available for social investment and consumer spending, and this increasingly compromised popular support for the non-democratic system.

Gorbachev's attempts to push through modernization left the pro-Soviet Eastern European Communist governments weak in the face of growing popular demands for reform. This led to the successive collapse of Communist regimes in Eastern Europe in 1989, and to the emergence of multi-party politics and free elections. In 1990, East and West Germany were reunited. In 1991, the Soviet Union was dissolved, as its former constituent republics, such as Ukraine, gained independence. From the 2000s, however, Russia under Vladimir Putin sought to claw back its loss of power, intervening militarily in Georgia in 2008 and in Ukraine from 2014.

Decolonization

THE PARTITION OF INDIA

Change in Europe was matched by changes in Europe's overseas empires. In 1947, exhausted after World War II, and no longer so committed to imperialism, the British renounced control over India. In discussion with the Jawaharlal Nehru, the main Hindu political figure, and the Muslim League's leader, Muhammad Ali Jinnah, the British Viceroy Lord Mountbatten devised the partition of India into two units – a Hindu-majority India and a Muslim Pakistan. This hasty and ill-planned division led to an upsurge in communal violence between Hindus and Muslims, with approximately one and a half million killed and another 14 million fleeing as refugees. Pakistan's borders essentially fell where Islam was dominant, although India imposed control over part of Muslim Kashmir.

More populous and wealthier, India acted as a regional power, fighting Pakistan in 1965, and in 1971 defeating it while helping East Pakistan become the new state of Bangladesh. India also occupied the Portuguese possessions in India in 1961, sent troops into Sri Lanka to help against insurgents, and confronted China in the Himalayas. Albeit with a period of 'Emergency' authoritarianism in the 1970s, India remained under civilian rule, but in Pakistan the military alternated in power with civilian governments.

Right: Muhammad Ali Jinnah, leader of the Muslim League, encouraged Lord Mountbatten to partition the Indian subcontinent into two units based on religion – India and Pakistan

THE MIDDLE EAST

Britain withdrew, too, from its UN-mandated control over Palestine in 1948, weary of acting as arbiter between Muslims and the growing Jewish population. The Middle East was of particular economic significance due to its role in oil production, and the foundation in 1948 of the state of Israel, largely by Jewish refugees from Europe, led to an attempt by Israel's Muslim Arab neighbours to destroy the new country. In the resulting war from 1948 to 1949, Israel won and a flood of Arab refugees fled from the new state. Victory over Egypt in 1956 was followed in 1967 by the Six-Day War, in which Israel conquered territory from Egypt, Jordan and Syria. Part of this was eventually returned, but Israel was left in control of the West Bank of the River Jordan and, with that, of a large Palestinian population that challenged its stability.

Below: During the Six-Day War of 1967, Israel conquered territory in Egypt, Jordan and Syria, bringing a large Palestinian population into its state on the West Bank and Gaza Strip

LEAVING AFRICA

Decolonization in Africa gathered pace from the late 1950s. Support within the imperial powers for imperialism declined, while an upsurge in colonial nationalist movements posed increasing problems, most notably for states that wished to rest imperial rule on consent, not force. Britain gave independence to its African colonies from 1957 (with Ghana being the first) on, while, in 1960, France granted independence to most of its African possessions bar Algeria, while Belgium abandoned the Congo.

The major attempts to maintain colonial control were made by France in Algeria in 1954–62 and by Portugal in Angola and Mozambique in 1961–74, but they failed as they could not crush the nationalist opposition. Although undefeated in battle, the French were unable to end guerrilla action in Algeria in what was a very costly struggle. French moves were actually often counter-productive in winning the loyalty of the bulk of the population. In all these cases, the Cold War was an important context for the conflicts, with the Soviet Union and China increasingly backing the insurrections.

Above: Kwame Nkrumah of Ghana became the first sub-Saharan African leader to achieve independence

The same was also true of the struggle to overthrow the independent, 'white'-ruled states in southern Africa: South Africa and Southern Rhodesia (now Zimbabwe), each of which was based on rule by the white minority. Liberation movements in the region drew support from Communist powers, although the overthrow of white rule in South Africa and of its discriminatory apartheid system, occurred after the end of the Cold War. This end reflected, instead, the domestic instability that stemmed from opposition to apartheid, the economic burdens of sanctions imposed by the USA and the European Union, and the belief among important elements of the white population that it was necessary to achieve progress through reform. In 1980, black majority rule was established in Zimbabwe, while elections held in South Africa in 1994 under a universal franchise led to victory by the African National Congress, the former liberation movement.

Africa in Independence

Independence brought its own challenges for the newly independent states. The continent soon became a battleground for the two superpowers. The first prime minister of the Congo, Patrice Lumumba, was assassinated for his perceived pro-Soviet sympathies. In some cases, tensions between ethnic groups broke out into war. In Nigeria, violence against the Igbo people led to the proclamation by Colonel Chuwuemeka Ojukwu in 1967 of the Republic of Biafra in the country' south-eastern region. The violent civil war lasted three years and attracted significant international attention. It was the first in a series of African conflicts that have followed independence.

The rapid rise in Africa's population has put immense pressures on the resources of the continent. Nigeria, Africa's most populous state and currently the 7th most populous in the world, is due to pass that of the United States (currently third) by 2050. Already, there has been a marked fall in land availability: from 0.5 hectares (1.2 acres) of cultivated land per person in 1965 to 0.28 (0.7 acres) in 1995. This pressure was disguised by widespread urbanization. The proportion of Nigerians living in an urban area rose from a fifth in 1963 to more than a third in 1991: by the 2010s, the largest Nigerian city, Lagos, was adding half a million people annually. Across Africa, pressure on land has caused environmental pressures and ethnic tension in rural areas. Soil loss was a major problem, with wind and water erosion hitting hard. There was a degrading of marginal farmland, especially in Namibia, Ethiopia and along the *sahel* belt south of the Sahara, and each of these suffered desertification. There was widespread drought in the *sahel* from the 1980s, which led, for example, many Mauritanians to abandon nomadic herding and move to live in the cities.

The rise in population, and the size and diversity of the continent, makes the economic success and political stability of Africa difficult to judge overall. Alongside current instances of growth and stability, such as Botswana, Zambia and Tanzania, come areas of acute instability, notably the *sahel* belt from Mali to South Sudan, as well as Congo. The combination of institutional weaknesses and widespread corruption has hit the politics of many states. In Lagos, there is terrible congestion, corruption, a poor power supply and a lawlessness that has led to vigilante groups keeping the peace for payment.

Economic disparities are a problem. Fewer than one in six of the African population was using the Internet by 2012. Chinese technology and investment is helping, for example with the spreading use of mobile phones, but much of the economic production continues to be of primary goods, and chronic underemployment or unemployment, as in Egypt and South Africa, are greatly exacerbated by rapid population growth.

Above: Lagos has grown rapidly since independence, reaching the status of Africa's largest city by 2012 with a population of 21 million according to the Lagos State government

Left: Deng Xiaoping enacted economic reforms that aided China's rapid development

The Rise of China

The end of World War II did not bring stability to East Asia. Once Japan was defeated, hostilities between the Guomindang and the Communists quickly resumed. With support from 50,000 US military advisors, the nationalists quickly retook the areas that had been occupied by the Japanese and in 1946 launched attacks on the Communist forces. In 1947 they seized the Communist capital of Yan'an, but it was a short-lived victory. Decisive victories for the Communists in the Huaihuai and Pinjin campaigns in 1948–49 forced the nationalist leader Chiang Kai-shek to retreat with his forces to the island of Taiwan.

The Communist People's Republic of China was proclaimed on 1 October 1949 with Mao Zedong as its leader. Under Mao, China launched a series of radical reforms. Between 1958 and 1962 the 'Great Leap Forward' campaign collectivized agriculture and aimed to transform China into an industrial society. The Cultural Revolution, which began in 1966, hoped to achieve just as dramatic a change in the cultural life of the country as the Communist Party sought to instil its values in every walk of life.

After the death in 1976 of Mao Zedong, there was a marked shift in policy. Communism lost its radical edge and became an official creed that adapted to capitalism, although a ruling group in the Chinese Communist Party retained power. In the 1980s, Deng Xiaoping, the new leader, pushed through economic liberalization and modernization measures. Freeing prices, permitting private businesses, giving farmers the right to retain surpluses, and attracting foreign investment, all helped ensure a boom that also owed much to the availability of foreign markets. China's GNP rose greatly, notably in the coastal areas in the south. Its plentiful labour supply helped China gain important comparative advantages over other exporters, and these advantages attracted inward investment. There were heavy costs, however, in terms of environmental degradation, social inequality and rising corruption. China became the world's second largest industrial producer in the 2000s and the largest by the 2010s.

In the late 1990s, talk of Asian dominance and of the challenge to the USA came to focus on China in place of Japan. From the 2000s, power-projection became a major theme in Chinese policy and this was pushed more firmly in the 2010s with ambitious plans for naval expansion and overseas bases, and with assertive policies in the East and South China seas. Remaining a one-Party state, China sought to offer an alternative system of values to that of the USA, and achieved considerable success in winning support, notably in Africa.

The Politics of Land Reform

In many countries, the ownership of land, previously held in a highly inegalitarian and hereditary fashion, was dramatically changed after World War II, continuing a pattern seen in the Soviet Union in the 1920s. Communist regimes pushed through 'land reform' in order to create a new social politics in which groups judged reactionary, particularly landowners, were dispossessed and collectives, which were regarded as progressive – the poor peasantry – were rewarded. It was believed that these changes would raise agricultural productivity, but, instead, they led to a centrist

and often inefficient managerial regime.

In China, land was redistributed from landlords to poor peasants under the 1950 Agrarian Reform Law, but collectivization was pushed hard from 1954 and peasants lost their land in the 'Great Leap Forward.'

Land reform took place in Japan in the late 1940s (although imposed by the American occupying power), as in Mexico after the 1910 Revolution and India following independence in 1947, creating (at least in theory) a buoyant peasantry of individual proprietors.

The USA after the Cold War

In the 1990s, the USA achieved a remarkable position of ascendancy. There was a rise in its percentage of the world's GDP, contributing to an increasing gap in per capita income between the West and the rest, and in the American share of global exports, which rose to 17.7 per cent in 1999. In contrast, Mexico faced a financial crisis in 1994–95, much of Asia a liquidity crisis in 1997–98 and Russia one of debt non-payment in 1998. These crises indicated the strains, in the shape of large-scale financial volatility, created by extensive investment and the major rise in liquidity, but also, because it survived, revealed that the financial system was stronger than in the 1930s. The USA played a key role in this survival, acting as a market to other states. In 2017, it had a record goods deficit with China: $375 billion.

THE SKYSCRAPER
Developed originally in the USA, notably in New York, skyscrapers reflected high land values and modern technology, especially rapid lifts. In turn, skyscrapers became an international style for city centre office buildings and hotels. These skyscrapers proclaimed a city's status, as in Hong Kong with the juxtaposed buildings of the Hong Kong and Shanghai Banking Corporation, the Bank of China and the Standard Chartered Bank.

The Rise of the Modern Consumer

The economic growth that characterized large areas from the mid-19th century, and notably after World War II, left most of the population in the 'developed world' with more disposable wealth, and also with more leisure time in which to spend it, accelerating the shaping of society by its expenditure patterns. American living standards were on average 82 per cent higher in 1973 than in 1948. During that period, median American family income rose on average by three per cent per annum; output per hour in the American business sector alsorose by more than three per cent per annum. Across the West, staples – food, housing, heating – absorbed a smaller percentage of the average budget, and this was further encouraged by the rise in labour participation rates that stemmed in large part from a higher percentage of married female workers.

The ability of people to define themselves through spending accentuated the rise of the money economy which had itself increased with mass urbanization. Fashion, cost and respectability helped determine choice, which was shaped by design and advertising, which tended to make products and activities national and international.

Traditional methods of advertising – on billboards, on the sides of buses, in shop windows and via 'sandwich boards' – were supplemented by more novel methods: colour photography and commercial television and, from the 1990s, the Internet. Advertising focused on entire countries and helped make products and activities national rather than local.

There was also an increasingly powerful international dimension to selling and advertising, which itself encouraged economic growth. This international

The dashing new Corvette (left) and the Bel Air Sport

Chevy puts the _purr_ in performance!

Above: Cars were the quintessential consumer good and by the late 20th century it became the expectation of every American family to own one

dimension owed something to the appeal of foreign products and to the enhancement of product ranges and possibilities through global technological developments, such as of synthetic fibres.

It became common throughout wealthier societies to replace goods even when they were still functional, or indeed to use products that were not functional, such as, in the 2010s, to wear jeans with holes. This situation contributed to the growth in rubbish, which had dire environmental consequences, notably with the greater production of plastic, which took many years to biodegrade, leading to the appearance of massive patches of discarded plastic in the oceans.

Popular Culture

From the 1960s, fashions, clothes and popular music began to stress youth culture and there was an emphasis on the individual and his or her ability to construct their own particular world. Songs and films featured sexual independence. Hedonism focused on free-will, self-fulfilment, and consumerism.

Youth culture, feminism, drugs and sexual liberation were international themes, and novel gender and youth expectations and roles commanded attention. At the same time pre-existing cultural and social norms ensured that there were very different responses, both public and governmental, to divorce, abortion and homosexuality.

The creation of artistic works continued to draw on different forms and to transcend boundaries, discarding established classifications and conventions. Radical intellectual influences contributed to a sense of flux. Structuralism, a movement that looked to the French anthropologist Claude Lévi-Strauss and the French literary critic Roland Barthes, treated language as a set of conventions that were themselves of limited value as guides to any underlying reality. This looked towards the Postmodernism that became influential in the 1980s. Existentialism, a European post-World War II nihilistic philosophical movement, closely associated with Martin Heidegger and Jean-Paul Sartre, stressed the vulnerability of the individual in a hostile world and the emptiness of choice.

In lifestyles, American popular culture had far more of an impact. Encouraged by the role of American films and television programmes, and of American-derived products in consumer society, the mystique of America as a land of wealth and excitement grew greatly in the 1950s, especially in Western Europe, Latin America and Japan. There was also a content to American culture that was democratic, accessible and populist, one seen in American films and television, and in music such as that of Leonard Bernstein and Aaron Copland, that spanned classical and popular idioms.

In the 1960s, social, cultural and intellectual changes hit, and in many cases swept away, earlier taboos. The introduction and rapid spread of the oral contraceptive pill from the late 1950s, for example, made it easier than ever before to separate sexuality from reproduction.

Right: The fashion of the 1960s reflected the wider culture of individuality that characterized the decade

Above: Elvis Presley was the iconic star of the rock and roll movement that emerged in the 1950s

Music

Consumer choice linked to a range of social developments including the emergence of the youth consumer. There was a widespread wish and ability to create an adolescent identity – not to be younger copies of their elders – and to reject the opinions of parents. This was particularly seen with the development of popular music, a genre increasingly focused on the young. This was true of 'rock and roll' in the 1950s and of 'Pop' in the 1960s. Stars such as Elvis Presley (American) and the Beatles (British) became iconic figures who defied traditional conventions of behaviour. The music generally lacked much sophistication or skill, but it lent itself to being listened to through new technologies such as transistor radios.

Television

In 1926, John Logie Baird gave the first public demonstration of television technology and in 1936 the world's first public television broadcasting service began in Britain. Its further development was held back during World War II, but affluence and credit helped ensure that television ownership across the West then shot up. In Britain, 75 per cent of the population had regular access to a television set by 1959. In 1986, there were 195 million televisions in the USA, which became the global centre of television culture, compared to 26 million in Brazil, 10.5 million in India and 6.6 million in Indonesia. In the 1990s, the already increased number of terrestrial television channels was supplemented by satellite channels. Television succeeded radio as a central determinant of the leisure time of many, a moulder of opinions and fashions, a source of conversation and controversy, an occasion for family cohesion or dispute and a major household feature. It became a force for change, a great contributor to the making of the 'consumer society' and a 'window on the world', which demanded the right to enter everywhere and report on anything. Television also increasingly became a reflector of popular taste.

In turn, satellite television brought cross-border influences that hit monopolies of control of information. Islamic fundamentalists sought to prevent or limit the spread of information about Western life, and television was banned by the Taliban regime in Afghanistan.

Right: John Logie Baird first demonstrated the television in 1926, but it was not until the 1950s that television ownership became widespread

Feeding the World

An unprecedented rise in the global population meant an unprecedented rise in the demand for food. This rise was generally met. Indeed, severe failures in food provision, in the form of famine, were the consequence of war, radical agrarian policies in command economies or extreme environmental conditions, High consumption in developed countries, where obesity became a serious health issue, was not matched elsewhere.

THE GREEN REVOLUTION

Growth in agricultural production in much of the world was concentrated in the second half of the 20th century. Thanks to the 'green revolution,' especially the widespread distribution of improved crop strains, the extensive use of chemical fertilizers and pesticides, mechanization and increased use of irrigation water, the figure for the average amount of grain available per person rose from 135 kilos in 1961 to 161 in 1989.

In Brazil, mechanization led to an increase in agricultural production in the last decades of the century. It also promoted a social and geographical switch away from small family farms and towards agribusinesses with large farms, especially in the *cerrado* region of the interior south of Amazonia. Large fields were more amenable to mechanization, and crop strains and layouts that could be readily harvested by machine were developed. The social cost in Brazil, however, was a crisis in traditional farming.

The environmental consequences of the 'green revolution' were very serious. The monoculture that came from an emphasis on a few high-yield strains lessened biodiversity and provided a food source for particular pests, while the nature of agricultural practice led to soil erosion and depletion.

FACTORY FARMING

Rising incomes led to greater demand for meat and fish and the yield of meat per acre became a major consideration. This led to a move away from beef cattle, which were generally fed on pasture, to animals that could be fed more intensively from feedlots throughout the year, especially pigs and chickens. The latter led to 'factory farming' with animals kept, in high-density, in buildings throughout the year.

Food

In the 1950s, the return to prosperity generally meant more of the same: increased consumption of the proteins and carbohydrates that were the staple of much of the Western diet. The nutritional standard of life in the developed world rose and daily calorie supply per capita was especially high in North America, Western Europe and Australasia.

From the 1960s, the national diet in these areas was increasingly affected by new ingredients and by dishes introduced from foreign countries. Italian, Chinese and Indian restaurants expanded outside their home areas, while American fast-food chains, such as McDonald's, became ubiquitous.

There was a willingness to try new dishes, and far more information on how to prepare them became available. Households were no longer prepared to accept inherited recipes or one biblical cookbook. Instead, they purchased several and consulted information technology, while cookery programmes became particularly popular on television. Refrigeration transformed eating habits by allowing the preservation of foodstuffs. Seasons were banished for consumers who wanted year-long supplies of products. The growth of convenience food, made possible by deep freezers and microwave ovens, provided a major market for new dishes.

Daily calorie supply, in contrast, remained particularly low in sub-Saharan Africa, South Asia and parts of Latin America. Famines occurred, as in Ethiopia. In addition, traditional foodstuffs and means of preparing food continued to be important. Moreover, cultural differences, such as religious taboos on the eating of pork or beef, proved resistant to change.

Below: From the 1960s on, new cuisines were introduced to the national diets in North America and Western Europe, from Italy, China and India among other places

Right: Protecting the natural environment became a major issue from the 1950s as the consequences of industrial production began to be understood

Environmentalism

The idea of the world as a terrain to shape, and a commodity to be used, was challenged from the 1950s by the proposition that it was a biosphere, operating in an organic fashion and using natural feedback mechanisms to sustain life. The globe was now presented as an environmental system affected by human activities, such as atmospheric pollution. It became possible to track and dramatize the movement of air- or water-borne pollutants. Books such as *Silent Spring* (1962) by the American ecologist Rachel Carson highlighted the environmental threat posed by pesticides, especially DDT.

Population growth, economic development and greater affluence all put pressure on the environment. Carbon dioxide emissions, the result of burning forests or fossil fuels, notably coal, and acid deposition, a consequence of sulphur and nitrogen production from industrial processes, all increased. Indeed 'acid rain' damaged woodland and hit rivers and lakes.

Pollution had the capacity to affect distant environments, both in the countries where the pollution originated, especially in upland areas, and in other countries.

The assault from pollution was varied. Lead emissions from traffic affected air quality. Consumer society produced greater and greater quantities of rubbish, much of it non-biodegradable and some of it toxic. Plastic waste in the oceans entered the human food-chain via algae and fish.

DEFORESTATION

Deforestation accelerated in the 20th century. Satellite data provided evidence of deforestation. Between 1970 and 1995 about ten per cent of the world's natural forests were lost. Looked at differently, between 1960 and 1990 the developing world lost about 450 million hectares of forest.

Whereas in temperate zones, such as Canada and Scandinavia, there was extensive new planting, this was not the case in the Tropics, where land hunger and the desire to exploit forest resources prevailed. In Brunei, much forest was cleared in order to permit cultivation for palm oil.On the Indonesian island of Java, the very rapid growth of the population far surpassed that of agricultural production in the first four decades of the century. This led to very small landholdings, as well as to deforestation and soil exhaustion, a process that occurred in many other parts of the world.

Below: Deforestation accelerated significantly in the 20th century due to new technology and the world's rapidly increasing population

DAMS

A product of ideology and politics, dams were seen as sources of controlled water flow, both for water consumption and for the hydro-electric power that, from the 1950s, was presented as a safe alternative to nuclear power in replacing fossil fuels. Nature could be tamed. Across the world, dams became symbols for its future. This was true of such major projects as the dams in the Tennessee River valley and across the west of the USA, most spectacularly the Hoover Dam, the dams on the River Don in the Soviet Union, the Snowy Mountains scheme in Australia, the Aswan dam in Egypt, the Cabora Bassa dam in Mozambique, and the Three Gorges dam on the Yangtze River in China. Major dams continue to be built. Ethiopia is constructing a huge one on the Blue Nile, and there are disputes with Egypt and Sudan downriver over the quantity of water they will receive.

Below: The Three Gorges Dam on the Yangtze River is a spectacular instance of adapting the environment to our own uses

CLIMATE CHANGE

As population has risen and land use been transformed, the ability of forests to act as huge carbon sinks has fallen. The build-up of greenhouse gases has been rising since the Industrial Revolution, which led to a vast increase in the use of fossil fuels such as coal and oil, whose burning releases carbon dioxide into the atmosphere.

This builds up in the atmosphere and stops heat escaping from the planet, encouraging the melting of polar ice as well as destructive changes in climate. The earth's surface temperature has risen steadily from the mid-1970s: from 1975 to the end of the century, temperatures rose by about half a degree centigrade.

Climate change contributed to anxiety about modernization and posed serious issues for international diplomacy. Attempts to reach agreement on limiting carbon emissions saw bitter quarrels in which the USA, China, India and the European Union found it impossible to agree. The Kyoto Protocol of 1997 was rejected in 2001 by the USA, which argued that it disproportionately benefited developing countries, and in 2017 the USA opposed an agreement on climate change reached in Paris in 2015.

Demographics

MIGRATION

Rates of migration rose in the 20th and 21st centuries in response to pull and push factors. The pull factors came in the forms of economic opportunity and improved transport routes, the push factors from armed conflict, political, ethnic or religious persecution, poverty often linked to population growth, and natural disasters such as droughts and floods. Patterns of migration were varied and complex. Much was within countries, in particular from countryside to city, and to areas of greater opportunity, notably the coastal cities of China, the major cities of India and Japan, and the Sun Belt in the USA. In Japan, the population moved from rural areas to Tokyo and Osaka.

Right: The arrival of the *Empire Windrush* near London in 1948 marked the beginning of a new era of immigration

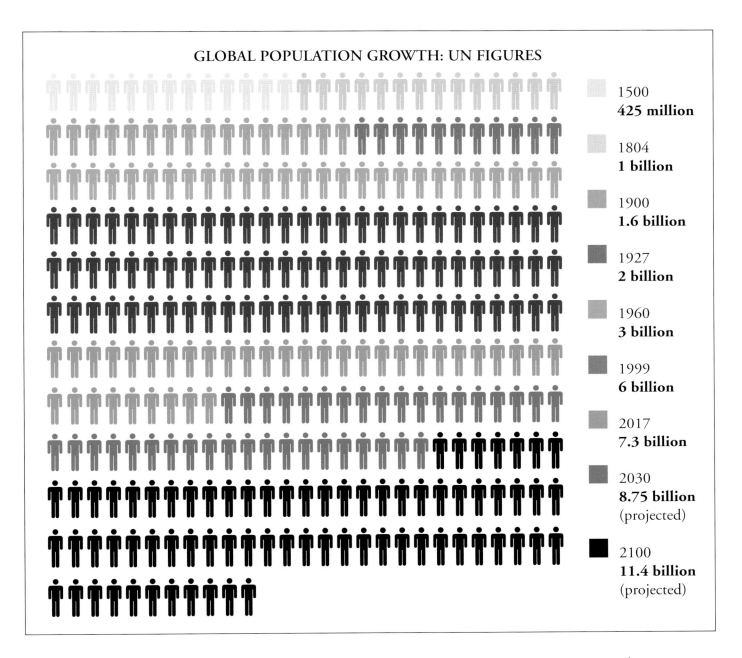

GLOBAL POPULATION GROWTH: UN FIGURES

	1500 **425 million**
	1804 **1 billion**
	1900 **1.6 billion**
	1927 **2 billion**
	1960 **3 billion**
	1999 **6 billion**
	2017 **7.3 billion**
	2030 **8.75 billion** (projected)
	2100 **11.4 billion** (projected)

Migration between countries created more controversy. Migrant workers, such as Portuguese going to France, Turks to Germany, and Indians to the Gulf, created fewer issues than those posed by migrants fleeing persecution who cannot return home. The problems posed, in truth or fear, by immigrants with very different cultures made the latter category more controversial.

In the 2010s, the rate of immigration from Central America to the USA, and from the Middle East and Africa to Europe, became politically highly charged. Some commentators advanced a sense of identity under threat and the situation was made more problematic by the current marked rise in world population, which is predicted to continue despite the fall in population in some countries, notably Japan (and possibly, by 2030, China).

Earlier hopes that the population would top-out at 9.5 billion in 2050, thanks to women being encouraged by education to limit their family size, have proved flawed and high rates of population growth persist in many areas and among more religious sections of communities. This is a subject that still concerns economic planners worldwide.

The City of the Future

The United Nations predicts that while more than half of the world's population of seven billion lived in cities in 2012, by 2030 the number of city-dwellers will be more than five billion. There are projections that three-quarters of the global population by 2050 will be living in cities, with most of the increase occurring in Asia and Africa. Indeed, the world now has 34 megacities with populations of over ten million. Of the 20 biggest cities in 2015, the top eight and six of the others are in Asia.

The need for new cities – China alone requires hundreds to cope with migration from the land – is a major factor driving research into more and better sustainable forms of urban development. A key solution is that of the cheap, mass-production construction of urban high-rises, which require only modest amounts of land. Shanghai has more than 1,000 buildings with over 30 storeys. It is a stunning example of the speed with which a city can be turned from a regional centre into a bustling, international megacity. Shanghai represents the 21st-century city as the agent of modernization and change, as Amsterdam was in the 17th century, London in the 18th and early 19th, and New York for the 20th. However, in Shanghai, there was massive demolition of the earlier city as well as the forced resettlement of hundreds of thousands of people, practices more generally true of Chinese urbanization. The challenge of urban living grows rapidly as population numbers rise and the resulting environmental strains become more intense.

Right: Shanghai continues to develop at a rapid pace. Cities are growing ever larger and building both upwards and outwards to house their growing populations

Modern Science

HEALTH CARE AND THE DEVELOPING WORLD

The major developments in improved health care occurred in the second half of the century, driven by an improved repertoire of drugs. Public health improved as the understanding of disease control became better and more widespread, and policies developed to ensure greater access to health care, child immunization programmes and better nutrition. The dramatic increase in food production in India and China as a result of the 'green revolution' lessened the impact of famine.

Global immunization programmes organized by the World Health Organization (WHO, established in 1948) were directed at diseases such as measles and tuberculosis. In 1948–66, the WHO was responsible for 180 million vaccinations against tuberculosis.

The major change in life expectancy in most developing countries from the 1950s owed much to the fall in infant mortality. Significant decreases in China and India were particularly important and, by 1999, life expectancy there had risen to 70 and 63 respectively. Rapid population growth constitutes one of the main shaping forces in the global history of the last three-quarters of the century.

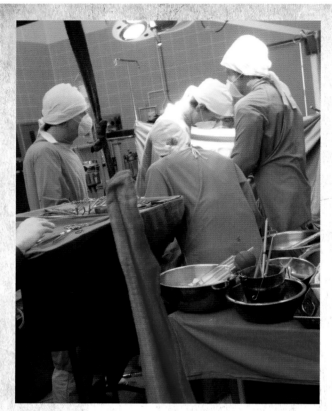

Above: The first heart transplant was performed in South Africa in 1967

TRANSPLANTS

Transplants, a dramatic branch of surgery, were tried in the 19th century, including the development of a successful technique for corneal transplants. Further attempts in the 20th, for example with renal (kidney) transplants were hampered by the failure until the 1930s to understand the basis of organ rejection, while patients were often too ill to survive the operation. These problems were overcome from the 1940s. Renal transplants became possible as patients could be kept alive on dialysis, and kept free of infection by antibiotics. The first kidney transplant was carried out in Chicago in 1950. Bypass and transplant heart surgery became possible in the 1960s, with the first human heart transplant performed in 1967 and the first heart-lung transplant followed in 1981. The transplantation of human organs was transformed from an experimental, and often fatal, procedure into a routine and highly successful operation.

Above: The World Health Organization has led many global immunization campaigns since its creation in 1948

CARS

In the developing world, there was a spread in car manufacturing and a marked increase in ownership. In the developed world car ownership rose during the 1950s as wartime austerity and controls ended, and with the car industry helping to drive economic growth. From the 1960s, first Japan and later Brazil and South Korea developed important manufacturing capacity. By 1990, there were nearly 600 million cars in the world and the following decade saw an important shift toward car ownership in China. On Easter Island in the Pacific, there was only one car (a jeep) in 1956, but over 3,000 (equal to the island's population) in 2000.

The car became one of the distinctive features of the human world. Pollution as a consequence worsened, contributing greatly for example to the terrible air quality in Beijing, Cairo and Delhi, while 'the sound of horns and motors' referred to in T.S. Eliot's poem *The Waste Land* (1922) became more insistent. In 2017, drivers in Los Angeles, the most congested city at peak travel, spent an average of 102 hours annually in congestion during rush hour.

Greater personal mobility for the bulk, but by no means all, of the populated world led to lower-density

HIGHWAYS

Long-distance, multi-lane roads designed to provide effective high-speed routes, first appeared in Germany from 1935 and were taken up more widely after World War II. The most important was the development of the American interstate highway system from the 1950s. This replaced long-distance passenger rail services and offered a free-on-the-point-of-use national network. The first British motorway opened in 1958 and the Trans-Canada Highway followed four years later.

housing and affected the development of leisure. Car ownership brought a sense, maybe an illusion, of freedom and an access to opportunities and options for many. The division of the population into communities defined by differing levels of wealth, expectations, opportunity and age became more pronounced. An obvious aspect of being poor was to have less mobility.

Below: The huge growth in car use has resulted in polluted and congested cities such as Los Angeles

Goods that changed the world – Computer Chips

The dramatic change in the size of computer equipment made it a feature of offices and households across the world. The miniaturization of electronic components made it possible to create complete electronic circuits on a small slice of silicon, an effective and inexpensive way to store information. The integrated circuit was invented in 1958, the first hand-held calculator in 1966, and the Intel 4004, the first microprocessor chip, in 1971. In 1965, Gordon Moore, the co-founder of the company responsible, predicted a dramatic revolution in capability as a result of the doubling of the number of transistors per integrated circuit every 12 to 24 months.

Miniaturization was to be a crucial element in the popularity of new consumer goods, such as mobile phones, laptop computers and mini-disc systems, as portability became an adjunct of the dynamic quality of modern mobile society. Keyboardless, handheld

Above: The microprocessor has changed the way people work and interact with each other

Below: The development of the fibre-optic cable greatly increased the volume of messages that could be transferred from one machine to another

computers followed. Meanwhile, the growing number of business and personal computers facilitated the use of electronic mail and access to the Internet. Improvements in network-computing, with programs running on different machines to co-ordinate their activity, ensured that interconnected machines could operate as a single much more powerful machine, removing the need for a supercomputer. A range of technologies was at play, including fibre-optic cables, which increased the capacity of cable systems and the volume of telephone and computer messages they could carry.

ROBOTS

By the end of 1999, 750,000 robots were in use in manufacturing around the world. They were most common in car manufacturing, particularly in Japan and, after that, the USA, Germany, Italy and France. Not a single country in Africa, Latin America or South Asia appeared in the list of the 20 countries with the most robots. As with computers, robots benefited from improvements in their capabilities and from better production systems that reduced their cost and helped to raise their productivity.

Above: Robots now play a major role in manufacturing, particularly in the automobile industry, but their use remains predominantly located in the USA, Japan and Western Europe

How we travel – Space

The rapid leap from heavier-than-air flight with the Wright Brothers in 1903 to the Soviet *Sputnik* rocket in 1957 clearly demonstrated the accelerating nature of change. The mapping of the Moon by orbiting satellites was followed, on 20 July 1969, by the first manned Moon landing as part of the American *Apollo 11* mission, which had been launched into space by a massive *Saturn V* rocket. 600 million people watched the landing live on television. The previous December, on the *Apollo 8* mission, the astronauts became the first humans to see the earth rise over the moon.

Unmanned missions were also important. Two *Viking* probes, launched in 1975, landed on Mars in order to search for life, but did not find any. The American *Voyager* mission launched in 1977 sent back pictures from the outer planets. It sent back radio signals at the speed of light which bore spectacular images such as those of Neptune in 1989. In 1990, the Hubble space telescope was launched, providing astronomers with even better images of distant galaxies. The discovery of the first extrasolar planets in the 1990s was followed by the discovery of thousands more.

The massive increase in the human ability to scrutinize the moon and then the planets and stars did not lead to the transforming discoveries that had been anticipated in much fiction as well as in films such as *2001: A Space Odyssey* (1968), and *Alien* (1979). Interest in aliens, but also a tendency to treat them as if human, was shown in the great popularity of series such as *Star Trek* and *Star Wars*.

Above: Unmanned missions like the *Voyager* have played an important role in improving our understanding of space

Left: The Moon Landing on 30 July 1969 was televized live to an audience of 600 million

UNDERSTANDING MATTER

Given the ease of creating apparently realistic phenomena, the extent to which current and future technology, especially that of 'virtual reality,' may blur distinctions between the human perception of fact and, on the other hand, 'fiction' or stimulated reality, is unclear. A different perspective was suggested by the research into the nature of matter and the universe, and thus of time in space and space in time, offered by a combination of enhanced astronomy, the Large Hadron Collider (an advanced particle accelerator) and quantum theory. The last implied that remote particles could 'know' how others were behaving. The theory opened up possibilities of complex information systems, including perhaps signals travelling faster than light (which had been believed impossible), and thus of conceivably going into the past. Thus, theoretical developments were linked to an understanding of the universe that offered a new assessment of time and space. While controversial, these ideas appear to be joining together time and space anew.

Right: The Large Hadron Collider has provided confirmation of new theories of matter and particle physics, including the existence of the Higgs Boson

CONCLUSIONS

The future of humanity appears set by two major trends: the rapid rise in population and the human impact on the environment. Together they have created what has been termed the Anthropocene, an age in which human activities have a global effect on the planet's ecosystems. It is a global change: simultaneously seen around the world but also affecting relations between different parts of the world.

The past repeatedly, and insistently, leads to the present, and sets the context, parameters and drive for, and into, the future. What is modern to one generation generally (although not always) dates rapidly. The term modernity tends to assume a process of modernization – becoming modern – and makes that into the central theme and organizing principle of study. This does violence to the variety of the past and the complexity of the processes of change. It can also be misleading as such an approach

Below: Is this a time of religious decline or religious fervour? It depends on where you look

is inherently both overly focused on the present and misleadingly clear. The recent history of religion might be considered as one of its marginality (in China, Western Europe, Australasia), or of the resilience and growth of religious commitment and accompanying divisions, which is the case in much of the rest of the world, notably in Africa and the Americas. Compared to 1900, or every earlier century, should we emphasise environmental degradation and moral bleakness, or the fall of most empires, the challenging of conservative social practices, particularly insofar as women are concerned, and the advance, in at least some countries, of political and religious freedoms?

Modernization can be charted in major changes such as the arrival of mass literacy and urbanization. These advances, which were essentially those of the 19th and 20th centuries, were prefigured by the importance and consequences of printing in the early-modern West because, unlike in China and Japan, printing there was linked to religious change, politicization and

PRINTING.   Plate II.

1. *Ruthvens Press*. 2 & 3. *Bacon & Donkin's Press*.

Above: The printing press led the way to mass literacy and provided the impetus for religious change, politicization and the spread of scientific advances

the large-scale dissemination of scientific and intellectual advances. For these reasons, modernization began in the early-modern West, developed greatly in the 19th century, notably as industrial development led to large-scale urbanization, and affected most of the world's population by the close of the 20th.

In South Asia and sub-Saharan Africa, modernization is very much a work-in-progress, and the contrasts are striking. India, an economy with very rapid growth, also still has a large number of people with little literacy, as well as a caste system and a harsh attitude toward women.

From the 19th century, it became possible to create what had hitherto existed only in the world of fiction, such as with space-travel. Stories continue to offer important clues not only to anxieties, but also to the hopes of the age. The idea of creating new and artificial life-forms became increasingly insistent. In addition to the humanoids of films such as

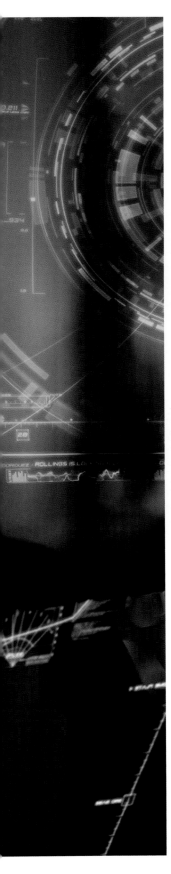

Above: Movies like *The Terminator* express the potential dangers of artificial intelligence

Left: Humans in the future are likely to use technology to enhance their brains and bodies and provide them with new ways to interact with their environment

Metropolis (1927) and *The Terminator* (1984) came troubling super-intelligent computers that seized control from humans, as in *2001: A Space Odyssey* (1968). In the 2010s, the rise of AI (Artificial Intelligence) became the basis of much anxiety, as also did concern about the instability expressed in social media.

Referring to the crisis and fall of Communism in Eastern Europe in 1989, Ronald Reagan argued: 'Technology will make it increasingly difficult for the state to control the information its people receive.' Thanks to such developments, established political, social and economic loyalties and alignments coexist with rapidly developing linkages and demands.

If future humans incorporate, possibly through implants, cloning or developing skills, an enhanced degree of mechanical characteristics, then the ability to handle more information, although difficult, may be part of this transition. This may realize, in a different form, some of the potential discussed in the 20th century. Neurological change has already been discerned, with brains rapidly adapting to the electronic age, as they did earlier to print. The change in the human environment created, and creates, new opportunities and pressures. Such adaptation will be necessary because these pressures will include the demands on resources and opportunities posed by a rising population, not least because there will be a very varied geopolitical spread of such opportunities and demands.

Humans will have to adapt to a rapidly-changing environment. Climate change will present major challenges. This will be the case across the world and at the individual level as well as that of communities. Providing adequate resources will be a key problem, but so also will be managing the ecosystem so that the quest for resources does not cause catastrophic damage. This will involve trade-offs between individual satisfaction and collective disciplines, and such compromises are far from easy. There are problems of understanding, of decision-making and of implementation. It is to be hoped that humans will have acquired the intellectual capital to deal with the major issues that doubtless lie ahead.

There is scant sign of meaningful international co-operation in resolving these problems. The entire period from 1945 has been one in which there have been attempts, on the global or regional levels, to secure co-operation on a greater range of subjects than ever before. Yet, so far this has proved elusive. Whether that can change is unclear. The omens are very varied. The species may outperform its governance, but it may not.

Right: Space may represent the next frontier for humanity. Ongoing issues with climate change, political conflict and overpopulation may make new solutions more important than ever

Index

PICTURE CREDITS